MURDER AND MYSTERY IN BOSTON

MURDER and MYSTERY in BOSTON

**Edited by
Carol-Lynn Rössel Waugh,
Frank D. McSherry, Jr. and Martin H. Greenberg**

DEMBNER BOOKS • New York

DEMBNER BOOKS
Published by Red Dembner Enterprises Corp.,
80 Eighth Avenue,
New York, N.Y. 10011

Distributed by W. W. Norton & Company, Inc.,
500 Fifth Avenue,
New York, N.Y. 10110

Copyright © 1987 by Carol-Lynn Rössel Waugh, Frank McSherry, and Martin H. Greenberg.

Library of Congress Cataloging in Publications Data

Murder and mystery in Boston

   1. Detective and mystery stories, American.
2. Boston (Mass.)—Fiction. 3. American fiction—
Massachusetts—Boston. I. Waugh, Carol-Lynn Rössel.
II. Greenberg, Martin Harry. III. McSherry, Frank D.
PS648.D4M853 1987   813'.0872'083274461   87-14361
ISBN 0-934878-95-1

Design by Antler & Baldwin, Inc.

CONTENTS

LUCKY PENNY

LINDA BARNES

Lieutenant Mooney made me dish it all out for the record. He's a good cop, if such an animal exists. We used to work the same shift before I decided—wrongly—that there was room for a lady PI in this town. Who knows? With this case under my belt, maybe business'll take a 180-degree spin, and I can quit driving a hack.

See, I've already written the official report for Mooney and the cops, but the kind of stuff they wanted: date, place, and time, cold as ice and submitted in triplicate, doesn't even start to tell the tale. So I'm doing it over again, my way.

Don't worry, Mooney. I'm not gonna file this one.

The Thayler case was still splattered across the front page of the *Boston Globe*. I'd soaked it up with my midnight coffee and was puzzling it out—my cab on automatic pilot, my mind on crime—when the mad tea party began.

"Take your next right, sister. Then pull over, and douse the lights. Quick!"

I heard the bastard all right, but it must have taken me thirty seconds or so to react. Something hard rapped on the cab's dividing shield. I didn't bother turning around. I hate staring down gun barrels.

I said, "Jimmy Cagney, right? No, your voice is too high. Let me guess, don't tell me—"

"Shut up!"

"*Kill* the lights, *turn off* the lights, okay. But *douse* the lights? You've been tuning in too many old gangster flicks."

1

"I hate a mouthy broad," the guy snarled. I kid you not.

"*Broad,*" I said. "Christ! *Broad*? You trying to grow hair on your balls?"

"Look, I mean it, lady!"

"*Lady's* better. Now you wanna vacate my cab and go rob a phone booth?" My heart was beating like a tin drum, but I didn't let my voice shake, and all the time I was gabbing at him, I kept trying to catch his face in the mirror. He must have been crouching way back on the passenger side. I couldn't see a damn thing.

"I want all your dough," he said.

Who can you trust? This guy was a spiffy dresser: charcoal-gray three-piece suit and rep tie, no less. And picked up in front of the swank Copley Plaza. *I* looked like I needed the bucks more than he did, and I'm no charity case. A woman can make good tips driving a hack in Boston. Oh, she's gotta take precautions, all right. When you can't smell a disaster fare from thirty feet, it's time to quit. I pride myself on my judgment. I'm careful. I always know where the police checkpoints are, so I can roll my cab past and flash the old lights if a guy starts acting up. This dude fooled me cold.

I was ripped. Not only had I been conned, I had a considerable wad to give away. It was near the end of my shift, and like I said, I do all right. I've got a lot of regulars. Once you see me, you don't forget me—or my cab.

It's gorgeous. Part of my inheritance. A '59 Chevy, shiny as new, kept on blocks in a heated garage by the proverbial dotty old lady. It's the pits of the design world. Glossy blue with those giant chromium fins. Restrained decor: just the phone number and a few gilt curlicues on the door. I was afraid all my old pals at the police department would pull me over for minor traffic violations if I went whole hog and painted "Carlotta's Cab" in ornate script on the hood. Some do it anyway.

So where the hell were all the cops now? Where are they when you need 'em?

He told me to shove the cash through that little hole they leave for the passenger to pass the fare forward. I told him he had it backwards. He didn't laugh. I shoved bills.

"Now the change," the guy said. Can you imagine the nerve?

I must have cast my eyes up to heaven. I do that a lot these days.

"I mean it." He rapped the plastic shield with the shiny barrel of his gun. I checked it out this time. Funny how big a little .22 looks when it's pointed just right.

I fished in my pockets for change, emptied them.

"Is that all?"

"You want the gold cap on my left front molar?" I said.

"Turn around," the guy barked. "Keep both hands on the steering wheel. High."

I heard jingling, then a quick intake of breath.

"Okay," the crook said, sounding happy as a clam, "I'm gonna take my leave—"

"Good. Don't call this cab again."

"Listen!" The gun tapped. "You cool it here for ten minutes. And I mean frozen. Don't twitch. Don't blow your nose. Then take off."

"Gee, thanks."

"Thank *you*," he said politely. The door slammed.

At times like that, you just feel ridiculous. You *know* the guy isn't going to hang around, waiting to see whether you're big on insubordination. *But*, he might. And who wants to tangle with a .22 slug? I rate pretty high on insubordination. That's why I messed up as a cop. I figured I'd give him two minutes to get lost. Meantime I listened.

Not much traffic goes by those little streets on Beacon Hill at one o'clock on a Wednesday morn. Too residential. So I could hear the guy's footsteps tap along the pavement. About ten steps back, he stopped. Was he the one in a million who'd wait to see if I turned around? I heard a funny kind of *whooshing* noise. Not loud enough to make me jump, and anything much louder than the ticking of my watch would have put me through the roof. Then the footsteps patted on, straight back and out of hearing.

One minute more. The only saving grace of the situation was the location: District One. That's Mooney's district. Nice guy to talk to.

I took a deep breath, hoping it would have an encore, and pivoted quickly, keeping my head low. Makes you feel stupid when you do that and there's no one around.

I got out and strolled to the corner, stuck my head around a building kind of cautiously. Nothing, of course.

I backtracked. Ten steps, then *whoosh*. Along the sidewalk stood one of those new "Keep Beacon Hill Beautiful" trash cans, the kind with the swinging lid. I gave it a shove as I passed. I could just as easily have kicked it; I was in that kind of funk.

Whoosh, it said, just as pretty as could be.

Breaking into one of those trash cans is probably tougher than busting into your local bank vault. Since I didn't even have a dime left to fiddle the screws on the lid, I was forced to deface city property. I got the damn thing open and dumped the contents on somebody's front lawn, smack in the middle of a circle of light from one of those snooty Beacon Hill gas streetlamps.

Halfway through the whisky bottles, wadded napkins, and beer cans, I made my discovery. I was doing a thorough search. If you're going to stink like garbage anyway, why leave anything untouched, right? So I was opening all the brown bags—you know, the good old brown lunch-and-bottle bags—looking for a clue. My most valuable find so far had been the moldy rind of a bologna sandwich. Then I hit it big: one neatly creased bag stuffed full of cash.

To say I was stunned is to entirely underestimate how I felt as I crouched there, knee-deep in garbage, my jaw hanging wide. I don't know what I'd expected to find. Maybe the guy's gloves. Or his hat, if he'd wanted to get rid of it fast in order to melt back into anonymity. I pawed through the rest of the debris. My change was gone.

I was so befuddled I left the trash right on the front lawn. There's probably still a warrant out for my arrest.

District One headquarters is off the beaten path, over on New Sudbury Street. I would have called first, if I'd had a dime.

One of the few things I'd enjoyed about being a cop was gabbing with Mooney. I like driving a cab better, but, face it, most of my fares aren't scintillating conversationalists. The Red Sox and the weather usually covers it. Talking to Mooney was so much fun, I wouldn't even consider dating him. Lots of guys are good at sex, but conversation—now there's an art form.

Mooney, all six-feet-four, 240 linebacker pounds of him, gave me the glad eye when I waltzed in. He hasn't given up trying. Keeps telling me he talks even better in bed.

"Nice hat," was all he said, his big fingers pecking at the typewriter keys.

I took it off and shook out my hair. I wear an old slouch cap when I drive to keep people from saying the inevitable. One jerk even misquoted Yeats at me: "Only God, my dear, could love you for yourself alone and not your long red hair." Since I'm seated when I drive, he missed the chance to ask me how the weather is up here. I'm six-one in my stocking feet and skinny enough to make every inch count twice. I've got a wide forehead, green eyes, and a pointy chin. If you want to be nice about my nose, you say it's got character.

Thirty's still hovering in my future. It's part of Mooney's past.

I told him I had a robbery to report and his dark eyes steered me to a chair. He leaned back and took a puff of one of his low-tar cigarettes. He can't quite give 'em up, but he feels guilty as hell about 'em.

When I got to the part about the bag in the trash, Mooney lost his sense of humor. He crushed a half-smoked butt in a crowded ashtray.

"Know why you never made it as a cop?" he said.

"Didn't brown-nose enough."

"You got no sense of proportion! Always going after crackpot stuff!"

"Christ, Mooney, aren't you interested? Some guy heists a cab, at gunpoint, then tosses the money. Aren't you the least bit *intrigued*?"

"I'm a cop, Ms. Carlyle. I've got to be more than intrigued. I've got murders, bank robberies, assaults—"

"Well, excuse me. I'm just a poor citizen reporting a crime. Trying to help—"

"Want to help, Carlotta? Go away." He stared at the sheet of paper in the typewriter and lit another cigarette. "Or dig me up something on the Thayler case."

"You working that sucker?"

"Wish to hell I wasn't."

I could see his point. It's tough enough trying to solve any murder, but when your victim is *the* Jennifer (Mrs. Justin) Thayler, wife of the famed Harvard Law prof, and the society reporters are breathing down your neck along with the usual crime-beat scribblers, you got a special kind of problem.

"So who did it?" I asked.

Mooney put his size twelves up on his desk. "Colonel Mustard in the library with the candlestick! How the hell do I know? Some scumbag housebreaker. The lady of the house interrupted his haul. Probably didn't mean to hit her that hard. He must have freaked when he saw all the blood, 'cause he left some of the ritziest stereo equipment this side of heaven, plus enough silverware to blind your average hophead. He snatched most of old man Thayler's goddamn idiot artworks, collections, collectibles—whatever the hell you call 'em— which ought to set him up for the next few hundred years, if he's smart enough to get rid of them."

"Alarm system?"

"Yeah, they had one. Looks like Mrs. Thayler forgot to turn it on. According to the maid, she had a habit of forgetting just about anything after a martini or three."

"Think the maid's in on it?"

"Christ, Carlotta. There you go again. No witnesses. No finger-prints. Servants asleep. Husband asleep. We've got word out to all the fences here and in New York that we want this guy. The pawnbrokers know the stuff's hot. We're checking out known art thieves and shady museums—"

"Well, don't let me keep you from your serious business," I said, getting up to go. "I'll give you the collar when I find out who robbed my cab."

"Sure," he said. His fingers started playing with the typewriter again.

"Wanna bet on it?" Betting's an old custom with Mooney and me.

"I'm not gonna take the few piddling bucks you earn with that ridiculous car."

"Right you are, boy. I'm gonna take the money the city pays you to be unimaginative! Fifty bucks I nail him within the week."

Mooney hates to be called "boy." He hates to be called "unimaginative." I hate to hear my car called "ridiculous." We shook hands on the deal. Hard.

Chinatown's about the only chunk of Boston that's alive after midnight. I headed over to Yee Hong's for a bowl of wonton soup.

The service was the usual low-key, slow-motion routine. I used a newspaper as a shield; if you're really involved in the *Wall Street Journal*, the casual male may think twice before deciding he's the answer to your prayers. But I didn't read a single stock quote. I tugged at strands of my hair, a bad habit of mine. Why would somebody rob me and then toss the money away?

Solution Number One: He didn't. The trash bin was some mob drop, and the money I'd found in the trash had absolutely nothing to do with the money filched from my cab. Except that it was the same amount—and that was too big a coincidence for me to swallow.

Two: The cash I'd found was counterfeit and this was a clever way of getting it into circulation. Nah. Too baroque entirely. How the hell would the guy know I was the pawing-through-the-trash type?

Three: It was a training session. Some fool had used me to perfect his robbery technique. Couldn't he learn from TV like the rest of the crooks?

Four: It was a frat hazing. Robbing a hack at gunpoint isn't exactly in the same league as swallowing goldfish.

I closed my eyes.

My face came to a fortunate halt about an inch above a bowl of steaming broth. That's when I decided to pack it in and head for home. Wonton soup is lousy for the complexion.

I checked out the log I keep in the Chevy, totaled my fares: $4.82 missing, all in change. A very reasonable robbery.

By the time I got home, the sleepiness had passed. You know how it is: one moment you're yawning, the next your eyes won't close. Usually happens when my head hits the pillow; this time I didn't even make it that far. What woke me up was the idea that my robber hadn't meant to steal a thing. Maybe he'd left me something instead. You know, something hot, cleverly concealed. Something he could pick up in a few weeks, after things cooled off.

I went over that backseat with a vengeance, but I didn't find anything besides old Kleenex and bent paperclips. My brainstorm wasn't too clever after all. I mean, if the guy wanted to use my cab as a hiding place, why advertise by pulling a five-and-dime robbery?

I sat in the driver's seat, tugged my hair, and stewed. What did I have to go on? The memory of a nervous thief who talked like a B movie and stole only change. Maybe a mad toll-booth collector.

I live in a Cambridge dump. In any other city, I couldn't sell the damned thing if I wanted to. Here, I turn real estate agents away daily. The key to my home's value is the fact that I can hoof it to Harvard Square in five minutes. It's a seller's market for tar-paper shacks within walking distance of the Square. Under a hundred thou only if the plumbing's outside.

It took me a while to get in the door. I've got about five locks on it.

Neighborhood's popular with thieves as well as gentry. I'm neither. I inherited the house from my weird Aunt Bea, all paid for. I consider the property taxes my rent, and the rent's getting steeper all the time.

I slammed my log down on the dining room table. I've got rooms galore in that old house, rent a couple of them to Harvard students. I've got my own office on the second floor, but I do most of my work at the dining room table. I like the view of the refrigerator.

I started over from square one. I called Gloria. She's the late-night dispatcher for the Independent Taxi Owners Association. I've never seen her, but her voice is as smooth as mink oil and I'll bet we get a lot of calls from guys who just want to hear her say she'll pick 'em up in five minutes.

"Gloria, it's Carlotta."

"Hi, babe. You been pretty popular today."

"Was I popular at one-thirty-five this morning?"

"Huh?"

"I picked up a fare in front of the Copley Plaza at one-thirty-five. Did you hand that one out to all comers or did you give it to me solo?"

"Just a sec." I could hear her charming the pants off some caller in the background. Then she got back to me.

"I just gave him to you, babe. He asked for the lady in the '59 Chevy. Not a lot of those on the road."

"Thanks, Gloria."

"Trouble?" she asked.

"Is mah middle name," I twanged. We both laughed and I hung up before she got a chance to cross-examine me.

So. The robber wanted my cab. I wished I'd concentrated on his face instead of his snazzy clothes. Maybe it was somebody I knew, some jokester in mid-prank. I killed that idea; I don't know anybody who'd pull a stunt like that, at gunpoint and all. I don't want to know anybody like that.

Why rob my cab, then toss the dough?

I pondered sudden religious conversion. Discarded it. Maybe some robber was some perpetual screwup who'd ditched the cash by mistake.

Or . . . Maybe he got exactly what he wanted. Maybe he desperately desired my change.

Why?

Because my change was special, valuable beyond its $4.82 replacement cost.

So how would somebody know my change was valuable?

Because he'd given it to me himself, earlier in the day.

"Not bad," I said out loud. "Not bad." It was the kind of reasoning they'd bounced me off the police force for, what my so-called superiors termed the "fevered product of an overimaginative mind." I leapt at it because it was the only explanation I could think of. I do like life to make some sort of sense.

I pored over my log. I keep pretty good notes: where I pick up a fare, where I drop him, whether he's a hailer or a radio call.

First, I ruled out all the women. That made the task slightly less impossible: sixteen suspects down from thirty-five. Then I yanked my hair and stared at the blank white porcelain of the refrigerator door. Got up and made myself a sandwich: ham, Swiss cheese, salami, lettuce and tomato, on rye. Ate it. Stared at the porcelain some more until the suspects started coming into focus.

Five of the guys were just plain fat and one was decidedly on the hefty side; I'd felt like telling them all to walk. Might do them some good, might bring on a heart attack. I crossed them all out. Making a thin person look plump is hard enough; it's damn near impossible to make a fatty look thin.

Then I considered my regulars: Jonah Ashley, a tiny blond southern gent; muscle-bound "just-call-me-Harold" at Longfellow Place; Dr. Homewood getting his daily ferry from Beth Israel to MGH; Marvin of the gay bars; and Professor Dickerman, Harvard's answer to Berkeley's sixties radicals.

I crossed them all off. I could see Dickerman holding up the First Filthy Capitalist Bank, or disobeying civilly at Seabrook, even blowing up an oil company or two. But my mind boggled at the thought of the great liberal Dickerman robbing some poor cabbie. It would be like Robin Hood joining the sheriff of Nottingham on some particularly rotten peasant swindle. Then they'd both rape Maid Marian and go off pals together.

Dickerman *was* a lousy tipper. That ought to be a crime.

So what did I leave? Eleven out of sixteen guys cleared without leaving my chair. Me and Sherlock Holmes, the famous armchair detectives.

I'm stubborn; that was one of my good cop traits. I stared at that log till my eyes bugged out. I remembered two of the five pretty easily; they were handsome and I'm far from blind. The first had one of those elegant bony faces and far-apart eyes. He was taller than my bandit. I'd ceased eyeballing him when I noticed the ring on his left hand; I never fuss with the married kind. The other one was built, a weight lifter. Not an Arnold Schwarzenegger extremist, but built. I think I'd have noticed that bod on my bandit. Like I said, I'm not blind.

That left three.

Okay. I closed my eyes. Who had I picked up at the Hyatt on Memorial Drive? Yeah, that was the salesman guy, the one who looked so uncomfortable that I'd figured he'd been hoping to ask his cabbie for a few pointers concerning the best skirt-chasing areas in our fair city. Too low a voice. Too broad in the beam.

The log said I'd picked up a hailer at Kenmore Square when I'd let out the salesman. Ah, yes, a talker. The weather, mostly. Don't you think it's dangerous for you to be driving a cab? Yeah, I remembered him, all right: a fatherly type, clasping a briefcase, heading to the financial district. Too old.

Down to one. I was exhausted but not the least bit sleepy. All I had to do was remember who I'd picked up on Beacon near Charles. A hailer. Before five o'clock, which was fine by me because I wanted to be long gone before rush hour gridlocked the city. I'd gotten onto Storrow and taken him along the river into Newton Center. Dropped him off at the Bay Bank Middlesex, right before closing time. It was coming back. Little nervous guy. Pegged him as an accountant when I'd let him out at the bank. Measly, undernourished soul. Skinny as a rail, stooped, with pits left from teenage acne.

Shit. I let my head sink down onto the dining room table when I realized what I'd done. I'd ruled them all out, every one. So much for my brilliant deductive powers.

I retired to my bedroom, disgusted. Not only had I lost $4.82 in assorted alloy metals, I was going to lose fifty dollars to Mooney. I stared at myself in the mirror, but what I was really seeing was the round hole at the end of a .22, held in a neat, gloved hand.

Somehow, the gloves made me feel better. I'd remembered another detail about my piggy-bank robber. I consulted the mirror and kept the recall going. A hat. The guy wore a hat. Not like my cap, but like a hat out of a forties gangster flick. I had one of those: I'm a sucker for hats. I plunked it on my head, jamming my hair up underneath—and I drew in my breath sharply.

A shoulder-padded jacket, a slim build, a low slouched hat. Gloves. Boots with enough heel to click as he walked away. Voice? High. Breathy, almost whispered. Not unpleasant. Accentless. No Boston *r*.

I had a man's jacket and a couple of ties in my closet. Don't ask. They may have dated from as far back as my ex-husband, but not necessarily so. I slipped into the jacket, knotted the tie, tilted the hat down over one eye.

I'd have trouble pulling it off. I'm skinny, but my build is decidedly female. Still, I wondered—enough to traipse back downstairs, pull a chicken leg out of the fridge, go back to the log, and review the feminine possibilities. Good thing I did.

Everything clicked. One lady fit the bill exactly: mannish walk and clothes, tall for a woman. And I was in luck. While I'd picked her up in Harvard Square, I'd dropped her at a real address, a house in Brookline: 782 Mason Terrace, at the top of Corey Hill.

JoJo's garage opens at seven. That gave me a big two hours to sleep.

I took my beloved car in for some repair work it really didn't need yet and sweet-talked JoJo into giving me a loaner. I needed a hack, but not mine. Only trouble with that Chevy is it's too damn conspicuous.

I figured I'd lose way more than fifty bucks staking out Mason Terrace. I also figured it would be worth it to see old Mooney's face.

She was regular as clockwork, a dream to tail. Eight-thirty-seven every morning, she got a ride to the Square with a next-door neighbor. Took a cab home at five-fifteen. A working woman. Well, she couldn't make much of a living from robbing hacks and dumping the loot in the garbage.

I was damn curious by now. I knew as soon as I looked her over that she was the one, but she seemed so blah, so *normal*. She must have been five-seven or -eight, but the way she stooped, she didn't look tall. Her hair was long and brown with a lot of blond in it, the kind of hair that would have been terrific loose and wild, like a horse's mane. She tied it back with a scarf. A brown scarf. She wore suits. Brown suits. She had a tiny nose, brown eyes under pale eyebrows, a sharp chin. I never saw her smile. Maybe what she needed was a shrink, not a session with Mooney. Maybe she'd done it for the excitement. God knows, if I had her routine, her job, I'd probaby be dressing up like King Kong and assaulting skyscrapers.

See, I followed her to work. It wasn't even tricky. She trudged the same path, went in the same entrance to Harvard Yard, probably walked the same number of steps every morning. Her name was Marcia Heidegger and she was a secretary in the admissions office of the college of fine arts.

I got friendly with one of her coworkers.

There was this guy typing away like mad at a desk in her office. I could just see him from the side window. He had grad student written all over his face. Longish wispy hair. Gold-rimmed glasses. Serious. Given to deep sighs and bright velour V necks. Probably writing his thesis on "Courtly Love and the Theories of Chrétien de Troyes."

I latched onto him at Bailey's the day after I'd tracked Lady Heidegger to her Harvard lair.

Too bad Roger was so short. Most short guys find it hard to believe that I'm really trying to pick them up. They look for ulterior motives. Not the Napoleon type of short guy; he assumes I've been waiting years for a chance to dance with a guy who doesn't have to bend to stare down my cleavage. But Roger was no Napoleon. So I had to engineer things a little.

I got into line ahead of him and ordered, after long deliberation, a BLT on toast. While the guy made it up and shoved it on a plate with three measly potato chips and a sliver of pickle you could barely see, I searched through my wallet, opened my change purse, counted out silver, got to $1.60 on the last five pennies. The counterman sang out, "That'll be a buck, eighty-five." I pawed through my pockets, found a nickel, two pennies. The line was growing restive. I concentrated on looking like a damsel in need of a knight, a tough task for a woman over six feet.

Roger (I didn't know he was Roger then) smiled ruefully and passed over a quarter. I was effusive in my thanks. I sat at a table for two, and when he'd gotten his tray (ham-and-cheese and a strawberry ice cream soda), I motioned him into my extra chair.

He was a sweetie. Sitting down, he forgot the difference in our height, and decided I might be someone he could talk to. I encouraged him. I hung shamelessly on his every word. A Harvard man, imagine that. We got around slowly, ever so slowly, to his work at the admissions office. He wanted to duck it and talk about more important issues, but I persisted. I'd been thinking about getting a job at Harvard, possibly in admissions. What kind of people did he work with? Were they congenial? What was the atmosphere like? Was it a big office? How many people? Men? Women? Any soulmates? Readers? Or just, you know, office people?

According to him, every soul he worked with was brain dead. I interrupted a stream of complaint with "Gee, I know somebody who works for Harvard. I wonder if you know her."

"It's a big place," he said, hoping to avoid the whole endless business.

"I met her at a party. Always meant to look her up." I searched through my bag, found a scrap of paper and pretended to read Marcia Heidegger's name off it.

"Marcia? Geez, I work with Marcia. Same office."

"Do you think she likes her work? I mean I got some strange vibes from her," I said. I actually said "strange vibes" and he didn't laugh his head off. People in the Square say things like that and other people take them seriously.

His face got conspiratorial, of all things, and he leaned closer to me.

"You want it, I bet you could get Marcia's job."

"You mean it?" What a compliment—a place for me among the brain dead.

"She's gonna get fired if she doesn't snap out of it."

"Snap out of what?"

"It was bad enough working with her when she first came over. She's one of those crazy neat people, can't stand to see papers lying on a desktop, you know? She almost threw out the first chapter of my thesis!"

I made a suitably horrified noise and he went on.

"Well, you know, about Marcia, it's kind of tragic. She doesn't talk about it."

But he was dying to.

"Yes?" I said, as if he needed egging on.

He lowered his voice. "She used to work for Justin Thayler over at the law school, that guy in the news, whose wife got killed. You know, her work hasn't been worth shit since it happened. She's always on the phone, talking real soft, hanging up if anybody comes in the room. I mean, you'd think she was in love with the guy or something, the way she . . ."

I don't remember what I said. For all I know, I may have volunteered to type his thesis. But I got rid of him somehow and then I scooted around the corner of Church Street and found a pay phone and dialed Mooney.

"Don't tell me," he said. "Somebody mugged you, but they only took your trading stamps."

"I have just one question for you, Moon."

"I accept. A June wedding, but I'll have to break it to Mother gently."

"Tell me what kind of junk Justin Thayler collected."

I could hear him breathing into the phone.

"Just tell me," I said, "for curiosity's sake."

"You onto something, Carlotta?"

"I'm curious, Mooney. And you're not the only source of information in the world."

"Thayler collected Roman stuff. Antiques. And I mean old. Artifacts, statues—"

"Coins?"

"Whole mess of them."

"Thanks."

"Carlotta—"

I never did find out what he was about to say because I hung up. Rude, I know. But I had things to do. And it was better Mooney shouldn't know what they were, because they came under the heading of illegal activities.

When I knocked at the front door of the Mason Terrace house at 10:00 A.M. the next day, I was dressed in dark slacks, a white blouse, and my old police department hat. I looked very much like the guy who reads your gas meter. I've never heard of anyone being arrested for impersonating the gasman. I've never heard of anyone really giving the gasman a second look. He fades into the background and that's exactly what I wanted to do.

I knew Marcia Heidegger wouldn't be home for hours. Old reliable had left for the Square at her usual time, precise to the minute. But I wasn't 100 percent sure Marcia lived alone. Hence the gasman. I could knock on the door and check it out.

Those Brookline neighborhoods kill me. Act sneaky and the neighbors call the cops in twenty seconds, but walk right up to the front door, knock, talk to yourself while you're sticking a shim in the crack of the door, let yourself in, and nobody does a thing. Boldness is all.

The place wasn't bad. Three rooms, kitchen and bath, light and airy. Marcia was incredibly organized, obsessively neat, which meant I had to keep track of where everything was and put it back just so. There was no clutter in the woman's life. The smell of coffee and toast lingered, but if she'd eaten breakfast, she'd already washed, dried, and put away the dishes. The morning paper had been read and tossed in the trash. The mail was sorted in one of those plastic accordion files. I mean, she folded her underwear like origami.

Now coins are hard to look for. They're small; you can hide 'em anywhere. So this search took me one hell of a long time. Nine out of ten women hide things that are dear to them in the bedroom. They keep their finest jewelry closest to the bed, sometimes in the nightstand, sometimes right under the mattress. That's where I started.

Marcia had a jewelry box on top of her dresser. I felt like hiding it for her. She had some nice stuff and a burglar could have made quite a haul with no effort.

The next favorite place for women to stash valuables is the kitchen. I sifted through her flour. I removed every Kellogg's Rice Krispy from the giant economy-sized box—and returned it. I went through her place like no burglar ever will. When I say thorough, I mean thorough.

I found four odd things. A neatly squared pile of clippings from the *Globe* and the *Herald*, all the articles about the Thayler killing. A manila envelope containing five different safe-deposit-box keys. A Tupperware container full of superstitious junk, good luck charms mostly, the kind of stuff I'd never have associated with a straight-arrow like Marcia: rabbits' feet galore, a little leather bag on a string that looked like some kind of voodoo charm, a pendant in the shape of a cross surmounted by a hook, and, I swear to God, a pack of worn tarot cards. Oh, yes, and a .22 automatic, looking a lot less threatening stuck in an ice cube tray. I took the bullets; the loaded gun threatened a defenseless box of Breyers' mint chocolate-chip ice cream.

I left everything else just the way I'd found it and went home. And tugged my hair. And stewed. And brooded. And ate half the stuff in the refrigerator. I kid you not.

At about one in the morning, it all made blinding, crystal-clear sense.

The next afternoon, at five-fifteen, I made sure I was the cabbie who picked up Marcia Heidegger in Harvard Square. Now cabstands have the most rigid protocol since Queen Victoria; you do not grab a fare out of turn or your fellow cabbies are definitely not amused. There was nothing for it but bribing the ranks. This bet with Mooney was costing me plenty.

I got her. She swung open the door and gave the Mason Terrace number. I grunted, kept my face turned front, and took off.

Some people really watch where you're going in a cab, scared to death you'll take them a block out of their way and squeeze them for an extra nickel. Others just lean back and dream. She was a dreamer, thank God. I was almost at District One headquarters before she woke up.

"Excuse me," she said, polite as ever, "that's Mason Terrace in *Brookline*."

"Take the next right, pull over, and douse your lights," I said in a low Bogart voice. My imitation was not that good, but it got the point across. Her eyes widened and she made an instinctive grab for the door handle.

"Don't try it, lady," I Bogied on. "You think I'm dumb enough to take you in alone? There's a cop car behind us, just waiting for you to make a move."

Her hand froze. She was a sap for movie dialogue.

"Where's the cop?" was all she said on the way up to Mooney's office.

"What cop?"

"The one following us."

"You have touching faith in our law-enforcement system," I said.

She tried to bolt, I kid you not. I've had experience with runners a lot trickier than Marcia. I grabbed her in approved cop hold number three and marched her into Mooney's office.

He actually stopped typing and raised an eyebrow, an expression of great shock for Mooney.

"Citizen's arrest," I said.

"Charges?"

"Petty theft. Commission of a felony using a firearm." I rattled off a few more charges, using the numbers I remembered from cop school.

"This woman is crazy," Marcia Heidegger said with all the dignity she could muster.

"Search her," I said. "Get a matron in here. I want my four dollars and eighty-two cents back."

Mooney looked like he agreed with Marcia's opinion of my mental state. He said, "Wait up, Carlotta. You'd have to be able to identify that four dollars and eight-two cents as yours. Can you do that? Quarters are quarters. Dimes are dimes."

"One of the coins she took was quite unusual," I said. "I'm sure I'd be able to identify it."

"Do you have any objection to displaying the change in your purse?" Mooney said to Marcia. He got me mad the way he said it, like he was humoring an idiot.

"Of course not," old Marcia said, cool as a frozen daiquiri.

"That's because she's stashed it somewhere else, Mooney," I said patiently. "She used to keep it in her purse, see. But then she goofed. She handed it over to a cabbie in her change. She should have just let it go, but she panicked because it was worth a pile and she was just baby-sitting it for someone else. So when she got it back, she hid it somewhere. Like in her shoe. Didn't you ever carry your lucky penny in your shoe?"

"No," Mooney said. "Now, Miss—"

"Heidegger," I said clearly. "Marcia Heidegger. She used to work at Harvard Law School." I wanted to see if Mooney picked up on it, but he didn't. He went on: "This can be taken care of with a minimum of fuss. If you'll agree to be searched by—"

"I want to see my lawyer," she said.

"For four dollars and eighty-two cents?" he said. "It'll cost you more than that to get your lawyers up here."

"Do I get my phone call or not?"

Mooney shrugged wearily and wrote up the charge sheet. Called a cop to take her to the phone.

He got JoAnn, which was good. Under cover of our old-friend-long-time-no-see greetings, I whispered in her ear.

"You'll find it fifty well spent," I said to Mooney when we were alone.

JoAnn came back, shoving Marcia slightly ahead of her. She plunked her prisoner down in one of Mooney's hard wooden chairs and turned to me, grinning from ear to ear.

"Got it?" I said. "Good for you."

"What's going on?" Mooney said.

"She got real clumsy on the way to the pay phone," JoAnn said. "Practically fell on the floor. Got up with her right hand clenched tight. When we got to the phone, I offered to drop her dime for her. She wanted to do it herself. I insisted and she got clumsy again. Somehow this coin got kicked clear across the floor."

She held it up. The coin could have been a dime, except the color was off: warm, rosy gold instead of dead silver. How I missed it the first time around I'll never know.

"What the hell is that?" Mooney said.

"What kind of coins were in Justin Thayler's collection?" I asked. "Roman?"

Marcia jumped out of the chair, snapped her bag open, and drew out her little .22. I kid you not. She was closest to Mooney and she just stepped up to him and rested it above his left ear. He swallowed, didn't say a word. I never realized how prominent his Adam's apple was. JoAnn froze, hand on her holster.

Good old reliable, methodical Marcia. Why, I said to myself, *why* pick today of all days to trot your gun out of the freezer? Did you read bad luck in your tarot cards? Then I had a truly rotten thought. What if she had two guns? What if the disarmed .22 was still staring down the mint chocolate-chip ice cream?

"Give it back," Marcia said. She held out one hand, made an impatient waving motion.

"Hey, you don't need it, Marcia," I said. "You've got plenty more. In all those safe deposit boxes."

"I'm going to count to five—" she began.

"Were you in on the murder from day one? You know, from the planning stages?" I asked. I kept my voice low, but it echoed off the walls of Mooney's tiny office. The hum of everyday activity kept going in the main room. Nobody noticed the little gun in the well-dressed lady's hand. "Or did you just do your beau a favor and hide the loot after he iced his wife? In order to back up his burglary tale? I mean, if

Justin Thayler really wanted to marry you, there is such a thing as divorce. Or was old Jennifer the one with the bucks?"

"I want that coin," she said softly. "Then I want the two of you"—she motioned to JoAnn and me—"to sit down facing that wall. If you yell, or do anything before I'm out of the building, I'll shoot this gentleman. He's coming with me."

"Come on, Marcia," I said, "put it down. I mean, look at you. A week ago you just wanted Thayler's coin back. You didn't want to rob my cab, right? You just didn't know how else to get your good luck charm back with no questions asked. You didn't do it for the money, right? You did it for love. You were so straight you threw away the cash. Now here you are with a gun pointed at a cop—"

"Shut up!"

I took a deep breath and said, "You haven't got the style, Marcia. Your gun's not even loaded."

Mooney didn't relax a hair. Sometimes I think the guy hasn't ever believed a word I've said to him. But Marcia got shook. She pulled the barrel away from Mooney's skull and peered at it with a puzzled frown. JoAnn and I both tackled her before she got a chance to pull the trigger. I twisted the gun out of her hand. I was almost afraid to look inside. Mooney stared at me and I felt my mouth go dry and a trickle of sweat worm its way down my back.

I looked.

No bullets. My heart stopped fibrillating, and Mooney actually cracked a smile in my direction.

So that's all. I sure hope Mooney will spread the word around that I helped him nail Thayler. And I think he will; he's a fair kind of guy. Maybe it'll get me a case or two. Driving a cab is hard on the backside, you know?

THE PROBLEM
OF THE BOSTON
COMMON

EDWARD D. HOCH

It was a warm summer's afternoon and old Dr. Sam Hawthorne was pouring a bit of sherry at a little table on the back lawn, obviously enjoying the opportunity to be out of doors. "The air is so clear and fresh today," he commented. "When I was young it used to be like this all the time, even in the cities. Sometimes folks ask me if I ever solved an impossible crime in the city, and there were a couple over the years when business of some sort took me away from Northmont. The first one—a terrifying case—happened in Boston, in the late spring of 1928 . . ."

I'd gone to Boston with my nurse April (Dr. Sam continued), to attend a New England medical convention. It was my first opportunity to take a long drive in my new car—a tan Packard Runabout that had replaced my beloved Pierce-Arrow. Though the roads weren't nearly as good as they are today we made the drive in under two hours, and I was quite pleased with the Packard's performance. It was warm enough to ride with the top down, which April especially enjoyed. Some years back I'd taken her with me to an engagement party up at Newburyport and she still talked about the excitement of that auto trip. Now she was equally excited as we drove up to the fancy hotel facing the Boston

Common and the uniformed doorman hurried over to help us with our bags.

"Are you here for the medical convention, sir?" he asked.

"That's right. Dr. Sam Hawthorne from Northmont."

"Go right in and register at the desk. The bellman will take your bags and I'll park the car for you."

The first person we encountered in the lobby was gray-haired Dr. Craig Somerset, vice-chairman of the New England Medical Association. "Well, Sam Hawthorne! How've you been? How're things out in the country?"

"Fine, Craig. Good to see you again. This is my nurse, April. I brought her along to see the sights while I'm involved in all those dull meetings."

His look made April blush at once, but Craig Somerset was always the New England gentleman. "Nice to meet you, April. I hope you'll enjoy our city."

"I haven't been to Boston in ten years," she told him. "It's changed so much!"

"It has that," Dr. Somerset agreed. "This hotel wasn't even here ten years ago. There's a great view of the Common from the upper floors. A word of caution, though—don't walk across the Common in the early evening. We've had some trouble here in recent weeks."

"What sort of trouble?" I asked, assuming he spoke for April's benefit. "Someone molesting women?"

"More serious than that, I'm afraid." The lightness had gone out of his voice. "Three people have been murdered there, all in the early evening while it was still daylight. The killer seems to be absolutely invisible."

"I'll bet Dr. Sam could catch him," April said. "He's solved the most impossible-soundin' crimes you ever did hear of, back in Northmont."

"No, no," I protested. "I'm here for the convention, nothing more."

"And I want to talk to you about that," Somerset said. "I'd like you to fill a little gap in our program the day after tomorrow and speak to us on the problems of country medicine."

"I'm no public speaker, Craig."

"But you could do a fine job. It's an area of medicine most of these men know nothing about."

"Let me think about it overnight."

"How were the people killed?" April persisted, her curiosity aroused.

"It seems they were poisoned by a quick-acting substance injected into the skin," Somerset said. "The police are trying not to alarm the public, but I was called in as a consultant on the poison question."

"Back in Northmont I swear Sheriff Lens calls on Dr. Sam as much to solve crimes as the sick folk call on him to get healed."

"You're embarrassing me, April."

I'd completed the registration forms by that time and I could see the bellman waiting to show us up to our rooms. "We'll see you later, Craig."

In the elevator April remarked, "He thinks you brought me 'cause I'm your girl, Dr. Sam." Even the words made her blush.

"We won't worry about what he thinks." April was in her thirties, a few years older than me, and she'd been my nurse since I came to Northmont in 1922. She'd lost some weight since those earlier days but she was still a plain-looking country woman. I'd never thought about her romantically, though I did enjoy her company.

"Are you going to solve the murders for them?"

"No, I'm here to attend a medical convention."

But events were working against me. That evening, shortly after eight, the invisible killer claimed his fourth victim.

Dr. Somerset came to my door around 8:30, looking quite alarmed. "We'd like your help, Sam. There's been another killing."

"On the Common?"

"Yes, right across the street! Can you come down?"

I sighed. "Give me five minutes."

We crossed the street in silence to a spot just inside the Common where the body of a young woman lay sprawled against a tree. The police were busy photographing the scene, using flash powder in the beginning dusk. A burly detective who seemed to be in charge came over to us. "Is this your great sleuth, Dr. Somerset?"

"This is Sam Hawthorne, a physician from Northmont. He's here for the convention, and I understand he's had great success solving seemingly impossible crimes back home. Sam, this is Inspector Darnell."

I could see right away that this was no Sheriff Lens. Darnell was a big-city cop who obviously resented interference, especially from a country doctor. "Do you use a magnifying glass, Doc? Want to crawl around on the ground like Sherlock Holmes?"

"To tell you the truth I want to go back to my room."

Dr. Somerset was exasperated. "Look, Inspector, will it do any harm to tell Sam what you've got so far? He just might come up with an idea."

"Hell, we've tried everything else. What we've got now are four dead bodies. Two men, two women. This last one seems to be the youngest so far. One of the men was a drifter who panhandled in the park. Another was a young lawyer on his way home after working late at the office. Then there was a middle-aged woman out for a stroll in the early evening. And now this one."

"All poisoned?"

The detective nodded. "That's how Dr. Somerset got in on it. We needed a doctor's advice on the kind of poison. The autopsy showed the first three died of minute injections of curare, the South American arrow poison. That fact hasn't been released to the papers yet."

"Curare? On the Boston Common?" It was hard for me to believe. Even in medical school the subject of curare poisoning had been barely touched on. It wasn't something the average doctor ever encountered.

"Curare acts within a few minutes in humans, paralyzing the motor and respiratory muscles," Dr. Somerset explained. "The speed of death seems to depend somewhat on the size of the victim. A thousand-pound ox took forty-five minutes to die from curare in an experiment described in Charles Waterton's book *Wanderings in South America*."

"You know a lot more about curare than I do," I admitted.

"That's why I was called in by Inspector Darnell." He was staring down at the dead young woman. "It's a particularly insidious poison for the killer to use, because there is no pain and very little warning to the victim. There is some double vision and inability to swallow, then asphyxiation as lung muscles are affected. Admittedly it's a painless death, but it's also one that gives the victim no opportunity to call for help."

"How was the poison administered?" I asked. "With a hypodermic needle?"

Inspector Darnell knelt by the body and turned back the collar of the dead woman's white blouse. A tiny feathered dart protruded from the skin of her neck. "It's so small she might never have felt it—or if she did she thought it was an insect bite. In two of the earlier killings we never found the darts. The victims must have felt them hit and brushed them to the ground as one would a pesky mosquito. In the first killing the dart was snagged in the victim's clothing."

"A dart gun of some sort?" I suggested. "An air pistol might have a fairly long range."

"In South America the natives use blowguns six feet long," Dr. Somerset said.

"I can't picture a murderer using one of those," I said. "He wouldn't stay invisible for long. Have all the killings been at this time of day?"

"All in the evening, but before dark. We doubled the police patrol after the second killing, and filled the Common with plainclothes men after the third one. Now I guess we should close it to pedestrians altogether."

"I'd advise against that," Somerset argued. "The killer would simply move elsewhere, or wait for the Common to reopen. You want to capture him, not scare him off."

"We're finished with our pictures," one of the detectives told Inspector Darnell. "Can we move her?"

"Sure. Take her away."

"Any identification in her purse?" I asked.

"Rita Kolaski, a nurse at Boston Memorial. Probably on her way to work."

The Inspector moved away from us without a goodbye, following the covered stretcher to the street. I turned to Dr. Somerset and said, "I really don't see how I can help here, Craig. Back home in Northmont I'm dealing with people and places I've known for six years. I know the way they live and how they think. I'm out of my element here. Boston people even talk different."

"I'm only asking you to look for something the rest of us might be missing, Sam."

"The killer is a madman, there's no doubt of that. And it's hard enough to catch anyone who's rational."

"Sleep on it, Sam. If you think you can help us in any way, see me after the first session in the morning."

They walked back to the hotel and Somerset asked the doorman to get him a taxi. "Aren't you staying here?" I asked, surprised.

The doorman ran down to the corner blowing his whistle for a cab, and Somerset fished a coin from his pocket for a tip. "No, I'm staying at home. My wife insists on it."

Up in my room I sat for a long time by the window overlooking the Common, watching the lights of the policemen as they searched the area of the killing. After a time I pulled down the shade and went to bed.

Another Common Killing, the morning paper screamed in a bold black headline. April read the story over breakfast and I admitted that Somerset had come to my room for help.

"You were over there, Dr. Sam? You saw the body?"

"I've seen a lot of bodies, April."

"But in the city like this—"

"She'd have been just as dead in Northmont."

"You've got time before the first session. Take me over and show me where it happened."

There was no talking her out of it, so we crossed busy Tremont Street and I showed her the spot where Rita Kolaski had died. We strolled farther into the park then, past the burying ground and all the way to the soldiers monument. Then we turned west, walking across Charles Street to the Public Garden that adjoined Boston Common.

"Look at the swan boats!" April exclaimed as we came to an artificial lake. "The people pedal them with their feet!"

She was like a child on Christmas morning, and I took her for a ride around the lake in one of the swan boats, knowing I'd miss the first session of the convention. Afterward we walked along the Arlington Street side, past the Washington monument and on up to Beacon Street. Presently, circling around the north side of the Common, we came to the State House with its golden dome glistening in the morning sun.

"The morning paper says the first body was found over on this side of the Common," April said.

"It doesn't concern me."

"Honestly, sometimes you can be so stubborn!"

"We're here to enjoy the city, not to solve murders. Come on, tonight I'll take you to the movie at the new Metropolitan Theatre. They say it's a regular palace."

We walked back across the Common, which was almost empty for ten o'clock on a weekday morning. The newspaper scare headlines were apparently having their effect. April left me at the hotel to do some shopping and I went upstairs just in time to catch the end of the opening session.

Dr. Somerset caught me on the way out. "I have a noon meeting with the Inspector. Care to sit in?"

"This business really isn't for me, Craig. April and I walked around the Common this morning. It's like a foreign country to me."

"There's one thing about the murders we didn't tell you last night," Somerset said, lowering his voice. "The killer has been in communication with the police."

"Just like Jack the Ripper."

"Exactly. Come along and you can see the letters."

Somerset knew how to pique my curiosity. There was no way I could turn down that invitation. I sat through the second morning session only half attentive, listening to a professor from Harvard Medical School discuss the latest polio research. The subject was much in the news that month, since Al Smith had just asked polio victim Franklin D. Roosevelt to run for governor of New York.

I offered to drive Somerset to police headquarters in my new Packard but he insisted we take a cab. They were easy to get at the stand near the hotel and during the day at least there was no need to tip the doorman. Riding up Tremont, I watched the faces of the people we passed, wondering if one of them might be the killer. In Northmont I would have known their names. Here they were strangers. In Northmont I might have had a half-dozen suspects. Here, the whole city of Boston was suspect.

"This is your city, isn't it, Craig?"

"Always has been. You should set up practice here and you'd learn what medicine is all about."

"Oh, I'm learning that."

"Six years in the country! Are you going to spend your life in Northmont?"

"Maybe."

"We've got three-quarters of a million people in Boston, Sam, and we need more good young doctors like yourself."

"Why?" I asked with a smile. "Is Boston the hub of the universe?"

"It could be. How many cities do you know that have daily steamship service to New York?"

"Maybe your killer comes up from New York by boat every week."

"No," Somerset answered seriously, "he's from this area."

We alighted from the taxi and walked up the steps of Police Headquarters. Off in the distance I could see the pointed tower of the custom house, the city's tallest structure. I had to admit that Boston had a certain charm. It was different from the simple country charm of a place like Northmont, but no less appealing.

Crime here was also different. The letters that Inspector Darnell spread out on the desk before me could only have been described as the work of a madman. *Last evening was the first of the Common killings! There will be more! Cerberus!* And another: *Two dead and more to come! Boston will remember me! Cerberus!* And a third: *Another must die because of what you did! Remember me! Cerberus!*

"And last night's killing?" I asked.

"Nothing yet." Darnell sighed and relit the stub of a dead cigar. "It's probably in the mail."

"These haven't been released to the press?"

The Inspector shook his head. "This sort of maniac thrives on publicity. We're trying to give him as little as possible."

"I agree completely," Somerset said. "The public doesn't even know the killings are connected, though it's bound to come out soon."

"The mayor wants to close the Common completely till this Cerberus is caught, but as you heard last night Dr. Somerset has advised against that."

"You need to capture him, not just send him into his hole."

I was studying the notes, but I could make nothing out of them. "I can't help you on this," I said. "I have no idea who he could be."

"That's not what we want you for," Craig Somerset said. "We want to know how he's doing it."

Inspector Darnell nodded agreement. "*How*, Dr. Hawthorne. We already know *who* he is."

* * *

I must admit their words took me aback. "You know who the killer is and you haven't arrested him?"

Craig Somerset smiled. "It's not like Northmont, Sam. In the city a man can hide out for months without ever being found."

"I didn't spend the whole of my life in Northmont, you know. Just the last six years. I know what city life is like."

But did I, really? Had I been away from it too long?

Inspector Darnell cleared his throat. "You must realize, Dr. Hawthorne, that what we tell you must go no further than this room. The lives of innocent people could be endangered if this Cerberus becomes aware that we know his identity."

"It was the curare that led us to him, of course," Craig Somerset explained. "It's not the easiest substance in the world to obtain, and once it was identified as the cause of death I began checking around at various hospitals and research centers in the Boston vicinity. As you may know, Sam, research is under way to find uses for curare as a muscular relaxant. It's a difficult task, because even in tiny doses it seems to cause nausea and a drop in blood pressure. But I found a research lab in Cambridge that's been running tests with the poison. About six months ago a quantity of curare disappeared from their lab, along with a part-time research assistant named George Totter."

"Why would he take it?" I asked.

It was Darnell who answered. "They laid him off. The research was being done under a grant from a local charity. When the money ran out, the research had to stop. Apparently Totter wrote to the city for more funds, but they ignored him. He made the remark to a co-worker that maybe they'd pay attention if a few people in Boston died of curare poisoning. Shortly after that he disappeared, and the lab discovered a vial of the poison was missing too."

"How much was in the vial?" I asked.

"Enough to kill twenty or thirty people. They didn't report it at the time because nobody believed Totter capable of murder. But when Dr. Somerset started checking for missing curare the story came out quickly enough."

"Is there any other possible source of the poison?"

Somerset shook his head. "It's highly unlikely. As you know, curare comes from the bark of various South American trees. The lengthy and laborious process is a deeply guarded secret among certain native families and tribes. Some attempt has been made to duplicate the process in a laboratory, but thus far researchers must depend on the real thing, brought in from the jungles. Our killer must be using a laboratory supply, and this lab in Cambridge is the only one that has it in this whole area."

"All right," I said, "I'll accept this man Totter as your killer. And I'll accept the fact that he could remain hidden in Boston for months. Now tell me why you can't stop him from killing these people."

Darnell ground out the stub of his cigar. "The darts are fired from either an air pistol or a blowgun. If he's using an air pistol of some sort he could probably be fifty feet away and still hit his target."

"Farther than that," I suggested.

"No, not with these hand-made wooden darts. We've tried it. After fifty feet they start wobbling and tumbling in the air. With a blowgun the effective range is only twenty-five feet. And there's our problem. These killings have been in broad daylight, in a park at the very center of a large city. There are no out-of-the-way trails or heavily wooded places in the Common. It's roughly an irregular five-sided park that's only seventeen hundred feet across at its widest point. You can see from one side to the other. There's no place to hide, except behind a tree or statue, and there are people constantly passing through—especially in the early evening hours on spring days like this."

"A blowgun disguised as a cane?" I suggested. "It would take just an instant for the killer to raise it to his mouth."

"Maybe for the first two killings it could have been something like that, but the park was filled with plainclothes police when the third victim got it. Yet nobody saw a thing." He picked up a folder on his desk. "Rita Kolaski, last night's victim, was actually under surveillance at the moment she was killed."

"What?" This was news to Dr. Somerset, and he reacted with surprise.

"I just learned of it this morning. She was suspected of being party to a Volstead Act violation. Two Treasury agents were following her in hopes she'd lead them to her boy friend who's been running boatloads of liquor in from Nova Scotia. She crossed Tremont Street at the corner beyond your hotel and entered the Common at exactly 8:10. There was still plenty of daylight and both agents had a good view of her. They

were especially watchful of anyone who came close because they were
waiting for a contact with the boy friend.

"But nothing at all unusual happened. No one even glanced at her.
Nothing was pointed in her direction. She'd been walking in the park
for only about two minutes when her walk became unsteady. She paused
to lean against a tree and then collapsed. Our plainclothes men moved in
at once, but it was too late. The Treasury agents filed a report with their
superior and a copy was sent to me this morning."

"Surely she must have felt the dart hit her," I argued.

Darnell held up one of the feathered wooden shafts, half the length
of a matchstick. "Notice there's the point of a common pin embedded in
the wood. Don't touch it, there's still poison on it. When the dart hit it
would feel like little more than a pinprick. She might have reached up to
her hair, but the Treasury men would think nothing of that."

"I can't believe this pin point could carry enough curare to kill a
person so quickly," I said. "Besides, what if she'd brushed it off her
neck before the poison could act?"

"She didn't, and she died. We don't know how many people this
Totter—or Cerberus—might have fired at. Maybe there's a dozen more
that brushed the dart off and lived. All we know is that four of them
died."

"Just where on the Common were the bodies found?" I asked.

Darnell referred to a large-scale wall map where four red pins
dotted the green area of the Common. "The first one, Pete Jadas, was
found on the other side of the Common near the State House. He was a
former wrestler who'd fallen on hard times and taken to panhandling.
Simon Falk, a young lawyer who'd been working late at his Tremont
Street office, died right here, about in the middle of the Common. The
third victim, a waitress named Minnie Wiser, died here, on the next
walkway over from Rita Kolaski."

"Wrestler, lawyer, waitress, nurse," I mused. "I guess there's no
pattern there."

"No pattern at all. He kills whoever happens to be handy."

I was staring at the map, but it wasn't telling me a thing. "What
about that Cerberus signature?"

"A dog with three heads," Darnell snorted. "Greek mythology!"

"A dog from Hades," Somerset added.

"He must have chosen that name for a reason."

"What is reason to a madman?"

"All right," I said, getting up to leave.

"Where are you going?" Darnell asked.

"For another stroll on the Common."

It was the lunch hour now and the walks were more crowded. On benches people sat and chatted. One man was reading about the latest murder in the newspaper, but nobody seemed terribly concerned. They didn't know about the poisoned darts, or the letters from Cerberus.

I crossed over Charles Street to the Public Garden and went down to watch the swan boats again. That was when I noticed the man with the picnic hamper. He was dark and heavy-set, with unfriendly eyes, but the thing I especially noticed was the way he kept his right hand beneath the lid of the hamper at all times. He might almost have been holding something.

Like the trigger of an air pistol.

Whatever it was, he didn't look the sort who'd come here for a picnic. When he started walking back toward the Common, I followed, wishing that Inspector Darnell had shown me a photograph of George Totter.

The man's right hand was out of the hamper now, but still near its lid. I stayed just a few steps behind, watching that hand. When it moved, when the lid came up again, I ran forward. I needed only the briefest glimpse of the gun within and I slammed my fist down on the lid, pinning his hand inside. He let out a gasp of pain and released his grip on the hamper.

Then, before I knew what was happening, a second man spun me around from the rear. I felt a glancing blow to the side of my head and everything went black.

I must have been unconscious for several minutes.

When I finally came to, with a throbbing headache, I saw a circle of men bending over me. One of them was Inspector Darnell. "What in hell were you trying to do?" he demanded.

"I—"

"That was one of my plainclothes men you jumped on!"

"I'm sorry."

"You should be! If Totter was anywhere around you certainly scared him off!" He helped me to my feet and brushed the dirt from my suitcoat. "In the future you'd better stay off the Common, Dr. Hawthorne. If we need your help we'll call on you."

I mumbled more apologies and moved away, feeling like a fool. I just wasn't used to the ways of big-city police. Back in Northmont, Sheriff Lens could hardly be expected to fill the town square with deputies because he had only a couple of part-time men whom everybody knew. Here in Boston it was different, maybe too different for me. Had six years in Northmont changed my perceptions that much?

I found April in front of the hotel, asking the doorman for directions to Paul Revere's House. "I figured I might as well see some historical sights while I'm here," she said. "Want to come along?"

"I don't think so, April."

I turned my head and she noticed the bruise where the second cop had hit me. "What happened to you?"

"Just a little accident."

"Let me get you upstairs and wash that! Did you fall?"

"I'll tell you about it."

She listened to my tale with much clucking as she bathed the bruise with cold water. "You're not even safe from the police in this city!" she decided.

"Don't be too hard on them, April. It really was my fault."

"Well, a gun in a picnic hamper! What were you to think!"

"They called Inspector Darnell right away. They must have thought they had the killer." I told her what I'd learned.

"Don't they have a picture of this fellow Totter?"

I shook my head. "And only a general sort of description."

I opened my medical bag and found a powder to take for my headache. Then I settled down to relax. Almost at once there was a knock at the door. April opened it and Craig Somerset hurried in. "I just heard what happened. Are you all right?"

"I guess I'll live."

"Good God, they didn't have to slug you with a blackjack!"

"I suppose they thought I was the killer."

"Darnell is sorry about it."

"So am I."

"The afternoon mail brought another letter from George Totter."

I came alert at once. "If it really is Totter. What does it say?"

"Darnell let me make a copy to show you. Mailed just before

midnight from the main post office." He held out a page from his notebook and I read: *Four down and more to come! I won't wait so long next time! Cerberus!*

"What is Darnell's plan to do next?" I asked.

"Keep watching the Common. Hope they can spot him the next time. What else is there to do, except close up downtown and throw the city into a panic?"

"There were two Treasury men watching the fourth victim and they didn't see a thing. What makes Darnell think he'll see the killer next time?"

"Sooner or later—"

"Sooner or later! Doesn't Darnell realize he's dealing with an invisible man? Someone like Chesterton's postman who's there but isn't there?"

Craig Somerset pursed his lips. "Could it be one of the plainclothes men assigned to the park?"

"Stranger things have happened. But if Cerberus—"

"What is it?"

"Just an idea. That map on Darnell's wall showing the location of the killings—do you think we could borrow it? Or make another?"

"What for, Sam?"

"You asked me to speak to the convention on the problems of country medicine. Suppose I speak instead on curare poisoning."

"What? But you're no expert—"

"I think I've learned enough these last two days. Let's see, I'm scheduled to speak late tomorrow afternoon. Is that right?"

"Four o'clock."

"Good. I think I'll spend the morning out at that research lab, brushing up on curare." As an afterthought I said, "And be sure to post the topic of my talk on the schedule in the lobby. I want as large an audience as possible."

As the time for my speech drew near, April was beside herself. "What if the killer learns you're givin' this talk, Dr. Sam? He might pick you for the next victim!"

"Now don't you worry your head, April. I'll be all right."

But she stuck by my side all the way down to the second floor, where a big meeting room had been assigned for my talk. I looked out on the rows of chairs, just now receiving the first arrivals, and felt just the least bit apprehensive. But to be honest I think I was more afraid of speaking in public than of the murderer. Directly behind me the large curtained windows looked out on the Common across Tremont Street.

"He could be down there in the park, watchin' us through binoculars right this minute!" April said, obviously worried.

"I think he's a lot closer than that," I said, watching the doctors file in. I was surprised to see Inspector Darnell take up a position near the door. Somerset had obviously alerted him to the subject of my talk, in order to obtain the map I needed.

Exactly at four o'clock, with the room more than three-quarters full, Craig Somerset strode to the podium. "Are you ready, Sam?"

"Ready as I'll ever be."

He turned to the audience and spoke loudly so that his voice would carry through the room. "Gentlemen—and I note a few ladies with us today as well—our speaker this afternoon is Dr. Sam Hawthorne, a relatively young man who has spent his six years as a physician in caring for the ills of the people of Northmont, about two hours' drive from here. Yes, Sam Hawthorne is a country doctor—the backbone of our medical practice. He was planning to speak to us today on the problems of medical practice in a small town, but as most of you know he's chosen to change his topic. In recent weeks four persons have died on the Common across the street from this hotel. Only today the police admitted to the press that all four died of curare poisoning. And it is that poisoning—so rarely encountered in general practice—which is the subject of Sam Hawthorne's talk."

When he'd completed the introduction I stepped to the podium and began to read from my notes, covering a history of curare and the early experiments by Charles Waterton in Dutch Guiana. Then I touched on the Boston-area experiments before getting to my main point.

"You see behind me, on my left, a large-scale map of downtown Boston. The points where the four curare victims died are clearly marked. But as you know from my previous remarks, curare does not kill instantly. You might say, the police have said, that a poison which kills within a few minutes is instant enough. But the truth is that a person can walk all the way across the Common in a few minutes. I've done it.

"The idea occurred to me that the invisible killer the police are seeking might not be roaming the park seeking out victims at all. His poisoned darts might all be fired from one location, and it might have been the dying victims who moved rather than the killer. Looking at this map, is such a possibility feasible?"

There was a stir of interest from the audience and I saw Inspector Darnell straighten up in the back row. I glanced over at April and hurried on. "We've already seen that the speed with which curare kills depends very much on the size and weight of the victim. An average person lives only a few minutes. A thousand-pound ox lives forty-five minutes. I checked the weights of the four victims this morning, but even without knowing them I could make certain guesses.

"The first victim, a drifter who'd been a wrestler, was found on the far side of the Common near the State House. My guess was that a former wrestler might be the heaviest of the victims—since the others were a young lawyer and two women. In that I was correct. He weighed the most, and therefore—assuming the curare doses to be about equal—would have taken the longest to die."

I could see I had them now. The doctors were hanging on every word, and all my early nervousness had vanished. "The young lawyer was found in the middle of the Common, and the two women closer to this side. The latest victim, being the smallest of the four, died the quickest. She was actually observed entering the Common from Tremont Street, just down at the corner here. The lawyer, we know, was coming from his office on Tremont Street. The waitress and the ex-wrestler both could have entered the Common from Tremont as well.

"I submit to you, Inspector Darnell, and to my distinguished audience, that the invisible killer is not in the Common at all, but right here on Tremont, hitting his victims *as they enter the park*."

My wind-up after that was anti-climactic. I couldn't give them the name of the murderer, so I ended with a few generalities about police work in poisoning cases, and then stepped back while Dr. Somerset said a few words of thanks. Doctors from the audience were grouped around me at the end, asking questions, but after a few pleasantries I made my escape.

"You were great, Dr. Sam," April assured me. "I can see Inspector Darnell coming our way."

"Come on, let's get out of here."

"Dr. Hawthorne!" Darnell called. "Let me have a word with you! I'm sorry about yesterday."

"That's all right."

"That was a very interesting theory. You seemed to be saying that the killer might be someone right around here. But how—"

"I have to go now." I broke away and headed for the elevator. If my idea was right, I could be in great danger.

Craig Somerset was hurrying after me too, but I jumped between the closing doors of the elevator and left him standing there with April and the Inspector. I knew it would be only a few moments before they caught the next elevator and came after me.

Downstairs I hurried across the lobby and out into Tremont Street. "Get me a cab, will you?" I asked the doorman.

"Certainly, sir."

He stepped behind me and blew his whistle and I felt the pinprick of a bite on my neck.

That was when I moved, as fast as I could, plucking the tiny dart from my skin and throwing myself on the uniformed doorman. Darnell and April and Somerset came through the revolving door as I wrestled the doorman to the sidewalk.

"Here's your killer!" I shouted. "Mr. George Totter, in person! April, there's a hypodermic needle in my right-hand pocket with an antidote for curare poisoning. I need it—hurry!"

What with all the police business and newspaper interviews after that, it wasn't till the drive back to Northmont the next afternoon that April and I had any time alone. "What a foolish thing to do!" she berated me. "Setting yourself up as a target for that madman!"

"Someone had to do it, April. The police were content to wait for the next victim, but I wasn't. I figured that the curare speech, advertised in the lobby, would attract his attention. But I probably wouldn't have risked it if that research lab hadn't given me a hypodermic full of an antidote they've been testing."

"Who would have thought of the doorman!"

"Once I established the victims had probably entered the Common from the Tremont Street side I started looking for somebody who was stationed there regularly. The doorman, whistling for taxis—sometimes even going up to the corner to get them—was in a perfect position to fire those darts at people crossing the street to enter the park. People saw him put something to his mouth and blow, but it was such an innocent gesture for him that they never noticed it. His whistle—a long slender one similar to the ones London bobbies use—had a tube like a short pea shooter taped to it. The tiny darts would be inaccurate at more than five or ten feet, but the point was he could get quite close to his victims before firing. He chose people heading for the Common so they'd die there. In his confession he said he'd fired more than a dozen darts in all, but some missed and the others were brushed off by the victims before the poison could take effect."

"Dr. Sam, you purposely ran ahead of us all in the hotel yesterday. You knew he was going to try for you and you didn't want us in danger."

"I was sure he would try. All the killings were in the early evening, so I figured it was the doorman who came on duty in the late afternoon. He knew I was the curare speaker and I thought I'd offer him a tempting target."

"You were that sure it was the doorman?"

"People like that want to be caught, April. Totter was telling the police who he was in those notes he sent, only they didn't understand him. Cerberus was a three-headed dog from Hades all right—he guarded the entrance! The word is sometimes used to signify a watchful guard or doorkeeper."

"You did pretty good in the big city, Dr. Sam."

"But it's good to be home."

"And that's how I caught the Boston Common killer," Dr. Sam Hawthorne concluded. "He was invisible only because nobody noticed him. But this sherry is invisible because the bottle is empty! Come inside and I'll give you another small—ah—libation. And if you have time I'll tell you about what I found back in Northmont that summer— an impossible murder right in our general store."

THE DIPPING OF
THE CANDLEMAKER

HAYDEN HOWARD

On a frosty morn, when a rigid gentleman, wigg'd, powder'd, and exhaling vapors like a dragon, stamp'd into our printing-house with his red cloak flung back in anger, I smiled secretly at the stick of type I was composing. For here was Colonel Clinton of the Assembly.

Now, thought I, it is my brother James's turn to bend the knee!

While breaking our fast, we had fallen into another of our disputations, and he, unwilling to admit himself trapp'd in contradiction by my devious Socratic inquiries, beat me passionately, which I took extreamly amiss; and, thinking my apprenticeship to him very tedious, I was wishing for some means of shortening it.

Most merrily I listen'd to Colonel Clinton berate him for some political piece lately appearing in our weekly newspaper. Yet I admired my brother for refusing to give up the name of its author who had made so free with our Massachusetts Assembly.

As the Colonel's threats crimson'd my brother, I began to fear the loosing of his too-ready fist. In this uneasy year of King George, 1722, to strike a member of the Assembly would mean something worse than the pillory.

But my brother was, for the moment, saved; such an outcry arising from Queen Street that both men rush'd to the doorway. I glanced at my

38

work, an advertisement for the sale of several Palatine maids, time of most of them five years. Tho' my brother might beat me again, I set aside my composing stick and ran after them on to the cobblestones. For the shouting had grown from "Seize him" to "Murder, murder most foule!"—which made me most curious.

All Boston seem'd running: hardy ropewalkmen, unkempt 'prentices, grimy pewterers jostled by His Majesty's grenadiers flush'd as red as their coats from grog, and good-wives scurrying with their gowns above their ankles and their tongues awagging. I was surprised to see the mob revolving beneath the wooden boot that advertised the shoemaker's stall; they were clamouring around the old cobbler and the huge Irish 'prentice lad as he held as easily as a partner in a dance.

The lad, Dennis O'Leary, apprentice to the candlemaker, stood meekly downcast, while round them, leaping like a bewigg'd frog in his excitement, shouted the candlemaker's tenant, little Warwick Lowther, a silversmith whose voice was the largest part of him: "Murder, he has murder'd his master!"

"Here, man, be silent!" Colonel Clinton snapp'd, and order'd that the lad be march'd back to the candlemaker's to view his abominable crime and confess to save his soul.

Thinking to remain out of my brother's notice, I follow'd at the coattails of the crowd, Dennis was shaking his red locks in confusion, in obvious denial as they propell'd him into the cavernous shop and into its dim after-part, where their numbers obstructed my curiosity.

Above their heads the rafters rose steeply to the high wall which divided the house in halves. I knew the ground floor of the other half to be the sleeping quarters of the candlemaker, named Mr. Gill, and his intemperate uncle, and also of Dennis. Above it was a garret, reach'd by the narrow staircase fix'd to this side of the wall and tenanted by little Warwick Lowther, silversmith, and his wife and brood of six or seven.

I climb'd upon the silversmith's table in the fore-part of the shop, being careful not to upset his neatly hammer'd porringers, sauce boats, wall sconces, and candlesticks, and wondering that some knave might not take this opportunity to steal them. For, lately, many Boston houses had been enter'd for their silver. A coldness slosh'd upon my shoe. I perceived I had jostled a pail of fresh beer, but thought no more of this as I stared over the heads of the crowd at a most unnatural sight.

Beneath the horizontal spokes of Mr. Gill's candle-dipping

machine, the mammoth kettle of wax seem'd stuff'd with the blue broadcloth from which coats are sewn. Two bulbous lumps of the cloth droop'd over the edge of the kettle, and from them hung gray woolens, narrowing to white stockings, which terminated in large leather shoes.

"Draw him out," the Colonel order'd.

With a greasily osculating sound, the candlemaker's shoulders and head were withdrawn from his kettle. The breathless room sweeten'd with the fragrance of bayberry wax. A horrid sight Mr. Gill's corpse made, with the greenish wax flowing downward on his features as if he were a waxwork during the Great Fire.

Around his hips, which had been at the surface of the kettle, the harden'd wax gave him strange proportions. And a wag blurted: "Silversmiths oft hammer their thumbs, but never before has a candlemaker dipp'd himself."

Some titter'd, some reproved, all talk'd. My brother thrust his hand into the kettle, but instantly withdrew it, the pan of coals beneath not being wholly expired. Recoursing to the poker, he hook'd out Mr. Gill's sodden wig. Never one to remain a modest spectator, he thrust it at Dennis O'Leary's nose, shouting: "Confess, I say! Here is the evidence. Blood upon your master's wig."

Altho' this show'd Mr. Gill had been struck down, I wonder'd that my brother was so easily convinced of Dennis's guilt. For a head bleeds whether struck by an apprentice or another. And I lean'd forward to hear the Irish lad's denial.

"God witness, sir," Dennis cried, "I found him thus—when I return'd from the *Sailor's Pleasure*. He'd sent me for a pail of beer. I would o' pull'd him out. But Mr. Lowther rush'd at me. He shouted 'Murder' and—chased me into the street."

"He fled from his conscience," the little silversmith retorted, his own fair and freckled complexion as flush'd as the boy's.

"See the terror of guilt upon the lad's face," my brother added.

Colonel Clinton silenced them with a dagger'd glance. I, too, was angered by my brother, believing his opinion to be poison'd against all apprentices. And, further, I consider'd Dennis my friend, lately we having done much walking together at dusk along the ship-wharves, exchanging our grievances.

I knew full well the mindless drudgery of candlemaking, my own father being a tallow chandler, and I his unwilling helper, boiling tallow, straining tallow, pouring tallow into moulds, until I was twelve and he, detecting I would run away to sea, apprenticed me to my brother to learn the printing trade. My brother had since treated me, I consider'd, no better than a bound-boy. I did not acknowledge that my overweening tongue was the chief cause of this. And Dennis now seem'd a symbol of myself persecuted.

I resolved to speak up for him, tho': those who in quarrels interpose, must often wipe a bloody nose. Prudently, I climbed down from the table so that my brother might not see who had spoken.

"Witness how the wax has harden'd about the waist," I cried. "From this I deduce that Mr. Gill has been a long time in his kettle, cooling. Yet we know the lad has but recently return'd. Here, on the table, his pail of beer still has a head on it."

This last turn'd the heads of the crowd, and my brother, with knitting brows, recognized me.

" 'Tis true!" the old cobbler exclaim'd. "The boy had pass'd my bench with his pail of beer and before twenty pegs were driven I heard shouts of 'Seize him' and he return'd like a cut-purse pursued."

Even little Warwick Lowther clapp'd his hand to his wig. " 'Tis true! My apologies. When I left my wife and children and came on to the stair, I observed the boy bending strangely over his master down there, and I rush'd to interfere. 'Twas only his flight that convinced me of his guilt."

The little silversmith made his way to his landlord's apprentice and, reaching up, placed his hand upon the lad's shoulder. "Tho' Dennis has been employ'd here but a short time, I have observed him to be mild of temper. Yet there is another with whom my landlord often exchanged blows."

"Blossom!" the apprentice gasp'd.

"Aye, Mr. Gill's uncle it well may be," Warwick Lowther replied.

All look'd about. Blossom Gill was so called for the grog blossoms studding his corpulent visage. An old man and living on his nephew's charity, nevertheless he would not take orders in good spirit from the candlemaker, and their quarreling could be heard even to our printing-shop, particularly when they had both been taking spirits of another order.

"Look for Blossom under the horses' legs," my brother laughed.

"He should have return'd by now," Warwick Lowther suggested, "if he were innocent. After the lad set out for the *Sailor's Pleasure*, a very considerable walk, Mr. Gill ask'd his uncle to fetch the cart, for they would go bayberrying on the morrow. Blossom retorted for him to fetch it himself. And tho' it is less than a hundred paces from this rear doorway to the wheelwright's, they were still squabbling when I ascended the stairway to take my tea in a less blasphemous atmosphere."

The little silversmith raised his forefinger with the questioning gesture of a minister of the gospel. "If Blossom set out for the cart, why did he not return before the boy? The expectation of beer would have quickened his pace. You can see the cart is not at the rear doorway. Therefore, I fear Blossom persisted in his refusal to fetch it, and blows were exchanged. Then rage overcame all mercy. Murder! Affrighted by his deed, the old man has fled."

"After him! Before he escapes to the ships!" my brother cried.

"Silence!" Colonel Clinton's voice cracked over the mob like a carter's whip, and he directed some men to run to the Long Wharf, others in the direction of the Fort, still others toward the Common and the Charles River, and a final group, including my brother James and myself, to inquire at the wheelwright's, then search the nearby taverns and stables.

But he call'd me back. I must remain to watch that nothing be stolen from the shop. To this I was not averse, my curiosity to examine the mark of the blow, to infer the weapon employ'd, to search the shop for it, being far greater than any boyish urge to fox-hound through the streets after a drunken old man.

At the front of the shop, on Warwick Lowther's work bench, none of the hammers and mallets show'd blood. In the main door, however, I noticed the long iron key to have been left carelessly in the lock. Since any knave might remove it, in order to return stealthily by night and attack the silversmith's strong-box, I took the key out, and shook my head. For its crude bit had but a single notch. The lock was single-warded. A child could have pick'd it.

I carried the key to Dennis, who sat upon the staircase with his face buried between his hands so that his red hair appear'd to be a pile of flame above them. When he look'd up, I ask'd him kindly: "Did your master, forgetting, leave his key in the door?"

"It is my key," he blurted. "Mr. Gill gave it to me, God rest his soul. Unlock'd the door, I did, and saw Mr. Gill's legs hanging from the kettle. I set down the pail and rush'd to pull him out, forgetting the key."

"Was there a reason the shop was not open for trade?" I ask'd.

"I know it not," he sighed. "I was surprised the door would not open, and quickly unlock'd it. For Mr. Gill and his uncle seem'd always impatient for their beer. Believe me, I found my master thus!" Fear raised the pitch of his voice. "You shan't tell of the threats I made against him whilst you and I walk'd on the ship-wharves?"

"Empty threats are common among apprentices," I said slowly, eyeing the trapezoid of sunlight that lay from the rear doorway across the wax'd floor, the huge kettle, and the base of the candle-dipping machine. "Was the rear door also closed?"

"My head was pounding too fast for me to notice such little things," Dennis replied.

"Was there sunlight upon the kettle or upon your master's blue coattails?" I persisted.

"Aye!" the Irish lad exclaim'd, wonderingly. "Into the dimness of the shop I came, and the first sight that struck my eyes was a spot of bright blue."

"So the rear door was left open," I mused. "Is this usual?"

Dennis nodded. "It helps draw off the wax vapors."

"But is it usual, the rear door open when the front door is lock'd?" I continued, to which he shook his tousled head.

I would have ask'd him whether Blossom Gill and Warwick Lowther own'd keys to the door, but this seem'd certain. And, a mouth being better closed when there is no longer wisdom behind it, I held my peace and review'd the circumstances: the candlemaker dead in his kettle, Warwick Lowther above stairs drinking his tea, the front door lock'd, the rear door open. The weapon—here I realized I had been foolishly searching for it before examining the wound, which would show whether the weapon be sharp or blunt, light or heavy, smooth or irregular.

Before I could reach the corpse, Colonel Clinton shouted angrily: "Here, you, lad, where has Lowther gone? The villain, he has fled! Have you been asleep, you dolt?"

Tho' I had been instructed to watch the silver, not the silversmith, I flush'd and ran up the stairs to Warwick Lowther's garret. His wife, a slight, dark-hair'd woman much sagg'd from child-bearing, retorted he was not there and follow'd me down.

"All is safe, sir," I assured the Colonel, "for his wife and children are still here."

Colonel Clinton's eyes narrow'd at Mrs. Lowther, and he mutter'd: "Nevertheless, men have deserted their families to preserve their own necks."

"Mr. Lowther has gone with the others," she rebuff'd him bravely, "to search for that evil old man. Fight, fight, it is all those two kinsmen did. I should have known it would end this way. Their drunken voices rose nightly to our quarters as if they were shouting up a hollow tree."

Embarrass'd, hoping the little silversmith had not deserted, leaving her to fend for six or seven young ones, I knelt beside the corpse. Mr. Gill's waxen face had now harden'd so that he seem'd a man frozen in green ice, and I peel'd away the greenish wax adhering to his closely tonsured yellow hair. The indentation on the back of his skull, I would have wager'd a sovereign, was made by the curved and bluntly pointed end of the poker.

Since my brother had employ'd the poker to retrieve the deceased's wig, blood could no longer be seen upon it. And I wonder'd if there might be certain chemicals which, applied to even the smallest trace of blood, would give off an accusing smoke or other indication that there was the victim's life-blood.

Even more useful, I ponder'd, would be a white powder which, sprinkled on the suspect's hand, would be distinctively color'd by the oil of his skin. The same white powder being sprinkled on the handle of the poker would turn a like colour if the villain had gripped it. But, replied the less fanciful side of my intellect, a murder weapon is immediately pass'd around by the curious, so that a useless rainbow-colour'd powder would invariably be the result.

What would completely simplify this life-and-death problem, I mused, and rule out all danger of faulty human deductions, as well as the need for the foregoing inventions, would be a clockwork mounted beside a horn which concentrates the suspect's voice upon a brass cymbal. Perhaps experiment would show that when a man utters a lie, his voice produces such unnatural vibrations that the cymbal, tuned to them alone, would vibrate. This motion could be transmitted by means of a lever to the clockwork, which would then strike a chime, infallibly declaring the falsehood.

I stood up and examin'd the bleach'd wig hairs clinging to the once or twice dipp'd wicks on the dipping frame above the kettle. Since invention of the foregoing mechanisms, if possible at all, would require more time and knowledge than was presently at my disposal, I determined that my truth-machine must be constructed of Pure Reason, systematically applied. For, having interceded once in this inquiry, my youthful pride would not permit me to withdraw from it.

Yet, I warn'd myself, I must not hazard an opinion as to the identity of the murderer. Rather, I should arrange the evidence as if it were columns of figures, and let the sum totals finally determine the guilt. Otherwise, I will tend to notice and consider mainly the evidence pointing toward the most likely suspect, and thereby risk building a false case. This is because, being a reasonable creature, I am able to find reasons for anything I have decided to believe. And today a man's life is at stake.

Turning, I observed on the next frame of wicks a few strangely short hairs of fiery red. And glancing covertly at my Irish friend, I felt my resolve of mathematical detachment sorely tax'd.

At least the red hairs are on a different frame from the white wig hairs, I puzzled, and turn'd again to the candle-dipping machine.

It consisted of a large cart-wheel mounted horizontally atop a stout post higher than my head. The rim had been saw'd out, leaving the six spokes, and loop'd from the end of each spoke by a leather strap was a dipping frame of cross'd dowels, with long wicks hanging from them nearly to the kettle.

In operation, each frame, in its turn, was taken down by hand from its spoke and lower'd, its wicks descending into the liquid wax, then hung up again for the wax to harden, the machine being turn'd so that the next frame might be then taken down.

Thus, I would have expected the murderer's hair, as he bent the candlemaker into the kettle, to have brush'd against the *same* frame of wicks as did Mr. Gill's white wig.

Yet I wonder'd if Dennis might have dallied outside with his empty pail until the old man finally went for the cart and the silversmith mounted to his garret. Then the strong lad might swiftly have return'd, struck down and drown'd his master in wax, lock'd the front door so that no customer might enter and discover the body too soon, then hurried to the *Sailor's Pleasure*.

The other two would testify he left before them, and because of the hardness of the wax and the head on the beer when he return'd to discover the body, it would seem the murder had been done some time before, in his absence.

I could see the streaks of wax gleaming on Dennis's red hair. Yet this is not conclusive, I argued, for he works often at the dipping machine. Further, he would have expected the old man to return before him. Still further, he would not have fled in such a guilty manner when Warwick Lowther rush'd down the stairs at him; yet one never knows how one will react with his life in the balance.

I must cease these suppositions, I thought sternly, and gather more substance. A house is not constructed by first hammering together the roof in empty air.

Examining the double-boilers on the hearth, I reflected that making bayberry candles would be less onerous than pouring tallow ones as I had done. The excursions to gather berries would be pleasant, and boiling the wax from them would produce a woodsy fragrance rather than the slaughterhouse stench of boiling tallow. Because the bayberry wax shrinks on cooling, it cannot be pour'd in molds, and is therefore dipp'd—a pleasant, rhythmic labour like press-work. I began to think the candlemaker's apprentice complain'd too much.

And I toy'd with one of the greenish candles. It did not feel greasy, like a tallow candle. Tho' of more irregular shape than cast candles, a greater price was ask'd, for bayberry candles will not droop against the wall in hot weather, and the snuff is pleasant rather than foul. The smoke is consider'd an aid for parted lovers; each lighting a bayberry candle at the appointed hour, tho' the Atlantic Ocean separate them, the two smokes are believed to mingle.

I wonder'd that, with two to help him, Mr. Gill had not produced larger quantities of candles and thus offer'd really worrisome competition to my father. Above the mantel was painted the old rhyme:

> *A bayberry candle*
> *Burn'd to the socket*
> *Brings luck to the house*
> *And gold to the pocket.*

I doubted it had brought much gold to Mr. Gill's pocket. For laziness travels so slowly that poverty soon overtakes him. Yet the candlemaker was still known as a buyer of expensive trifles, and I wonder'd that Warwick Lowther's rent was enough to support Mr. Gill's continuing extravagance.

Thus I began to smell a dead mouse.

Indeed I now doubted that the little silversmith was capable of paying any rent at all. He was said to have fled Providence to avoid debtor's prison, and I thought it unlikely he would better his lot here, since many Massachusetts folk would as soon commission their silverware from a Papist, or Lucifer himself, as from a Rhode Island free-thinker. And Boston already housed an excellent silversmith.

With seven or eight mouths to feed, Warwick Lowther must scent the foul odour of a debtor's prison no matter which way the wind blows. Were he a larger, stronger man he might exchange his tools and silver for an axe, a plow, and oxen, and escape to the wilderness, westward into the valley of the Connecticut River, where Indians would take more than his wig. But that he had escaped from Providence with silver enough to make the articles display'd upon his table was puzzle enough for me.

Suddenly a portion of the mob flow'd back into the shop, their teeth showing with satisfaction, for they dragg'd Blossom Gill in their midst. Prominent among them, little Warwick Lowther bent a knee to the Colonel. "Sir, we discover'd him in a ditch behind the wheelwright's."

"Dead drunk," my brother James added, and the Colonel afforded my kin such an ill-temper'd glance he would have been wiser to have removed himself at once to our printing-house.

Hulking old Blossom sway'd between the pushing hands of his captors. He blink'd like an owl in the daylight, and when Colonel Clinton snapp'd at him: "Confess!" he fell heavily to his knees and the mob guffaw'd. The old man's limbs would not support him. The Colonel whirl'd about, unable to silence the mob, and pointed his ring'd hand at the body of Mr. Gill.

"You, sot, can you see what *that* is?" the Colonel cried.

There was no answer, for Blossom Gill had sunk his elbows and forehead to the floor, drunk as an Iroquois. Colonel Clinton, sliding forward like a dancing-master, kick'd him smartly. "Get up, I say!"

Disliking to see even a confirm'd drammer kick'd, even by a

gentleman, I put my arm under the old man's, my brother took the other, and we lifted Blossom upright. The Colonel then kick'd his leg with such force he near brought down the three of us. This seem'd, however, to waken the old man, and he mutter'd: "It ish my brother's son."

"Why did you not return at once with the cart?" the Colonel demanded.

"Wush waiting for it."

"In a ditch?" Colonel Clinton demanded. "Why did you not return? You knew the boy had been sent for beer!"

"Bottle of rum," Blossom gurgled. "Made my nephew give it to me, or I will go to the mashi-magistrate and we shwing together."

The Colonel's eyes narrow'd. "Smugglers, eh, like half of these people. So, you murder'd your nephew for a bottle of rum. Speak up, I say!"

"Not shmugglers," the old man mutter'd, but the mob had grown so noisy, I believe the Colonel thought Blossom had mouth'd some imprecation against him; for he deliver'd another savage kick.

"In the Name of the King, confess!" Colonel Clinton raged, and, receiving no answer, set to kicking him with such force the old man jerk'd in our arms like Kidd upon the gallows.

"Hold, sir," my brother protested, and express'd himself in somewhat contradiction to his own previously officious conduct. "Boston is no longer a hamlet without proper magistrates; therefore these men should be speedily brought before them. Private enquiry is usurpation."

This insulted the Colonel extreamly, and he turn'd to the mob. "Upon my orders, throw this fork-tongued printer's devil into the street!" And there being a few in every crowd who tug their forelocks and jump to obey the meanest order so long as it springs from someone they consider of exalted rank, my brother was dragg'd, loudly protesting, from the shop.

I was allow'd to remain, I think, because the Colonel had forgotten whose apprentice I was and, perchance, imagined me a useful lackey, though a half-wit. On my part, I resolved to disappoint him as to the latter.

"Pardon, sir," call'd the burly wheelwright who had jostled to the front rank. "The old man did come for the cart, but in fixen one spoke, I broken another. Wait he does, and drink. The wheel, when iss finished, the old man iss not there."

The colonel shrugg'd and again address'd Blossom Gill. "Confess, you toss-pot!"

The old man lolled against me as if requiring sleep, and I was reminded of a beast peculiar to this continent and call'd The Oppussum, which, when surrounded by huntsmen, feigns death, tho' whether through fright or cunning I do not know.

"Sir," Warwick Lowther politely interposed. "Note the bruise upon the old man's forehead. So often did the two of them come to blows, I fear'd it would end thus in tragedy. And note the stripes of wax upon his wig. No doubt these were acquired when he bent forward against the frame of wicks, while thrusting his nephew's head into the kettle."

"Quite correct," the Colonel replied, pleased. "I was about to announce the same conclusion. What do you say to that, sot?"

My own thought was this evidence was far from conclusive, since Blossom work'd often dipping candles, and wax upon his wig would have been more suspicious by its absence.

"I shay you'll shwing along 'o us, Warwick Lowther," the old man gurgled angrily, his grog blossoms lighting up like coals in a high wind. "You begging sho meek, please we let you go free to the wilderness and you'll never tell nor do us harm!"

Blossom Gill's mind seem'd fix'd on something that had been troubling him prior to the murder, for he raved on: "Ash this shilversmith where he got his silver, shir! I tell you, and roof over hish head. My nephew takes him in to melt and rework and sell the silver we have acquired, yesh, *acquired*, hah! But we do not trust this little man, and my nephew ashts him to accompany him through the window of the Reverend Dr. Mather, to acquire silver, and to fit his little neck in the noose so that Warwick Lowther dare not inform!"

As Blossom sagg'd against me, I wonder'd that his tongue had grown so quickly nimble for one so deeply sotted, and he gasp'd thinly: "I—I wanted no part of thish. From the firsht, I had no part in it, and I would have gone to the authorities, but my nephew would have kill'd me. He shouted at thish little silversmith, 'I already own you, body and soul.' And Lowther finally said he would go with him. Tho' I warn'd

against it, to-night is the night the window was to be forsh'd. But to-day
my nephew ish murder'd!"

"If these men were the silver thieves," Warwick Lowther shouted
clearly above the tumult, "I knew nothing of it."

"So your silver appearsh like shwallows from the mud, hah?"
Blossom Gill challenged. "You dare not unlock the shtrong-box and
show them Mr. Samuel Sewall's silver plate, much of it not yet melted
into lumpsh, hah?"

With his face red with anger beneath his white wig, the little
silversmith drew a brass key from his waistcoat and march'd to the
strong-box, which was of old oak, bound with much iron. He pointed a
white finger at Blossom, saying: "Now give up your key, old fox!"

I saw the strong-box wore three locks, and by the time Blossom
had dug his key from his small-clothes, Warwick Lowther had unlock'd
his. Blossom's key was a clumsy, single-notched one and took much
twisting before it would open its lock. The candlemaker's key could not
be discover'd in his pockets, and I consider'd offering to pick his lock,
but one's a fool who cannot conceal such wisdom. I held my peace and
join'd them in searching the corpse. About its neck was a loop of string,
which, being torn from its sheen of wax and drawn out, reveal'd the
third key.

When the lid of the strong-box was raised, we found only a bag of
foreign coins of small worth, a new silver spoon that had split from too
much hammering, and some ancient account books. The old man look'd
about wildly.

"Now you see he lies," Warwick Lowther said. "Ask the boy if
Blossom is not lying so that my neck be stretch'd for murder instead of
his own."

Dennis O'Leary, turning pale, mumbled he did not know. "I have
not work'd here long."

"A blind boy!" Blossom Gill spat. "Not shuprising. Likely he
help'd such a little man drown my nephew."

"Hang them all," a wag shouted. "That way they'll be equally
assured of justice."

"Hold," cried a hand-rubbing tavern keeper of long and dripping
nose, who had been probing about the dead man. "Colonel, Your
Grace, all is resolved. See how the blow bloodied the back of the head

rather than the top, as if the murderer could strike no higher. Therefore he was a little man. And only one of these three is short."

"Do not look so concern'd for your widow, silversmith," a wag shouted. "She can sell a child each year."

At this, I look'd up, and was not pleased to see on the staircase a whole row of little Lowthers, their faces aghast and flush'd red as their flaming red hair.

The Colonel, too, look'd displeased by this deduction of the tavern keeper, perchance having already determined Blossom Gill to be the murderer. And I was irritated by the tavern keeper's reasoning, which was weak, if not false, and resolved to confute it.

"I am puzzled, sir," I interceded loudly. "Would not a man bent over the kettle, dipping candle wicks, present the *back* of his head to attack from behind, no matter the assailant be a dwarf or a giant?"

"Exactly what I had decided," the Colonel declared. "There can be no doubt the murderer was this old house-pad. For a large, strong man was required to lift the candlemaker into his kettle."

This I doubted, the mouth of the kettle being no higher than a man's waist, so that the victim need only be push'd, rather than lifted. But I held my peace, for I was considering the more important matter of the young Lowthers' red hair. Their mother's hair was dark brown. Since I had never seen the silversmith without his wig, and since he was closely shaven and nearly hairless upon the wrists, I had never thought of him possessing hair, much less of it having color. Yet, unless Mrs. Lowther had deceived him seven times at yearly intervals, I now suspected his hair was as red as Dennis O'Leary's.

So many contradictory deductions having confused the mob, and having shortened the tempers of some, they began to shout in unison: "Throw them in the millpond. All three. Let the pond decide their guilt."

Truly, a mob is a monster, with many heads and no brains.

"Silence!" the Colonel shouted, a sudden perspiration gleaming on his brow. "We are not examining witches. This admitted thief and murderer shall be speedily arraigned before the magistrates." And he seized the old man's elbow.

But Blossom Gill stood fast, tho' swaying, and cried at the mob: "I am innocent as a babe! 'Tis thish Rhode Island receiver of stolen property has murder'd my nephew."

The Colonel dragg'd Blossom forward a step, but the mob would not open to let them pass. They preferr'd a Massachusetts thief to any foreigner from Rhode Island. But chiefly they desired a raree show, and a cluster of bawling ropewalkmen began to shout: "String up all three for silver thievery. We must go back to work. Let the murderer be discover'd and judged in the next world."

Colonel Clinton stood gaping like a fish, uncertain whether to bluster or retreat. The mob, which in a sense had been his creature at the beginning, was his no longer. Having sown wind, he was reaping whirlwind.

Dennis too was dragg'd into the midst of them, pale and protesting. And I guess'd they would not listen, tho' they must know full well that an apprentice is helpless to prevent an ill-doing to his master, and dare not blab. His master's word would be taken over his, and revenge against his master might seal an apprentice's lips forever.

Apologies would not interest the mob any longer. I knew I must give them words they would listen to, and thus I shouted: "Colonel, I have irrefutable proof of the murderer!"

"Hear, hear," the mob clamor'd, many of them laughing, which irritated me extreamly.

The Colonel, to my surprise, glared; but, uncertain of the temper of the mob, he did not interfere when I carried forward two frames of wicks.

"On this frame," I cried, "are long white hairs from what would seem to be the wig of the deceased. On the other are a few strangely short red ones."

Before I could explain the next step in my deductions, they laid hold of Dennis most painfully, ripping his clothing and even pulling out his long red hair. They show'd that a little understanding may be more harmful than none, shouting with joy as tho' they, the mob, had brilliantly solved the matter. Some even shouted for a rope.

I could not recapture their attention, and fear'd Dennis would be strung up before my eyes, the Colonel making no attempt to prevent it. Since all depended on this moment, I rush'd back to the kettle and scooped the iron shovel into the pan of blackened coals beneath. I raised the shovel full to shoulder height and, whirling, broadcast the warm coals upon the heads of the mob. Needless to say, this regain'd their attention.

At their angry bedlam I shouted: "Another of the three suspects has also red hair, but conceals it. Take off your wig, Warwick Lowther!"

And in doing so, he show'd that his seven children were his own, for his head was as red as theirs. Without the craven expression I had expected, he confronted the mob with his red stubble. Its colour seem'd the same as Dennis's unkempt red mop. The voices of the mob diminish'd.

"This fiddle-faddle about red hair, white hair, no hair, is of no consequence," Warwick Lowther stated firmly. "No doubt Dennis left his red hairs on the wicks while working at the dipping machine. No more candles were dipp'd after he was sent for the beer. Thus, his red hairs are still there, and innocently enough."

"But *these* red hairs are all peculiarly short," I replied. "Most hairs coming loose from a head are long and old, dried at the roots, perchance, like last year's tall weeds; whilst short hairs are, for the most part, cuttings, not uprootings. If you will very closely examine the short hairs on this wick, you will see that all of them lack the small root that is so often present when hair falls out naturally. By drawing hairs from your comb or brush between your fingers, you will frequently feel this tiny root. Since these hairs lack it, I believe them to be the short hairs that are scatter'd about after a visit to the barber. And since your stubbled hair is cut often, Warwick Lowther, in order that your wig be comfortable, I believe these short hairs to be from your head. And more of them will be found clinging inside your wig."

"Of no consequence," the little silversmith cried, shifting his feet rapidly, his voice rising to the excited pitch with which he had accused Dennis while leaping about him on Queen Street. "Plotter! The red hairs are on a different frame than the white ones! Any fool knows that the murderer, bending his victim into the kettle, would touch his head above his victim's, thus leaving his hairs on the wicks of the *same* frame."

Before I could dispute this, he shouted: "The hairs could not be mine—unless this old man treacherously glued them there. For my hair is always cover'd; I protect my head with a wig!"

As I stepp'd toward him, he cried: "Looking for stripes of wax on my hair, eh? You won't find them! For I have not been near the dipping machine, as the lad will testify. It is Blossom Gill who has wax upon his wig!"

And, whirling about, his own wig still clutch'd in his fist, Warwick Lowther show'd his back to me, and pointed an accusing finger at the old man. The mob seem'd even more confused, not many of them shouting, for most had tried to hear my explanation. But very few seem'd to have heard all of it, or understood it rightly.

Some ruffians came running back into the shop with a rope for Dennis. Others, whose wigs had been scorch'd by the coals, seem'd working up their anger to hang me alongside of the Irish lad. I had near despair'd of reasoning with the mob, when I remember'd that before me was a proof of Warwick Lowther's guilt which might convince even the dullest of them.

Since only a raree show would hold their attention, I leapt upon a bench and, waving my arms at the heavens, cried loudly and clearly: "Warwick Lowther, there is a witness to your crime!"

This recaptured their ears from their own voices. Of a sudden, their eyes seem'd like a myriad of shiny arrows drawn taut at me, and I began falteringly: "Good citizens of Boston—"

Then I realized if I reveal'd my final piece of evidence first, the explanation proving its importance might not be heard above the ensuing tumult. The silversmith might speak his way clear. With so unruly a mob, I must present my deductions in proper order for the grand total of them to be understood; and further I must present my thoughts entertainingly for them to be listen'd to.

"Warwick Lowther," I cried in a voice confident and strong for a humble apprentice, and continuous; for I fear'd interruption. "It is said that he who lies down with dogs shall rise up with fleas. Your bargain to handle suspicious silver, perchance in exchange for your use of the garret and shop, inevitably led you toward greater crimes. Mr. Gill decided you should be his accomplice in a robbery, that your increased guilt put you more fully in his power. To escape this, you waited till the old man and lad had gone out, then took off your wig, that it not be wax'd during the assault, and took up the poker; creeping behind Mr. Gill, you struck him down as he bent over his kettle."

"I say Holy Lightning shall strike you down!" Lowther cried.

"As you said yourself," I continued quickly, "the murderer bent his victim forward into the wax. You were careful that your head not touch the wicks above the kettle. And you hasten'd to lock the front door, that no customer enter and discover the body before the old man's return, for which you left the rear door open.''

Warwick Lowther shouted a denial. And I shouted back: ''You are a skill'd workman, sir, and speedily open'd the other two locks of the strong-box, and removed the incriminating silver to a hiding place unknown to the old man. I'll wager, on taking these locks apart, we shall find unnatural scratches caused by your pick-lock.''

At this, he swept up a fistful of tools, shouting he would break open the locks and prove me a liar. And I guess'd my prideful confidence had swell'd beyond my intellect; hastily, I overshouted him that, being a metal worker, he might as easily have filed his own keys, which surely proved the murder was not the result of a sudden rage.

''You plann'd that the old man discover the body,'' I shouted. ''As he pull'd it out of the kettle, you would rush down the staircase crying 'Murder,' and your word would be taken over his. For Blossom's conflicts with his nephew were well known, and it is consider'd that a besotted man is not a truthful one, and, further, much wax might have been smear'd upon his clothing. Perchance, you hoped to incite the mob to close Blossom's throat with a rope before he could make plain the nature of your dealings with Mr. Gill. For three can keep a secret only when two of them are dead.''

''But it was the lad he first accused,'' Colonel Clinton interposed somewhat sourly.

''Yes,'' I cried, ''the little silversmith waited and waited, and Blossom did not return. All the while, he knew Dennis was striding closer with the pail of beer. In his fright, no doubt, he forgot the wax was cooling and that he should go down to stir the coals. And finally he heard Dennis unlock the front door, and his last hope of the old man returning in time was gone. There seem'd naught to do but rush down the staircase and accuse Dennis in his stead.''

''False, false, 'tis a plot!'' Warwick Lowther was exclaiming, and the mob began to clamor so that I must exert my lungs to the utmost.

''When the hardness of the wax freed Dennis from suspicion, you swiftly and cunningly diverted it to the old man, who was not there to defend himself,'' I shouted, and then took a thrust at the Colonel for evicting my brother. ''You easily duped Colonel Clinton with your talk of a fresh battle between uncle and nephew, and of the stripes of wax

upon Blossom's wig. You were confident there was no wax upon your
own wig, and when I suggested your hair be red, you were not afraid to
show it, believing no wax to be on your red stubble. Perchance you
even look'd in a glass to be safe.

"Bring two looking-glasses," I cried.

When I bade him look at himself in one of them, he quickly did so,
and shrugg'd, no doubt relieved. But I moved the second glass to the
back of his head, as tho' I were his barber, and said: "Silversmith, when
you sprang back from the kettle, your freshly cut hair brush'd the frame
of wicks *behind you*. Yet you have assured this company you did not go
near the dipping machine."

He stared into his mirror like a pig poison'd, for he could see,
reflected in mine, the stripes of bayberry wax on the back of his red
head.

Then his freckled face became hard and calm, and he turn'd to me.
He stood very tall for such a short man. He stared upward through me as
tho' I were a mist. And, without apology or complaint, he sternly said:
"I did my best to feed my family."

Following his uplifted gaze, I, too, stared at the row of young
Lowthers upon the staircase, and I need not describe their uncom-
prehending and distraught expressions.

Like Icarus of mythology, I felt my triumph lose its wings.

The mob was sufficiently amazed by my deductions, and so
sober'd that Warwick Lowther was allow'd to be hang'd by the proper
authorities, which doleful event I did not attend. It cost me much unrest
and some of my books, which I sold to give help to the widow; and I
ponder'd that a fund ought to be set up, offering loans to those displaced
artisans who, tho' showing capability and industriousness, need a
respite from starvation in which to establish themselves. In later years I
was able to arrange such a fund for Philadelphia.

As for my return from the crowded candle shop, it was greeted by
my brother James's unreasonable fist. He set me to useless labors till
midnight . . . My now well known aversion to arbitrary power, which
a lifetime of public service has express'd, stems from my brother's
tyrannical treatment of me.

Bitterly upon my knees, I scrubb'd the press while, beyond the
flickering candles, glowering and smiling, James composed much satire
against the authorities. As a result, he was taken up and imprison'd for a

month. His discharge was accompanied by an order of the House that he "should no longer print the paper call'd the *New England Courant*." My brother's means of evading this order produced my own means of escape; for he return'd my apprenticeship indenture to me so that his paper might be printed for the future, as indeed for a time it was, under my own name, Benjamin Franklin.

AUTHOR'S POSTSCRIPT: The fictional adventure you have just read has its source in the early part of Benjamin Franklin's AUTOBIOGRAPHY (the Bigelow version). Remember that these events were supposed to have occurred in the America of 1722, which was a very different kettle of fish from, let us say, 1776; just before the Revolutionary War. The chief problems in 1722 were not with the British; they were with the French and Indians, they were the rivalries among the colonies themselves, and they arose from the ideological struggle between weakening Puritan theocracy (Cotton Mather did not die until 1728) and such "insidious European doctrines" as rationalism and scientific method. Complete independence from England was utterly inconceivable in 1722. The bonds tying the colonies and England were so close at that time that travel to England, for example, was as common as to the other colonies—and hardly more inconvenient!

IT WAS AN AWFUL SHAME

CHARLOTTE MACLEOD

"The Coddies gave a party just about a week ago.
Everything was plentiful, the Coddies they're not slow."

With an ever-so-knowing wink, Exalted Chowderhead Jeremy Kelling of the Beacon Hill Kellings raised his foaming flagon and quaffed. In accordance with time-honoured ritual, the other Comrades of the Convivial Codfish gulped in unison, then slapped their own tankards down on the emerald green tablecloth with one great, unanimous thwack.

"They treated us like gentlemen, we tried to act the same,
And only for what happened, sure it was an awful shame."

Again the tankards were raised, this time in gallant toast to the plump and pleasing person in kelly green who sailed into the room bearing the Ceremonial Cauldron. Behind her in single file marched the Highmost, Midmost, and Leastmost Hod-carriers.

As Mrs. Coddie, for such was her title, set the Cauldron in front of Jeremy Kelling, the three Hod-carriers clicked the poles of their hods smartly together, then stepped back in order of precedence to form a guard of honor behind their Exalted Chowderhead. Jem tied an oversize green linen napkin under his bottom chin, then went on with the incantation:

"When Mistress Coddie dished the chowder out, she fainted
on the spot.
    She found a pair of overalls in the bottom of the pot."

The Comrades had engaged many Mistress Coddies in their long and sometimes glorious history, but never one who swooned with more élan or finesse. As they rose in admiration of their recumbent hostess of the day, Comrade Bardwell voiced the consensus.

"By gad, this Mistress Coddie is a ring-tailed doozy with a snood on."

"Any objections or abstentions?" said the Exalted Chowderhead.

There being none, he raised the Ancient and Timeworn Overalls which had occasioned Mrs. Coddie's well-feigned swoon slowly from the cauldron.

"Fluke Flounder he got fighting mad, his eyes were bulging
out.
    He jumped upon the pi-an-o and loudly he did shout."

This year, Comrade Archer of the real estate Archers was Fluke Flounder. Despite his fourscore years and then some, despite the fact that he had to be boosted to the top of the Steinway by a dozen comradely hands, right loudly did Comrade Archer in good sooth manage to shout.

"Who threw the overalls in Mistress Coddie's chowder?
    Nobody spoke, so he hollered all the louder."

And, by George, he did. So did they all. In reasonably close harmony, making up in volume for what they lacked in tone, the Comrades bellowed their way through the ballad composed in 1899 by George Geifer and bastardized in 1923 by Jeremy's late uncle Serapis Kelling.

At the end of the first chorus, Mistress Coddie (actually Mistress Cholmondely of the Perkins Square Cholmondelys) recovered her senses with fine dramatic effect and rose to take away the Ceremonial Cauldron, into which the Exalted Chowderhead had again lowered the Ancient and Timeworn Overalls with due ceremony and pomp. Escorted again by the Highmost, Midmost, and Leastmost Hod-carriers, she bore away the sacred relics and returned with a tureen full of genuine codfish chowder.

Excellent chowder it was, and full justice did the Comrades do it. Not until the tureen was bone dry did they quit baling. And not until Jeremy Kelling had untied his green napkin from beneath his nether-most jowl did he realize he was no longer wearing his insignia of office.

"The Codfish," he gasped. "It's gone!"

"It fell into the Cauldron, you jackass," said Comrade Archer, who'd got his wind back after a bellyful of chowder and several more restorative flagons.

"I didn't hear it clink."

"Of course you didn't. You're deaf as a haddock and drunk as a skunk."

This was the kind of after-dinner speaking in which the Comrades delighted. They kept it up with variations and embellishments while their leader commanded the Keeper of the Cauldron to go get the goddamn thing and bring it back. This done, the Exalted Chowderhead personally shook out the overalls, fished in the pockets and down the mortar-crusted legs to the accompaniment of ribaldries most uncouth, and finally stuck his head into the empty pot.

"It's not there," he wailed.

"Then it's under the table, where you generally wind up, you old souse," shouted Archer the wit.

It was not. It wasn't anywhere. That cumbrous chain of heavy silver with its dependent silver codfish, so recently ornamenting Jeremy Kelling's neat little paunch, was now vanished like the chowders of yesteryear.

"You forgot to put it on," sneered the Highmost Hod-carrier. "Softening of the brain, that's all. Nothing to worry about. Let's have our Codly coffee."

All hailed this sage counsel except the Exalted Chowderhead. A relative infant among the Comrades of the Convivial Codfish, being yet on the sunny side of seventy, Jeremy Kelling had labored long to achieve high office. He'd worked his way up from Journeyman Bouncer to Leastmost Hod-carrier. He'd been Fluke Flounder for one halcyon term, during which he'd pulled a calf muscle leaping to the piano and strained a tonsil putting too much fortissimo into his shouts.

At every meeting and frequently in between, he'd dreamed of the day when he would wear the Great Chain, sit behind the Ceremonial Cauldron, and show these clods how to run a meeting. His installation had taken place only last month. This was the first time he'd got to officiate. How breathtaking had been the moment when the Great Chain was withdrawn from its secret hiding place by the Opener of the Shell and hung around his palpitating neck. At the end of the meeting, the Chain was supposed to be returned to its hiding place with the Secret Valedictory Chant. How the hell could he conduct the concluding ceremonies without the blasted Codfish?

Where, Jeremy asked himself as he sipped with less than usual relish at his whiskey-laden coffee under its cargo of whipped cream, had the damn thing got to? The Great Chain couldn't have fallen off. Its overlapping links had been clinched together forever and aye by an old-time artisan, there was no clasp to come undone. The only way to get it away from him would have been to lift it over his head.

Quod erat absurdem. An experienced toper like Jeremy Kelling could never have got drunk enough on a paltry few schooners of special dark to be oblivious to any such trick as that. Furthermore, he'd been in full view of all the Comrades ever since he'd donned the Chain, and there was not such unanimity of spirit among them that somebody wouldn't have ratted on anybody else who made so free with the revered relic.

As the Codly coffee mugs were replenished, speculation about the Chain's disappearance grew more imaginative. Everybody naturally accused everybody else of codnapping. They took to visiting the men's room in squads to make sure nobody was trying to sneak the Codfish off in his codpiece.

Mrs. Coddie, of course, was exonerated, firstly because she'd been under escort by the three Hod-carriers all the time, secondly because she'd been in her swoon during the time when the fell deed was most likely to have befallen, and thirdly because she proved to be somebody's mother.

At last a thorough search of the room was conducted, with all the members crawling around the floor on hands and knees, barking like a pack of foxhounds, but finding nothing. For the first time in the club's history, they had to close the meeting without the Valedictory Chant, though a few Comrades gave it anyway either because they were too befuddled not to or because they always had before and they damn well would now if they damn well felt like it.

Most appeared to regard the Great Chain's disappearance as a jolly jape and to be confident it would turn up at the April meeting pinned to the seat of the Ancient and Timeworn Overalls. Jeremy Kelling was not so sanguine. His first act on returning to his Beacon Hill apartment was to fight off the ministrations of his faithful henchman Egbert, who took it for granted Mr. Jem must be sick because he'd come home sober and perturbed instead of sloshed and merry. His second was to put in an emergency call to his nephew-in-law, Max Bittersohn.

"Max, I've lost the Codfish!"

"I knew a man once who lost a stuffed muskellunge," Max replied helpfully.

"Dash it, man, cease your persiflage. The Great Chain of the Convivial Codfish is a sacred relic. Like the grasshopper on top of Faneuil Hall," he added to emphasize the gravity of the situation. "It disappeared while I was removing the Ancient and Timeworn Overalls from the Ceremonial Cauldron."

"That was probably as good a time as any," said Max. "The Chain didn't fall into the pot, by any chance?"

"How the hell could it? I looked. Anyway, the thing was around my neck. I'd have had to fall in, too. Which," Jem added, "I did not. I'd have remembered. I'm not drunk. Egbert can testify to that."

"Put him on," said Bittersohn.

Egbert, to their mutual amazement, was able to vouch for his employer's unprecedented sobriety.

"It's very worrisome, Mr. Max. I've never seen him like this before. Except sometimes on the morning after," he qualified, for Egbert was a truthful man when circumstances didn't require him to be otherwise. "I think he might be described as shaken to the core."

"To the core, eh? Okay, let me talk to him again."

Max Bittersohn was a professional tracker-down of valuables that had been stolen, pawned by spouses faced with private financial emergencies, or otherwise detached from their rightful owners. Thanks to his expertise, he was able to extract from Jem a complete and perhaps even reasonably accurate account of what had happened. He offered words of cheer and comfort, then went back to his Sarah, who did not want to hear about her uncle's missing Codfish, she being a recent bride with other things on her mind.

In truth, Bittersohn himself gave little thought to Jeremy Kelling's dilemma until the following evening when Egbert dropped by to break the tidings that Mr. Jem had fallen downstairs and broken his hip. Sarah was horrified. Max was intrigued.

"Fell downstairs? How the hell did he manage that? Jem hates stairs."

"The elevator appears to have been stuck on the top floor, Mr. Max."

That was credible enough. The building where Jem and Egbert lived had an antique elevator about the size of a telephone booth, that wouldn't work unless it had been tightly latched by the last person who got out of it, which frequently didn't happen.

Jem's usual procedure in such cases was to bellow up the elevator shaft until somebody was goaded into going out and shutting the door properly. In desperate circumstances, however, such as when it was Egbert's day off and he'd run out of gin, Jem had been known to walk down the one flight of stairs from his second-floor apartment. This had been one of those times. Now he was over at Phillips House with a brand-new stainless steel ball where the hip end of his left femur used to be. Egbert thought Mrs. Sarah and Mr. Max would want to know.

"Of course we do," cried Sarah. "How ghastly! Bad enough for Uncle Jem, of course, but think of those poor nurses. What happened, do you know?"

"All I know is, I got home about five o'clock and found him sprawled on the floor of the vestibule, yowling his head off. He said Fuzzly's had called to say his whiskers were ready and they'd be closing soon, so he'd rushed out, found the elevator stuck, and gone cavorting down the stairs. There was no darn need of it, you know. I could perfectly well have gone and got them tomorrow morning but you know Mr. Jem. He wanted those whiskers."

"What for?" asked Max.

"The Tooters' railroad party," Sarah told him. "Uncle Jem was

going to dress up in Dundreary whiskers and Grandfather Kelling's old
frock coat, and impersonate Jay Gould."

"Did Jay Gould have Dundrearies?"

"Who knows? Anyway Uncle Jem was all in a dither about the
party. He's an old railroad buff like Tom Tooter."

"Do you mean model trains?"

"No, that's Tom's brother Wouter. Tom collects real trains. He has
his own steam locomotive and a parlor car with velvet-covered settees
and fringed lampshades. Also a dining car and a caboose."

"Any particular reason?"

Sarah shrugged. "I suppose he got them cheap. The Tooters have
always been in railroads. Anyway, Tom and his wife are having an
anniversary and Tom's rented the B&M tracks for the evening. They're
going to have a string ensemble playing Strauss waltzes and a fountain
spouting champagne."

"My God," said Bittersohn. "Jem will have apoplexy at missing a
bash like that."

"He was in a highly aggravated state of profanity when I left
him," Egbert agreed. "They were about to administer a sedative."

"I don't wonder." Sarah poured Egbert a tot of their best brandy,
for he was an old and beloved friend. "Here, have one yourself, then
Max will walk you home. Go to bed early, you're going to need your
rest."

"Truer words were never spoken, Mrs. Sarah."

"At least a broken hip ought to take his mind off that silly Codfish
for a while. He's been phoning every hour on the hour to see whether
Max has found it yet."

"As a matter of fact, his parting bellow was that I—er—call the
matter to Mr. Max's attention."

Max grinned. "In precisely those words?"

"Not precisely, Mr. Max."

"Tell him I'm hot on the trail. More brandy?"

"Thanks, but I ought to be getting along."

"Come on, then."

The two men set out to walk the short distance from Tulip Street to
Pinckney. "Who else is going to the party?" Max asked. "The whole
Codfish crowd?"

"No, I believe Mr. Jem was the only Comrade invited, except for the Tooters themselves, of course, and Mr. Wripp, who's recently had a cataract operation. Mrs. Tooter felt the outing would do Mr. Wripp good."

"No doubt," said Bittersohn. "What office does Mr. Wripp hold?"

"Mr. Wripp is a Formerly Grand Exalted Chowderhead. Being by now ninety-two years of age, he appears content to rest on past laurels. Oh yes, and Mr. Obed Ogham will be among those present. So maybe it's all for the best that Mr. Jem won't."

"Why? Don't he and Ogham get along?"

"None of the Kellings get along with Obed Ogham, Mr. Max. He's the bird who sued Mr. Percy Kelling for two dollars and forty-seven cents he claimed Mr. Percy overcharged him. That was after Mr. Percy's accounting firm had helped Ogham recover the five and a half million dollars Ogham's comptroller had been swindling him out of."

"Oh yes, the King of the Crumbs. How come he and Jem both belong to the same club?"

"There have always been Kellings and Oghams among the Codfish," Egbert explained. "Neither is willing to cede his ancestral right. Noblesse oblige, as you might say."

"But don't the Tooters know Jem and Ogham are feuding?"

"They're not exactly feuding, Mr. Max. I believe it's more a matter of maintaining a haughty silence in each other's presence."

Max found his mind boggling at the notion of Jem's maintaining a haughty silence in anybody's presence, but he was kind enough not to say so.

"Besides," Egbert went on, "Mr. Ogham and Mr. Wouter Tooter are this year's Highmost and Leastmost Hod-carriers respectively. It's not the done thing for one Hod-carrier to exclude a Comrade of the Hod from any of his routs and junkets, personal feelings notwithstanding. Comrade White, the Midmost Hod-carrier, would normally have been included, too, but he's just left for Nairobi on a business trip. Mr. Jem was to have escorted Mrs. White."

"Mrs. White's a good-looking, well-dressed woman somewhat on the buxom side and fond of a good time in a nonthreatening sort of way, right?"

"You know the lady, Mr. Max?"

"No, but I know Jem. And the rest, I suppose would be friends of the Tooters?"

"I expect they'll be mostly railroad buffs and members of Mr. Wouter Tooter's model railroad club. It won't be a large party, since the parlor car can't accommodate more than thirty or forty people comfortably."

"That sounds like a lot of money to spend on a relatively small affair, wouldn't you say?"

"Between you and me, Mr. Max. I think it's partly what they call public relations. Somebody's been spreading a rumor that the Tooter enterprises are in financial difficulties. I shouldn't be surprised if making a splash now is their way of squashing the rumor before their stock starts to drop."

"Very interesting. Well, here's the old homestead. Mind if I come up with you?"

"Thanks, Mr. Max, but you mustn't feel obliged."

"I want to see where it happened."

"Just a second till I find my keys. Ah, here we are. There's the staircase, you see, and Mr. Jem was on the floor at the foot."

"Marble floor, I see. Damn good thing he didn't go down head first. Who uses the stairs as a rule?"

"Nobody, unless the elevator gets stuck. I used to, but I have to say I find them more of a climb than I like nowadays."

"Did Jem say how he happened to use them today?"

"He said there was a power outage just as he received the phone call from the shop. The lights were out and the radio went off. That meant the elevator wouldn't be working either, of course. A very unfortunate coincidence. My mother always claimed bad luck came in threes. First the Codfish, and now this. What next, is what I'm wondering. Do you think we can count Mr. Jem's having to miss the party as the third piece of bad luck, Mr. Max?"

"I'm not sure we should count any of it as just luck. What happened to the clothes he was wearing when he fell?"

"I brought them home from the hospital and dropped them off before going on to your place."

"Good. Let's have a look."

The tiny elevator was sitting in the lobby, its folding brass gates meticulously fastened. Word of Jem's accident must have got around.

Max and Egbert squeezed in together and rode to the second floor.
Egbert fetched the clothes and Max pulled out a magnifying glass.

"Aha! See that, Egbert?"

"A grease spot on his pantleg? Mr. Max, you don't think I'd have
let Mr. Jem go around looking like that? He must have done it when he
fell."

"My thought exactly. There's grease on his shoe sole, too. Got a
good flashlight?"

"Oh yes, I always keep one handy."

"Come on then, let's see which stair got buttered."

It was Egbert who first noticed the brownish glob under the fifth
tread from the landing. "Would this be what you're looking for, Mr.
Max?"

Bittersohn rubbed a little on his finger and sniffed. "It sure as hell
would. Bowling alley wax, I'd say. It's been cleaned off the step with
some kind of solvent, but whoever did it forgot to wipe underneath,
probably because he was in a hurry to get away. I'll bet he was hiding in
the cellar while they were lugging Jem off. Let's go call on the
neighbors."

The first-floor people were away. On the third floor lived an elderly
lady, her cook and her maid. The lady was out playing bridge with her
maid in attendance because Herself didn't like going out alone at night,
the cook explained. "Can I give you a cup of tea in the kitchen, now?"

The two men were happy to accept. "I see your electric clock's
right on the dot," Max remarked as they sat down.

"Has to be," said the cook. "Herself likes her meals prompt to the
second."

"You haven't had to reset it lately?"

"No, I haven't touched it in ages, except to dust it now and then
when the spirit moves me."

Cook was plainly glad of company and ready to talk, but she didn't
have much to tell. The first-floor people were in Palm Beach, and had
been for the past two months. Her own household hadn't known about
Jeremy Kelling's fall until they heard him being taken away in the
ambulance. Herself considered him to have been struck down by a
Mighty Hand in retribution for his ungodly and riotous ways. Cook
personally thought Mr. Kelling was a lovely man, always so kind-
spoken when they happened to meet, which wasn't often because

Herself was of the old school and believed in servants using the back stairway. This very night, Mary the maid had been required to go down the back way, around the alley, and walk back up to the front door while Herself used the elevator in lone elegance. Mary might get to ride up after Herself when they got back, it being so late and good maids hard to come by.

"That's nice," said Max. "Thanks for the pleasure of your company. The cake was delicious."

"Would you be wanting a piece to take to Mr. Kelling, now?"

Egbert expressed the opinion that Mr. Jem would prefer a cake that had a bottle of Old Grandad baked into it, and they parted on a merry note.

Going back to Jem's flat, Max asked, "Egbert, would you have a recent picture of that Codfish crowd?"

"Scads of them, Mr. Max. Mr. Jem keeps an album of all the doings since he joined the club."

"Great. Where is it?"

New Englanders love to look at photograph albums, for some reason. They spent quite a while over this one. Jem had each photograph neatly labeled. He himself appeared in most of them wearing various appurtenances of office. The latest showed the Great Chain of the Convivial Codfish adorning his well-padded front.

"I'll take this," said Max.

Egbert was alarmed. "Mr. Max, if anything should happen to that album, Mr. Jem would have a stroke."

"I'll guard it with my life. Where's his invitation to that ungodly revel he was supposed to go on?"

"It's a ticket. Mr. Tooter had them printed up special. Can't ride the train without a ticket, you know." Egbert produced the precious oblong. "Is it a clue, do you think?"

"Who knows? Anyway, Jem won't be needing it now. Sleep tight, Egbert. Sarah will be over to the hospital at crack of dawn, I expect, so take your time in the morning."

Max took his leave, pondering deeply. The next day, leaving Sarah to comfort the afflicted, he first collected Jem's whiskers from Fuzzly's, dropped in on some pals at the Fraud Squad, lunched with a prominent member of the Securities and Exchange Commission who owed him a favor, had a chat with his Uncle Jake the lawyer, paid a call on a fair and buxom matron who was mystified, gratified, and eager to cooperate; and finally went home to placate his wife.

"Sorry I can't have dinner with you tonight, sweetie-pumpkin."

"And where are you off to, pray tell? What are you getting all dressed up for?"

"A train ride," he replied from the depths of a starched shirt. "Seen my studs lately?"

"You might try your stud box. Uncle Jem wants to know when in blazes you're going to catch his Codfish."

"Anon, I hope. One kiss, my bonny sweetheart, I'm off for a prize tonight. With the voluptuous Mrs. White, in case some kind friend thinks you ought to know."

"In that disgusting clawhammer coat? Where on earth did you get it?"

"Same place I got these." He put on Jem's Dundreary whiskers. "How do I look?"

"Don't ask. I'm going next door and cry on Cousin Theonia's shoulder. Mrs. White, indeed! I hope she singes your whiskers."

Mrs. White was ready and waiting when he went to pick her up. They had some trouble stowing her into the taxi on account of her bustle, feather boa, and a hat freighted with a whole stuffed pheasant; but at last they were able to proceed.

On Track Four at North Station, business was booming. A conductor in a stiff cap and brass-buttoned uniform was joyfully clipping tickets. Max recognized him from Jem's album as Tom Tooter, their host. Up ahead in the engine cab, a melancholy individual wearing a high-rise cap of striped ticking, greasy striped overalls, and a tremendous scrubbing-brush mustache leaned out to survey the throng flocking aboard. This could be none other than Wouter Tooter, throwing himself into his role.

Max himself received some puzzled glances as Mrs. White introduced him right and left as her dear, dear friend Mr. Jay Gould. People must either be putting him down as somebody they'd met before but couldn't place, or else making mental notes to have a quiet chat with Mr. White when he got back from Nairobi.

Mrs. Tom Tooter was doing the honours inside the parlor car, wearing silver lace over a straight-front corset, with white gloves up to her armpits and strings of pearls down to her knees. She looked a trifle nonplussed when Max made his bow, but pleased to have such a good-

looking man aboard even if his ginger side whiskers did clash rather
ferociously with his wavy dark hair. Luckily, Mr. Wripp tottered in just
behind him and had to be fussed over, so Max escaped without a
grilling.

The lights were dim enough to make all the ladies look charming
and all the men distinguished. There was no fountain splashing
champagne, but they did have a swan carved out of ice to chill the
caviar, and a bartender wearing red arm garters and a black toupee
neatly parted down the middle. Max got Mrs. White a white lady, which
seemed appropriate, then turned her over to her friends and went
prospecting.

Tom Tooter was in his glory. He'd changed his conductor's cap and
coat for a Prince Albert. He bagged at the knees and bulged at the
shoulders, but what did he care? Kings might be blest, but Tom was
glorious, o'er all the ills of life victorious. He couldn't possibly be the
man Max was looking for.

Mrs. Tooter kept glancing at her husband with fond wifely
indulgence and brushing imaginary specks off his lapels as women do in
public places where decorum forbids more overt displays of affection.
Max indulged himself for a moment in thinking that if Sarah were here,
she might be brushing specks off his lapels, then got on with his job.

Obed Ogham was easy to spot and would no doubt be a pleasure to
dislike. He was one of those loud, beefy men who trap people in corners
and tell them a lot of stuff they don't want to hear. Max stayed well clear
of him. He'd be the sort to ask personal questions of strangers.

Wouter Tooter was not in the parlor car. Various guests were asking
for him; no doubt cronies from his model railroad club as they wore
trainmen's caps with their false whiskers and old-fashioned clothes.
Tom said he was around somewhere and why didn't they come into the
dining car?

This was an excellent suggestion, Max found. Rows of tables with
snowy napery and genuine old railroad cutlery were set out around a
long center buffet laden with hams, roasts of beef, whole turkeys, hot
dishes under metal covers the size of igloos, cold platters of every
description, and epergnes dripping with fruits, sweets, and exotic
flowers. Edward VII would have found it adequate.

Waiters hovered ready to fetch and carry. A wine steward wearing
a silver corkscrew on a heavy silver sommelier's chain circulated among

the tables murmuring recommendations through a well-trimmed but all-covering beard. He sounded as if he had a marble in his mouth. Max took one long, earnest look at the wine steward, then slipped out into the vestibule. When the man came through, Max tackled him.

"Mr. Wouter Tooter, I believe? Changed your overalls, I see."

"Who the hell are you?" mumbled the man.

"You'd better take that marble out of your mouth, Mr. Tooter. You might swallow it. To respond to your question, my name's Bittersohn and I'm a private detective sent by the Securities and Exchange Commission to guard Mr. Obed Ogham. They don't want anything to happen to him before he's indicted."

"Indicted? What for?"

"You don't really have to ask, do you? You know damn well Ogham's trying by highly illegal methods to scuttle your brother's firm so he can make a killing on the stock market. That's why you're playing wine steward tonight with the Great Chain of the Convivial Codfish."

Wouter looked down at his chest as if he thought it might possibly belong to someone else, and said nothing.

"That's why you deliberately disabled Jeremy Kelling, so that he couldn't come tonight and catch you wearing the chain. Your brother's too busy with the guests to notice, and old Mr. Wripp's too bleary-eyed from his cataract operation. Ogham might catch on, but he's not supposed to live long enough to rat on you, is he?"

"I don't know what you're talking about."

"Like hell you don't. You cut off the electricity in Jem's apartment yesterday afternoon and waxed the stairs. Then you put in a fake phone call from Fuzzly's, knowing that would send Jem charging out to get his whiskers. He'd find the elevator inoperative, gallop down the stairs, and take a toss, which he did. And you've got some kind of muck in your pocket right now that you're planning to drop into Ogham's wine as soon as he's drunk enough not to notice. You needn't bother. He's on his way to jail, though he doesn't know it yet. Your brother's business is safe and so are you, on two conditions."

"What conditions?" said Wouter sulkily.

"You leave Ogham alone and you show me how the hell you got that chain off Jem's neck."

"Oh." Light dawned on what little Max could see of Wouter's

lavishly disguised countenance. "I know you now. You're the bird who married Jem's niece. The pretty one who's always getting murdered."

"Right. And you're the wise guy who landed your buddy in the hospital with a broken hip."

"Well, hell, what was a man to do? I couldn't make Tom listen to reason. He simply refused to believe even that reptile Ogham would scuttle a Comrade. Jem won't mind once he knows I did it for Tom. I knew the old sculpin would land on his feet, he always does. This time he bounced on his backside first. Too bad, but it was in good cause. Surely you must realize that."

"Couldn't you just have asked Jem to stay away from the party?"

"Jem Kelling miss a bash like this? You must be out of your mind. I'd have had to explain why, then all Jem would have done was swagger in here, waltz up to Obed, and paste him straight in the mouth. He'd have to stand on a chair to reach that high, I expect, but he'd do it. You know Jem."

Max did know Jem, and he could not dispute Wouter's logic. "Okay, if you can make that sound sane to Jem, more power to you. What were you planning to fix Ogham's wagon with?"

"Just a Mickey Finn. I thought I'd make believe he'd passed out from too much booze, drag him to the observation platform supposedly to sober up, and shove him overboard. Then I'd take off my disguise and go back to being me."

"While Ogham was found suffering from minor contusions and rushed to the nearest hospital, where the doctors would start wondering how he got bunged full of chloral hydrate and your nice family train ride would turn into a major scandal. Nice going, Tooter."

"Well, damn it, I never committed a murder before. This seemed like a good idea."

"Take it from me, it stinks. Hand me the chloral and show me how you worked the Chain."

"Oh well, there's nothing to that." Wouter gave Max the little bottle, then took off the Chain. "You see, last year I was Opener of the Shell, which meant I had custody of the Great Chain. Just for fun, I split one of the links and inserted a tiny magnetic coupling to hold it together. You'd need a magnifying glass to see it."

"No problem." Max had one, of course. Wouter's craftsmanship was indeed masterful.

"It's worked by a remote-control switch. I meant to open it as a joke sometime, but when this foul business with Ogham came up, I got the idea of wearing the Chain and posing as a wine steward. No sense in going out and buying one when I'd never use it again, was there?"

"Hardly," said Max. He was feeling a trifle dizzy by now.

"You see, I'm Leastmost Hod-carrier this year. That means I get to stand behind Jem when he pulls the Ancient and Timeworn Overalls out of the Cauldron. This is all highly confidential, top-secret stuff, of course, so don't breathe a word to a soul. So anyway, then Mrs. Coddie swoons. I knew they'd all be watching her, so I released the Chain, grabbed it as it fell, and slid it down inside my own overalls. As soon as I could, I slipped into the men's room, put the Chain around my own neck under my clothes, and wore it home."

"Not bad," said Max. "How were you planning to get it back?"

"Frankly, I hadn't thought that far ahead. Maybe I could write old Jem a ransom note and deliver it myself. I could slink in wearing all this face fungus."

Wouter started peeling off false eyebrows and chinwhiskers. "Might as well get my money's worth out of it. Fuzzly's aren't expecting it back till tomorrow afternoon. In the meantime, I can put the Codfish back on the Chain. Had to switch it for a corkscrew, you know. I mean, without the Codfish, the Chain's just a chain."

"That did occur to me," said Max. "Also, since you fiddle around with model railroads, I thought you might be pretty good at midget switches and convenient power failures. If I may make a suggestion, you'd do better to send Jem the corkscrew and a bottle of something by way of penance."

"Damn good idea. I'll make it a case of burgundy. Speaking of which, now that I've resigned as wine steward, let's you and I go put on the feedbag. Then we can go up to the engine. Maybe the fireman will let us shovel some coal."

THE MASSACHUSETTS PEEP-O'NIGHT

S. S. RAFFERTY

As I watched the shameful procession go down the road under our second storey, front room windows at Witloe's Nook, I couldn't help but think that the people of Boston are hard put to learn a lesson. Here it was, exactly two years to the day, this being 5 March 1772, that British troops had to fire at a surly mob to quell what could have been a mass riot. Massacre indeed! Now here they were, these Bostonians, having a memorium march for the five *martyrs*. Ironically, things had never been better in these American Colonies since that black day. Trade was flourishing. Corn and wheat shortages in Europe had brought British specie into the colonies for the first time. Despite this moment of calm, nay, profitable tranquillity, these rascals who call themselves the Sons of Liberty had the audacity to create a street spectacle. It was an affront to the Crown and dangerous sport. What's the worse, one of the paraders marching by, head and shoulders above the rest, was none other than Captain Jeremy Cork, my employer and friend—the man I would make the richest man in the Americas.

I turned from the window shaking my head in consternation and went back to work on the ledgers. At least one of us was employing his time gainfully.

Since our arrival in Boston three weeks back, I was surprised to find that much of the usual anti-British oratory had abated, as radicalism usually does in the face of prosperity. Even at home, William Pitt himself had taken America to task. I prayed that this procession was merely a symbolic gesture carried off by the diehards as a futile and empty gesture. If only that damnable Sam Adams would shut his mouth—even if he now only spoke in whispers each night at the Green Dragon Tavern.

When Cork returned around midnight, I ignored him and went on reading my copy of the *Evening Post*.

"Did you enjoy the procession, Oaks?" he asked, slumping into a chair.

I peered over the top of the newspaper at him. He must have spied me at the window when he marched by, and he was out to trick me. But I have been with him too long, watched him interrogate too many suspects in his solution of his damnable social puzzles, to be trapped into mendacity.

"I saw it, not enjoyed it. As you would say, *that* was a leading question."

"How so? I was looking for a spectator's opinion. I thought it well organized and orderly."

"And futile. Look here at the news. My God, Captain, the colonies teem with good fortune."

"*Taxed* fortune."

"The Crown's privilege, sir. And if we are so oppressed by customs taxes, how do you explain Boston happily paying £8,921 in duties this past year? Why, even more indentured servants are running away these days. Serves their owners right though, half of those scamps are transported felons and not worth ten minutes trust. The newspaper is filled with reward advertisements. Now that's a sign that times are flourishing," I chuckled.

He didn't enjoy my jest at all, and showed it. "That is a good analogy, Oaks. Excellent! The Americans, all Americans, are in danger of becoming indentured slaves to the Crown. Mark my words. First customs duties, next Crown-paid judges, and then . . ."

"I say let the Crown pay the judges. It's a saving for us to get them off the colonies payrolls."

"Bad logic and more so . . ."

I was thankful for the rap at our door, for it saved me from another argumentative evening. Cork opened the door to admit a well groomed but plainly dressed man of thirty-odd. He was vaguely familiar to me, but I couldn't quite place him. One thing, however, sent my thanks for his arrival up the chimney-fire. He bore the unmistakable stamp of a lawyer, and they always mean trouble. I felt some relief when Cork addressed him as "Mr. Adams." Sam Adams is known to me, and it certainly wasn't him.

"This is Wellman Oaks," Cork said, introducing us. "Mr. John Adams."

Certainly he was familiar; he was John Adams, Sam's cousin, who had successfully defended the British soldiers in the "massacre" affair two years ago. Of course, Cork had considered the verdict of that trial faulty, since only two of the soldiers had been found guilty, and were allowed to plead right of clergy at Adams's request, thus escaping the gallows. Not that Cork is bloodthirsty, but he detests the legal concept that, because a man can read and write, he is excused of a capital crime. I say better to brand and transport the culprit than to clog the jails and gibbets. Obviously, John Adams agreed with my viewpoint.

"I am most pleased to meet an illustrious barrister, sir," I said, shaking his hand. Cork took his coat and stepped back to the door to call down for libations.

"If only I had the luxury of being merely a courtroom barrister, Mr. Oaks," Adams said to me, taking the seat I offered. He looked quite tired. "I'm afraid the American law practitioner is but a ladened donkey, being solicitor, barrister, research clerk and bill collector rolled into one. Ah, Cork, it wasn't necessary to serve drinks."

Cork came in from the door, a tray in hand. "Hospitality is my strongest card, sir. Apple Knock for Oaks and myself and a Whistlebelly Vengeance for you."

"Many thanks, Captain," Adams said, taking the mug up, "but I fear hospitality is not your strongest card. It's your ability as a detector that I'm here to solicit."

Heaven help us! I thought him a rational man, and here he drops a crime at our doorsill. Well, there's no going by appearances.

"Don't tell me your cousin Sam has gotten himself into a scrape over the processional?" Cork asked with a smile.

"If it were only that simple. Mind, that's not a rap on Sam. He's a

sound man, not a rabble rouser. No, the problem is most complicated—
and dangerous."

"My sentiments exactly," I said. "The procession should not have
taken place at all."

Adams looked at me strangely. "Mr. Oaks, I sense that you have
me out of perspective. Many people do, since I took up the defense of
the British soldiers. I am an American, sir, but I believe in the rule of
law, not courtroom passion. As for politics, I would rather remain
retired and cautious, minding my farm and my own business, but this
has nothing to do with the procession today. It does have much to do
with the future of Massachusetts."

Cork was sipping Knock and his eyes were sparkling, not from the
liquor, but from glee. He had a new case. Damn his dancing eyes.
"Well, let's to it, man," he said.

Adams took a deep breath and hooked his thumbs into his
waistcoat. "We have what appears to be a foul murder on our hands.
You are familiar with Major General Sir Francis Moran of His Majesty's
Army?"

"Well, well," Cork mused, "a Major General and a Knight to
boot. Oaks and I did him a service back in—what was it, Oaks?"

" '60's sir, during the French and Indian wars. The theft of the
Ishmael plan, you might recall. He was a Colonel then."

"Yes, of course. Oaks is a great recordkeeper, Mr. Adams. Has
Moran murdered or been done so?"

"He was poisoned. This very night, of all nights, at the home of
Titus Fairmont. A senior Crown officer murdered in the home of a
leading Tory, and with a member of the Royal Family visiting in the
house. The charge against Dobby Hayes will be more than murder, it
will be political assassination. You can see how that will bring it down
on the heads of the Sons of Liberty."

Cork raised a palm to halt him. "Mr. Adams, you are a skilled
lawyer now in the grip of emotion. It's understandable from the morsels
that you have proffered that the situation is grave but pray, man, order
your facts. A brief—a prolusion at least."

Adams wiped his brow. "Quite right, and I thank you for reining
me in. Very well, the facts, gentlemen, the facts."

The lawyer spoke now with courtroom precision, each pertinent
point followed in step by another, like well drilled troops.

Sir Francis had suddenly arrived in the colonies on what was purported to be an inspection tour, although his presence was viewed by local patriots as another slap in the colonial face, for Moran was a soldier of war, not an ambassador. This evening, he was to be feted at the home of Titus Fairmont, a wealthy Tory (Tory was Adams's term; I would have called him a Loyalist). At the same dinner was to be none other than the Marchioness de Waldengrave, a member of the Germanic aristocracy and cousin to King George's wife, Queen Charlotte. The royal lady was a current house guest of the Fairmonts. At the opening of the dinner, Sir Francis rose to give a toast to the King and, having drunk from his goblet, fell into a convulsion. A doctor was one of the guests, and he rushed to the Knight's aid, but it was too late.

"From the manner in which Moran died," Adams went on, "the doctor suspected poisoning, and tested the remains of the goblet on a cat, which also went into convulsions and died. However, there was no poison in the wine decanter or the other goblets, so it became obvious that the poison had been introduced into Moran's goblet by a third party, and Dobby Hayes came immediately under suspicion. Dobby is the Fairmont's footman and he had poured the wine. But what is worse, he is the brother of one of the men killed in the massacre two years ago."

"An act of retribution," I said.

"Yes, or so the authorities claim. In fact, they see Hayes as the instrument of a Sons of Liberty plot, since he is a fervent member of that society. Of course it's rubbish, but the British can use that excuse to crush the last bit of colonial peaceful resistance left. If they can brand us as skulking assassins—some sinister cabal—our friends in other colonies will disown any allegiance to the cause. Most of the members have fled the city for fear of arrest. My cousin Sam and John Hancock arrived at my farm in Braintree and suggested that I come and ask your help. Sam has a high regard for your ability as a fact-finder."

Cork stretched his legs out in front of him, seemingly taking up half the room. "It would be futile to try to prove that Hayes acted alone, Mr. Adams. The suspicion of a plot would always loom large, as they have for centuries."

"Sir, I would ask you to prove that Dobby Hayes did not do it at *all*. I stopped by the jail where he is held and was able to speak with him. He says he is innocent, and I believe him."

"Most culprits say that, sir, as you well know," Cork admonished our guest. "What amazes me is that, if he did do it, why not go for the bigger target?"

Both Adams and I shared puzzled looks.

"The Marchioness herself, gentlemen. If Hayes were a crazed madman seeking revenge on the British for having killed his brother, why not strike closer to the throne?"

"Kill a woman!" I was horrified.

"Madmen have poor manners, Oaks. I was merely making a point in Hayes's favor. Admittedly a weak one, however."

"Non-existent," Adams explained. "You see, the Marchioness took ill during the afternoon and was not at the dinner party."

Cork looked stern. "It is an intriguing challenge, but I, too, marched in the procession today and the authorities would hardly cooperate with me, Mr. Adams. I'll need facts. Who else was at the dinner? Who might have a grudge against Moran? I'll need to talk to people, probe them."

"I think you will be given welcome, Captain. I am told that a Major Phillip Tell is in charge of the investigation. He is known to you, is he not?"

Known to us! He is a pox on us. Major Tell has been our companion on many occasions. As King's agent-at-large, he has involved Cork and me in a number of cases which diverted us from coin-turning enterprises. Now he pops up again. And he pops up just when the Captain himself has given a plausible reason for not getting involved in this current affair. Damn, there's no escaping the man.

"Ah, Tell," Cork said with a grin. "That *is* different. He owes us some favors, eh, Oaks?"

"More like owing us £50,000 for all the times we've spent saving his neck."

He gave me that smirk-a-mouth of his and I knew we were off again on the hunt.

"Confound it, Cork," Major Tell rankled, "I know I owe you more than I can ever repay, but dammit all, man, this is not a backstairs murder. A distinguished officer—a man that was dubbed into the peerage by George III only a month ago, has been foully slain. I am not in concert with this plot theory, although I don't dismiss it, but this

Hayes fellow is guilty as sin. No one else could have done it, or have reason to."

"We've heard that many times before, old friend, and it doesn't always wash."

Cork had been at him for half an hour. We were in a small office off the jail's guardroom, having come there directly after parting from John Adams. He was off, I suspected, to inform his cousin and Hancock that Cork was at work. Tell had been courteous at first and even allowed us to speak with Hayes. But when Cork asked that all the dinner guests be assembled at the scene of the crime, Tell balked like an ox. Cork kept pressing him; he hadn't had that problem with Dobby Hayes, who was all talk and little sense.

"I'm for separation from Britain, Captain," Hayes told us in his cell after Cork had browbeaten Tell into allowing the interview, "but I'm not a fiend. I had no grudge against Sir Francis. I knew and liked him when he was Mr. Fairmont's guest back some eighteen years ago. He was just a Colonel then—gave me a sovereign when he left for Quebec. I actually admired the man."

"Times have changed, as well as attitudes, Dobby," Cork said with a shrug.

"You mean my brother's death," the prisoner said in disgust. "I had no affection for Davey, gentlemen. He was a King Street loafer, to my mind. When I came to the colonies, I worked out my time to Mr. Fairmont and he kept me on as the master of the servant hall. Would I repay him by killing a guest who had once been kind to me?"

As he spoke, I tried to study his face and eyes, as I knew Cork was doing. He certainly didn't look like a killer. Clean shaven, with a healthy complection, his chubby physique showing the munificence of the servant's hall table, Dobby Hayes looked the admirable footman, not the revengeful poisoner. Cork was digging.

"You were familiar with the guests?"

"To a fair turn, Captain Cork. 'T'weren't that many, since Sir Francis showed up unexpected."

"He just arrived at the Fairmonts' unexpectedly?"

"You might say that. The master, Titus Fairmont, had word that Sir Francis was to be in Boston Town and sent word to the General Staff that his house was open to the Knight. The Fairmont house is one of the finest about, as you may well know—finer even than Mr. Hancock's. Sir

Francis's ship was four days early and there he was, with bag and baggage, at our sill. You can imagine the chaos that caused with the help. Here we are with a knight of the realm newly arrived and a Marchioness getting ready to leave for New York. The laundry alone caused all manner of havoc, and on top of that, the mistress feels she must have a welcoming dinner party for Sir Francis. Thank heaven it turned out to be a small affair, with a grandiose ball planned for next week."

He stopped for a moment in thought. "Well, at least that's off the staff's back."

"And a murder charge clings to yours, Dobby," Cork reminded him. "Who was at the dinner?"

Dobby flicked a finger out and held its tip with his other hand, as if he were counting silverplate or bed linen.

"One, Sir Francis Moran; two and three were the master and mistress; four, the daughter of the house, Miss Priscilla; five, Mr. Milo Windam." He reversed hands. "Six, Mr. Colin Livingston; seven, the widow Chalmers; eight, Dr. Twilling, and Miss Rose Dribblon, a friend of Miss Priscilla's, makes nine."

"It seems Madam Fairmont is not socially skilled. There was one extra man at the table."

Dobby smiled benevolently. "Madam is no grand lady, sirs, but she tries her best. 'Sides, she planned on the Marchioness not getting ill and then it was too late in the evening to invite another lady."

"Yes, of course. Tell me, Dobby, did you lay the table yourself?"

"Aye, me and Sadie did. She's Mrs. Fairmont's personal maid and my wife, I'm proud to say."

"Are there no downstairs help?"

"Sally the cook, two scullies and a boy of all work. Couldn't trust them to do it right with a princess and a knight at the table. Used the best plate, we did, polished to a turn. If only I hadn't knocked the General's goblet as I reached to pour the wine, I wouldn't be here."

"How so?"

"That's when they say I put the poison in. You see, I had the decanter ready to fill his goblet when I tipped it a mite. It didn't fall over because I steadied it with my right hand. The General let it pass, but Madam gave me a look that seared my hide. When I steadied the goblet, they say I put the poison in."

"Did you?"

"No, Captain, 'pon my soul I didn't."

"Confound it, Cork," Tell was still raging against Cork's request for an assembly of witnesses. "Lord, man, Fairmont is a powerful personage—not to mention the Marchioness. I can't herd them together for your convenience and have you question them to death. The case is closed satisfactorily."

"Is it?"

"Of course it is. Who else would have reason to kill Sir Francis?"

"Of course you're sure it *was* Sir Francis who was the intended victim?"

"What the devil are you suggesting, Cork?"

"I mentioned to Oaks earlier that if Dobby Hayes wanted symbolic revenge, why not go after a bigger target—the Marchioness herself?"

The Major actually shuddered. "By the Duke's guns, Cork, that would have tumbled the beehive. But of course, the royal lady was not at the table."

"Which is precisely my point. Let us put Hayes aside for the moment. If he wanted to kill the Marchioness, he had ample opportunity during her visit. Let us assume for the moment that someone wanted the Marchioness dead."

"But she wasn't at the table!"

"Exactly, Tell, exactly. If she had been at the table, she would have had the seat of honor at Mr. Fairmont's right. But she had a last-minute spell of some sort, so obviously Moran would move up to that spot."

"Well, that's what did happen according to Mrs. Fairmont, but . . ."

"And suppose," Cork continued, "the poison was put in the goblet before the guests sat down to be served."

"*Before* the dinner?"

"When else, assuming Hayes is innocent?"

"That's preposterous, Cork. Sheer lunacy."

"No, Major, it is a possibility. Now, if someone attempted to take the Marchioness's life and was foiled by her sudden illness, is it not possible that he will try again? And if he succeeds, how will that stand in London?"

I'm sure, in his years of soldiering, the Major has lived through some dark moments, but if the expression now etched on his face was any indication, this was his greatest moment of despair. Cork can be relentless when he has found an opening and he drove home on his point. It took almost another hour, but finally Tell conceded that the murder should be investigated more fully. He would not, however, allow Cork to pursue the case openly. He finally agreed to Cork's suggestion that he pose as an *amicus curiae* who was helping to strengthen the case against Dobby Hayes.

As we walked back to Witloe's Nook and some needed sleep, I wondered how he was going to pursue one target while seemingly after another. I found out the next morning at ten, when we were admitted to the Fairmont home in Tell's company.

"Well, what more evidence would you ask for?" Titus Fairmont grumbled from his chair behind his massive oak desk. We had been shown into a small, well appointed room on the ground floor which served as the master's office. Fairmont's wealth was derived from a number of enterprises, and the papers and documents piled here and there gave evidence of his industry. Perhaps, I hoped futilely, some of this man's love of commerce would rub off on Cork. Fairmont was a spare fellow close on fifty years or so.

"Seems to me, Major," he went on, "that you got Hayes dead to rights. He slipped the poison in when he toppled the cup on orders from these damned troublemakers."

"Not quite dead to rights, sir," Cork injected. "Many a criminal case has fallen when the preparation was not thorough. The Major wants to be crack-sure that we have Hayes pinned."

"No one can fault you for that," Fairmont sighed. "I just hope you're not going to turn the house topsy-turvy. With Hayes in jail, things are confused enough."

"We shall be careful, sir,"Cork assured him. "Sir Francis was sitting to your right, as I understand. Did you observe Hayes's hands when he toppled the cup?"

"Can't say that I did. Too startled and embarrassed, I suppose. But I didn't have to *see* him. Man, he did it. My own footman!"

"Did you know he was a member of the Sons of Liberty, sir?"

"No, I did not! I knew his brother had been killed in that affair two years ago, but I always assumed Dobby to be a loyal subject."

"You were a friend of the General?"

"Not exactly. Well, yes, I guess you could say that. Knew him back during the French and Indian. He stayed with us a while before he went to Quebec. Then, of course, he went on to greater honors in Ireland and India."

"In addition to your family, you had other guests at table. A Miss Dribblon?"

"Rose Dribblon, a chum of my daughter. All agog over meeting royalty and a peer. Sort of scatterbrained like most of the young girls today. She wouldn't have noticed anything. And it was most fortunate that the Marchioness wasn't present to witness that awful thing. I can see her shocking the Queen with stories of how barbaric we are over here."

"How is Lady Caroline today?" Tell inquired.

"Tolerably well, considering all the chaos. I've convinced her to rest a few days before going to New York. If only she had left before Sir Francis arrived. Ah well, it's done."

"There was a gentleman named Colin Livingston here last night, too," Cork said, bringing the conversation back to pertinent points.

"Yes, he's new in these parts. Mighty successful for a young buck. Made a fortune in India and decided to come over here. We could use more like him, I can tell you."

"India, hey?" Cork was stroking his barba. "Must have known Moran out there."

"No, he says not. Seems he was in the north most of the time. He'd heard of Moran, of course. Who hadn't?"

"Yes, I also had his acquaintance. What of Milo Windham?"

"See here, Cork, I know you're supposed to be a genius at these things, but why all this interest in my guests?"

"Perhaps one of them saw Hayes put the poison in the goblet."

"Well, if they did, they would have said so last night." Fairmont's voice was showing irritation.

"They may not realize what they saw and I'll have to jog their memories."

Fairmont gave a sly wink. "Yes, I see your method. Not much to tell of Windham. Came here ten years ago and has done well in naval timber and such. Sound fellow. But the person to talk to is Cecily Chalmers. That woman notices everything. Her late husband was a friend of my father's. She's a hawk on details."

"I'll be sure to see her, sir," Cork assured him. "Now could we interview the lady of the house and your daughter?"

"Well if you want to waste your time, Captain, go right ahead. They're up in the sewing room doing more gossiping than sewing, I'll warrant. That flippitygibbet Rose Dribblon was back here at dawn, it seems, and they've been chirping about this affair like magpies ever since."

A serving girl called Nellie was summoned and she nervously led us up to the back of the house. Cork, en route, asked her where Dobby's wife Sadie was, and was told that she was below stairs.

"Poor woman's in a terrible state with the Hayes bein' dragged off. Put all the work on me and I'm dreadin' serving breakfast to the royal lady, having never been 'bout no great lady before. Here ye are, sirs."

The Fairmont sewing room was occupied by three well frocked ladies. Tell introduced us. Mrs. Fairmont was a plain woman with a touch of grey in her hair. Her daughter, Priscilla, favored neither parent, for she was a remarkably handsome young girl with well honed features and hair so blond and soft you were tempted to touch it. Her friend, Rose Dribblon, was a perky, pug-nosed imp with a coy smile. She truly was a bit of a magpie who tittered when she talked.

"I was at the other end of the table, of course," Mrs. Fairmont replied to Cork's question. "So my view was blocked by the centerpiece. Dobby was usually so correct in table service that I was shocked when he almost knocked over the goblet."

"He was nervous all day," Rose chirped. "Remember, Prissy, I mentioned it during the afternoon?"

"He was overworked, you mean!"

"Priscilla!" her mother chided her, "what will these gentlemen think of us? The servants aren't slaves. They were all nervous with such important people in the house."

"Oh, it's all so much bosh and bother over nothing," Priscilla stated firmly. "Royalty is a trick of fate. People born to the right parents."

"Priscilla!" Mrs. Fairmont was irked now. "I will not have that talk in your father's house. You must forgive my daughter, gentlemen. She expresses these wild views to bring attention to herself. An educated girl can be a burden."

She solicited our agreement and I, for one, gave it mentally. Cork, however, merely smirked.

"Just how did Dobby express his nervousness, Miss Dribblon?"

"In many ways, sir. I told him he had set the table wrong, and he told me I was wrong. Respectfully, of course, but . . ."

"You were wrong," Priscilla told her friend. "Even Her Royal Highness said so." Her reference to the Marchioness was definitely sarcastic. Rose's only rejoinder was to pout her mouth and say, "Oh pooh, Prissy."

Cork asked a few more questions which, to my mind, weren't pertinent, and we excused ourselves and retired to the hall.

"This all seems rather fruitless, doesn't it, Cork?" Tell asked impatiently. "We got nothing out of that encounter and I doubt we will with the others."

"You have lazy eyes, Major. You are committed to an assassination plot and can see nothing else, which is a pity. For myself, I have a thread of something, but it is not clear as yet."

"Well, the least you could do . . ." I was cut off by a resounding crash and a woman's voice screaming from upstairs.

"Look alive," Cork bellowed and made a bound for the back serving stairs. Tell and I followed with shocked obedience. My mind was ringing with Cork's prediction of the Marchioness being in danger. On the second floor landing we found Nellie, the serving girl, shaking uncontrollably. A breakfast tray lay on the floor outside an oak door, its former contents strewn about on the carpet.

"What happened, girl?" Tell demanded. He got nothing but more gasping sobs. Cork crossed the hall to the door and knocked on it.

"She threw a mirror at me, she did," Nellie pushed out the words. "Didn't know she was in her bath, sir."

In response to Cork's rapping, the door opened. In its frame stood an enraged woman in a satin morning wrapper. She was tall, dark-haired and fiercely beautiful.

"My lady," Cork said with a bow, "we feared for your safety, but it seems you were merely interrupted in your toilette. The girl meant no harm."

"She should be flogged. Don't you servants knock before entering a room?" The Marchioness's voice was sharp and officious.

The mention of flogging brought fresh wails from Nellie.

"Where is thy other servant, Sadie? At least she has some training, but *that* clod is impossible."

"My lady, I extend the apologies of the house, though it is not mine." Cork was being charming which he is devilishly good at where ladies are concerned. I had moved next to his side, wondering if I should genuflect, then dismissed the thought. The Marchioness's boudoir was obviously the master bedroom, given over to her for her stay. Near the fireplace was a high-backed French bathtub from which the lady had obviously just emerged in a rage.

"Who are you?" she demanded of my employer.

"Captain Jeremy Cork, at your service, m'am. We colonials take some time getting used to. May I suggest we send for another breakfast tray and set your room to rights?"

"You may be a colonial, sir, but you know your manners," she said, softening her look of disdain.

Nellie was set to scooping up the dropped tray while Tell and I, at Cork's suggestion, carried the portable bathtub out of the chamber. When we returned, Cork was sitting opposite her. She reclined on a chaise longue. Cork was oozing with concern for her comfort.

"Most distressing," the royal lady said. "My two ladies in waiting taken ill in Philadelphia and I am left to the ministrations of scullery maids. Then this dreadful death downstairs."

"Did you happen to know Sir Francis at court, m'am?"

She looked startled. "Well, hardly an acquaintance. These peers created by the sword are, to my mind, to be only tolerated. Of course, my dear cousin . . ." she cast her eyes at a miniature on the bedside table. It was a well executed portrait of Queen Charlotte. ". . . poor Charlotte must by her office suffer all courtiers, but I do not."

There was a knock on the door and a new tray and a new servant appeared. It was Sadie, Dobby's wife, to the rescue, which she handled expertly. We excused ourselves and left.

In a whisper, I said, "I hate to say it, but the Marchioness is a bit of a snob. I wonder if she really was ill last night at all."

"Probably thought the whole affair beneath her," Major Tell put in. "I'm relieved that you didn't mention your theory that the poison might have been meant for her."

"You do plan to protect her, however?"

"Do you think that necessary now, Cork?"

"Yes, a guard would guarantee her safety and protect *your* position should an attempt be made."

Tell agreed and left us to arrange for guards, and we descended the stairs and were let out of the house.

"Won't the sudden appearance of guards alarm her?" I asked as we strolled along.

"Oaks, that lofty lady will be pleased as punch. She'll love the spotlight and think it her due that she finally has an honor guard. But we have other trails to follow."

"To be sure, Colin Livingston. He may have run afoul of Sir Francis out in India, although Milo Windham seems to have had no relationship with the dead man."

"We shall see, old son, in due time, but for now, we seek the more important witness."

"Who, pray?"

"The hawk-eyed Widow Chalmers."

We made straight for the house pointed out to us by a servant back at the Fairmonts'. It sat in a side alley with its own small dooryard; more a large cottage than a town house.

The widow was quite old, but by no means feeble. She wore an old-fashioned dress with a matching cap on her cotton-white hair. Her eyes *were* quick and alert, much like a hawk's.

"Wondered when someone was going to get around to asking me some questions. Just 'cause a body's getting on don't think I don't see things, young man." She waggled a finger in Cork's direction.

"We share a bent for observation, madam," Cork said as we took chairs. "Too many people walk through life with their eyes half shut."

"Folks today, you mean. They wouldn't have lasted five minutes on the old frontier. Had to be alert in those days, watch every tree and bush for redskins."

"Had you met Sir Francis before last night, m'am?"

"Yes, when he was here back during the French and Indian."

"What was your opinion of him in those days?"

"Opinion!"

"Observation, then. Let me explain. I also knew Moran when he was a Colonel. Let me tell you what I saw. A dashing officer, a devilishly handsome blond Irishman with an eye for the ladies."

I expected the old lady to turn crimson at such a ribald description.

Of course, it was true, but why bring that up in front of this ancient widow? There was no embarrassment forthcoming, however. To my surprise, she gave a low cackle.

"He was all you say, I suppose, but that's a soldier's nature. You don't look a shrinking violet yourself, Captain Cork."

Cork smirked again and went on. "I was struck by something odd when at the Fairmont home this morning. I couldn't help thinking how heredity is strong and unerring."

"I agree that bloodlines will out," the widow said warily, "but I can't see where it figures in Moran's death."

"Really, Madam? I'm surprised you missed it, but no matter. Can you tell us exactly what happened at table last night?"

The old lady went through pretty much the same story of the fumbled goblet and Moran's drink of death. When we rose to leave, she looked straight into Cork's eyes. "I miss very little, sir, unless I care to. Some things should be overlooked, sir, and I trust you are a worthy gentleman."

"As worthy as conscience allows, m'am. Thank you and good day."

"That was quite a cryptic exchange. I trust I have missed something?"

"You usually do, Oaks. The old hawk has confirmed a suspicion of mine, first by her silence and then by her final appeal. Put some facts together, man. Moran was last here eighteen years ago when he lived in the Fairmont home."

"Yes, and you think something happened then. Why all this jabber about bloodlines?" The thought came back to me. When we had entered the sewing room, I had noticed that Priscilla Fairmont's handsomeness set her apart from both her father and her mother.

"By jing, Captain," I cried with amazement, "that child is the spitting image of a younger Francis Moran!"

"And she is eighteen years old, my lad."

"Is it possible? Mrs. Fairmont is certainly a proper Boston woman."

"Propriety be damned. Moran was a persuasive man and effective in war *and* love."

I shook my head in amazement. I know the human condition is fragile, but in Boston?

"Which one do you think, Cork? I'm for the wife. The wronged woman, and all that?"

"Or the revengeful daughter?"

"Oh no, she couldn't know her true parentage."

"Her eyes could have told her. But that goes for Fairmont himself," Cork explained.

"Yes, that makes more sense. He says he didn't know of Hayes's association with the Sons of Liberty, but he could have lied. Old Dobby would be suspect even if he hadn't tipped the goblet. By jing, you've done it again, Captain."

"Done what?"

"Solved the mystery, of course."

"Nonsense. I have put forward a conjecture that merely gives us a wider dimension to work with. There are some other facets that bother me. Let us see what some trolling in Colin Livingston's waters will bring."

When Titus Fairmont had described Colin Livingston as a young buck, he understated the case. He was almost a lad fresh to his maturity. But his youthful appearance was only skin covering. Inside the young fellow was a shrewd old man's insight and the bustle of his offices on Broad Street showed his business ability.

He, too, was fair-haired and blue-eyed, but his years in India had turned his skin nut brown, giving him a rugged appearance. He seemed to be engaged in the import-export trade and his clerks and warehouse men scurried about in an atmosphere of success which I admired deeply.

"Damndest thing I ever witnessed, I can tell you, gentlemen. Saw a fellow struck by a cobra out east who lasted longer than Sir Francis did. Certainly jarred the ladies, I can tell you. Don't mix in politics, haven't got the time, but this Hayes fellow seems to be the culprit. I can understand your wanting to build a stronger case, but I can help you little. Damn shame for the Fairmonts."

"You are a guest there often?"

"No," he smiled, "but I hope to be, as time goes on."

"Yes, Miss Fairmont *is* most attractive," Cork said. "What brings you to our shores, sir? I understand you found good fortune in India."

"The climate was not to my liking, sir. Bloody hot all the time, you know. The flaming sun would fry a man."

"Well, we appreciate your confirmation that Hayes had the only access to the lethal goblet, and we thank you."

We were on the street once more and I asked Cork if our final witness, Milo Windham, was next on the list.

"No, Oaks, but *list* is the appropriate word. We are off for the State House."

I followed like a loyal dog and when we reached the building in King Street, he made his way to the Board of Trade offices. Ten minutes later, with the help of a clerk prodded by a shilling, he had confirmed that there had never been a Colin Livingston registered with the East India Company in the last five years.

"Our young soldier could not enter trade out there without a registration."

"Soldier? You think he was a soldier out there?"

"He has a soldier's speech, punctuated with 'sirs' and army curse words. Perhaps Tell could trace him on the Army lists. In any event, we know he has a past."

"You know, Captain, he also could have knowledge of exotic poisons. The east abounds in them, I fear."

"Not likely an exotic poison, Oaks. Anyone can put his hands on rat killer. Well, let's go back to Witloe's Nook for a lunch."

"And what of Milo Windham?"

"Two birds with one stone, my lad. The gentleman has rooms there and I left a note this morning inviting him to join us. I asked him to extend our invitation to Dr. Twilling as well."

When Cork designs a lunch, it turns into a feast of no mean proportion. Of course, the table he had prepared was simple fare, by his terms. Consider a Leaping Joint, a specialty at Witloe's Nook, wherein a haunch of venison is slow simmered in Toggleberry sauce. This masterpiece is preceded by mounds of shucked oysters, corn chowder, baked taters with gobs of butter and the inevitable beans with slab pork. This is simple?

"My, my, this is a fine spread for a midday repast," Dr. Twilling said, peeping over his eye specs. One wouldn't expect a dour old man's attitude to hide a trencherman's ability. Milo Windham merely toyed with his food and I suspected he thought a luncheon that lavish was a total waste of money. I liked Windham at first sight. He was a no-nonsense man of commerce who sat down, checked his timepiece and informed Cork that he could spare only thirty minutes. He got to the point immediately.

"I know your reputation, Captain Cork, or should I say your escapades, where you rescue the seemingly guilty from the gallows and replace them with the true culprits. I further think that you intend to do so in this Moran affair. I wish you good fortune, sir, and stand ready to answer any question to the best and fullest of my ability. First, let me say I did not notice Dobby Hayes's mischance with the goblet. Second, I knew no one at the dinner except Fairmont himself, and I suspect I was there to be impressed for commercial reasons, not social. It was the first and, I might add, the last time I shall dine under his roof. Damned insulting to invite a man to witness a murder."

"Come now," Dr. Twilling said, "old Titus couldn't have known what a servant would be up to. He is the embarrassed party, if anyone. Here's a lady of the blood royal who has offered to aid his interests at court. I don't think the murder of a knight, almost in her presence, will predispose her to Titus Fairmont's commercial cause now."

"Yes, and I have lost two thousand pounds in the process."

"Two thousand pounds?" Cork asked.

"Yes. That is royalty for you. Seems the Marchioness is short of cash and Titus thought it would be a fine idea if we joined forces in a 'loan.' He called it a royal offering of friendship. Now she is so angry she'll probably do us more harm than good back in London."

"Gifts to the royal family are not uncommon," the good doctor said, savoring the joint.

"Pishes and poshes, Doctor. Well, Captain, I have but ten minutes left."

"I have what I want from you, sir."

"But you haven't asked me anything."

"Right you are, Mr. Windham. Very well, one question. Were you ever a registered agent for the East India Company?"

"How strange. The answer is yes. In the period 1758 through 1760, I was a London agent for that company, but I can't for the life of me see why that is pertinent."

"Believe me, sir, it is quite pertinent and I thank you for you candor. There is a lovely trifle for dessert if you can wait."

Windham declined and left for some money-making conference or other—an activity we should be pursuing, but we finished our meal instead.

"Tell me, Doctor," Cork asked over the trifle, which I admit was expensively delicious, "have you determined the nature of the poison?"

"I am no expert, but it 'pears to be a quick acting substance used on vermin. I learned only an hour ago that this Major Tell has discovered a tin of the stuff in the sub-kitchen of the Fairmont house. Seems Dobby had it ready to hand."

"Many kitchens have vermin, Doctor. I take it you attend to the Fairmont household's medical needs?"

"Have for twenty years."

"Would you say that Mrs. Fairmont is a vengeful woman?"

The doctor looked perplexed. "Vengeful? Mercy no. I wouldn't say so. Mild woman, that. You don't think she had anything to do with this?"

"Forgive the implication. I was just curious about her emotional stand."

"Well, I can tell you she is the most proper of womankind, a truly gentle nature, sir."

"Yes, I think you are right. More trifle, gentlemen?"

Later that day, just after dark, Cork started to act strangely. All afternoon he had sat silently drinking Knock. At one point, he left our rooms and returned an hour later with a queer smile on his face.

"You've hit on something," I said after the supper dishes had been cleared.

"It's a preposterous long shot, my friend, and quite dangerous if I am wrong."

"Then I shall share the peril equally, sir, as always."

"No, not this time, Oaks. I will need you in reserve."

He got up and went to his sea chest and, to my amazement, took out his long glass.

"Going star-gazing?" I chided.

"Yes, in a way. A good navigator fixes his position before an action. I shall be back within the hour."

But he wasn't. Nor was he by ten o'clock. My worry was increasing when about midnight, a frantic rapping came at the door. It was the Fairmonts' servant, Sadie Hayes, Dobby's wife. She was wide-eyed with agitation, and breathless.

"Your master has been taken by the sojers," she gasped. "Ye best come quick."

"Where, how?"

"Tarry not a moment. Come."

Twenty minutes later, we were at the Fairmont door and to my surprise, Major Tell opened it.

"Major, what's going on here? Where's Cork?"

"It's despicable, Oaks. To think that Cork is a common peep-o'night!"

"Cork peeping in ladies' windows! That's insane, Major, and you know it."

"Oh, I wish it were. He was caught by a member of the guard mount I put about the house. Having a fine old time for himself observing ladies in their boudoirs."

The shame of it fell over me like an odoriferous fog. The man I admired above all others had a baser side I had never known.

"Certainly it can be hushed up, Major?"

"How, man? He has demanded an immediate trial and, by God, he's going to get one. Judge Cooper is here at my request. That damned fool employer of yours has called character witnesses who don't even know him. I tell you, Oaks, the man's gone mad. Fairmont is livid that his women have been seen dressing for bed. And he'll prosecute to the limit."

I was appalled, of course, but also puzzled. Cork is no stranger to women preparing for bedtime, so why in heaven did he put himself in jeopardy? He is a loose living man, but no lecher. Or was he?

I became suspicious when I followed Tell into the main drawing room where Judge Cooper was to hold his informal court. There were all the guests of the tragic dinner—the Fairmont family, Rose Dribblon, the widow Chalmers, Colin Livingston, Dr. Twilling, Milo Windham and lastly, the Marchioness herself.

Rose Dribblon was saying to the judge, "I was horrified, your Honor, when I gazed into the garden and saw this *man* with a spy glass observing the house in moonlight. You are a filthy fellow, Captain Cork."

"Unethical, perhaps, young lady," Cork retorted and then turned to the judge. "Sir, shall we do the Bay Colony a service this night and solve a murder?"

Judge Cooper, a squat little man, looked galled. "Don't cloud the issue, Cork."

"Nay, sir, I'm the fresh breeze to dispel the fog. See here, we have put this royal lady to a great inconvenience. Before she leaves us tomorrow for New York, I think we should show her that we colonials are not the crude bumpkins we seem. Perhaps it will allay any hard feelings she would carry back to the Court of St. James."

"You mean you can prove conclusively that Hayes did it?" Titus Fairmont asked with glee. He obviously hoped to impress the Marchioness.

"I can prove the murderer out, sir." Cork said.

"Your Honor," Milo Windham joined his partner in protecting his investment, "perhaps we should hear him and take up the other charge later. Cork does have a knack in these affairs."

"This is most irregular," the judge mused aloud, "but if it would show our royal visitor that our courts are swift and fair . . ." He, too, was out to impress the Marchioness. "What have you to say for yourself, Cork?"

"Many minds full, sir; the winnowings of a hundred thoughts, dozens of conjectures and surmises and, at last, hopefully, a solution among the silt."

He was in high style, as he always is with an audience in attendance. So he had done it again. Contrived to bring things to a head by this peep-o'night ruse.

"Now let's to it," Cork went on. "In all fairness, we must put Dobby Hayes aside and explore other sectors. All here were in this house at the time of the murder and their names must be cleared beyond all doubt."

I thought Titus Fairmont would swallow his tongue as he spluttered and fumed. "This is unpardonable, Cork. I will not have my guests treated in this way."

"One of your guests was treated most shabbily and it cost him his life. Now, sir, if you will be quiet and let me proceed."

"Yes, Mr. Fairmont, let the man go on so we can be done with it," the judge said wearily.

"Thank you, sir." Cork bowed. "First, I asked myself what was the motive for the murder. Since Sir Francis had not been in the colonies for eighteen years, it would have to be for an old grudge. That would discount Messrs. Windham and Livingston, for they are recent arrivals. On the other hand, that would point to those people who knew him years ago; the Fairmonts, Widow Chalmers and, of course, Dr. Twilling."

I glanced from face to face. Fairmont glared, his wife sat impassively. Widow Chalmers stared dead ahead as if in a worrisome trance. Only Dr. Twilling spoke.

"And what possible grudge could I have, sir?" he asked indignantly.

Cork shrugged his shoulders. "It is only that you, as a medical man, are familiar with poisons and have access to them."

"I told you, it seems to have been rat poison which was found here in the house. What nonsense!"

"I agree, doctor," Cork replied. "I felt an eighteen-year-old grudge murder *was* nonsense. As nonsensical as Dobby Hayes committing murder to revenge a brother he didn't care two pins about."

The judge interrupted with a grump. "Seems to me, Cork, you've exonerated everyone."

"Yes, on the motive of revenge, although Colin Livingston was in that category for a while."

Livingston had a superior smile on his face. "Thank you for exonerating me, Cork. I appreciate it."

"Delighted, sir. You see, at first, I believed that you were an agent for the East India Company, but the records at the Board of Trade do not list you. However, records are marvelous things—one thing the British are expert in is the listing details. You were absent from the East India list, but I'm afraid Major Tell has found your name on the Army lists. Subaltern Colin Livingston of the 234th Light Horse—cashiered over a year ago."

Livingston started up out of his chair. "You scoundrel," he snarled. He then stopped and looked hopelessly at Priscilla Fairmont.

"No sir, *I* did not steal money from my brother officers—I suggest you are the scoundrel and, I might add, one without further prospects in this house."

The young man sank back into his chair, seething in silence.

"I say," the judge perked up, "there's a motive for you. This young scamp killed Moran to avoid being detected as a cad."

"Well done, your Honor," Cork congratulated him. "That crossed my mind. But all he had to do was refuse the invitation to dinner. Yet he came and met Sir Francis quite boldly. No, it won't wash. Generals pay little or no attention to the sins of junior officers."

"Well then, confound it, Cork, where does that leave us?" The judge was irritated at the fallacy of his theory and the verbal rigamarole Cork was spinning. I admit I was getting a bit sick of it myself.

"It leaves us with Milo Windham. No, pray, sir, don't bestir yourself. The same East India list that exposed Livingston verified your story that you never left England until you came here. Which brings us to my little experiment this evening with my long glass."

"You dirty man," Rose Dribblon chastised him.

"I told you before, young lady, the word is *unethical*, and my act was necessary, for if I had been wrong, it would have cost me my head."

He started pacing nervously around the room as he spoke, and I feared he had run out of excuses for his actions.

"You see, your Honor, you had it quite right about the murderer wanting to escape detection by Sir Francis, and she almost did."

To our horror, Cork reached over and savagely tore the bodice of the Marchioness's dress, baring her shoulder and breast.

The woman screamed. The judge said, "Good Lord," but the royal lady sat there, not embarrassed, but shaking with rage.

It was then that I noticed the target of Cork's horrendous act. There, on the high section of her breast, was a bright red scar—a brand forming the letter F. "F" for felon.

"Madam, I know not your true name. It could be any one of twenty printed in the runaway indentured columns. But we'll find out, my girl."

And find out we did, just a fortnight later. Tell brought the news to our dinner table at Witloe's Nook.

"It was a Sarah Wilson," he said, taking a seat. "Ran away from her owner in Baltimore over six months ago."

"And she had served at court?" Cork asked.

"Bless my soul, you're a conjuror, Cork, pure magician."

"No, her speech was too perfect; she had been around quality all her life."

"To be sure. She had been a servant at court and absconded with her mistress's jewels. A lady in waiting, I believe. Then that she-devil posed as the Queen's cousin in leading houses from Charleston to New

Port, borrowing money, promising royal offices. But you still haven't told us how you caught on to her."

"By elimination *and* one telling fact that everyone forgot."

Tell and I looked at each other in puzzlement.

"Sir Francis arrived four days early, did he not? She was trapped in the house. The sister of the Queen could not avoid a meeting with a knight of the realm, so she feigned illness."

"But the poison?"

"The young ladies told us she oversaw the laying of the table. She could coat her own goblet with poison knowing she wouldn't be there and that the one person who could expose her game would be moved to the spot."

"But you say elimination of suspects uncovered her," I said. "Surely no one would suspect a royal personage of murder."

Cork took a mouthful of roast goose and scoffed. "Put it together, Oaks. She travels without servants, becomes enraged when a servant enters her bath. Her only credential seemed to be a miniature of the Queen. I suspect *we* Americans *are* bumpkins."

"And you actually used your long glass to spy on her when she was preparing for bed?" Tell leered.

"You can thank Oaks for putting me onto the fact that she might have been a runaway servant. He, himself, said they were mostly branded felons allowed to plead right of clergy. In England, most women are branded on the breast or shoulder. All I had to do was test the theory with a little peep-o'night. Fortunately, it worked out."

"And if it hadn't?"

"We would have trailed her elsewhere, Oaks, a task I'm sure you would have enjoyed."

AUTHOR'S NOTE: Although this is a fictional story, the exploits of Sarah Wilson, who was probably America's first con woman, are quite true. She posed as the Marchioness de Waldegrave quite successfully in the major cities of the colonies during the late 1700s, although historical records disagree whether she posed as the "sister" or "cousin" to the Queen. In either case, she got away with it because there is no evidence that she was ever caught.

MULDOON AND THE NUMBERS GAME

ROBERT L. FISH

A few of those who believed in the powers of old Miss Gilhooley said she did it with ESP, but the majority claimed she had to be a witch, she having come originally from Salem, which she never denied. The ones who scoffed, of course, said it was either the percentages, or just plain luck. But the fact was, she could see things—in cloud formations, or in baseball cards, or in the throwing of bottle caps, among other things— that were truly amazing.

Muldoon was one of those who believed in old Miss Gilhooley implicitly. Once, shortly after his Kathleen had passed away three years before, old Miss Gilhooley, reading the foam left in his beer glass, told him to beware of a tall, dark woman, and it wasn't two days later that Mrs. Johnson, who did his laundry, tried to give him back a puce striped shirt as one of his own that Muldoon wouldn't have worn to a Chinese water torture. And not long after, old Miss Gilhooley, reading the lumps on his skull after a brawl at Maverick Station, said he'd be taking a long voyage over water, and the very next day didn't his boss send him over to Nantasket on a job, and that at least halfway across the bay?

So, naturally, being out of work and running into old Miss Gilhooley having a last brew at Casey's Bar & Grill before taking the bus to her sister's in Framingham for a week's visit, Muldoon wondered why he had never thought of it before. He therefore took his beer and sat down in the booth across from the shawled old Miss Gilhooley and put his problem directly to her.

"The unemployment's about to run out, and it looks like nobody wants no bricks laid no more, at least not by me," he said simply. "I need money. How do I get some?"

Old Miss Gilhooley dipped her finger in his beer and traced a pattern across her forehead. Then she closed her eyes for fully a minute by the clock before she opened them.

"How old's your mother-in-law?" she asked in her quavering voice, fixing Muldoon with her steady eyes.

Muldoon stared. "Seventy-four," he said, surprised. "Just last month. Why?"

"I don't rightly know," old Miss Gilhooley said slowly. "All I know is I closed me eyes and asked meself, 'How can Muldoon come up with some money?' And right away, like in letters of fire across the insides of me eyeballs, I see, 'How old is Vera Callahan?' It's got to mean something."

"Yeah," Muldoon said glumly. "But what?"

"I'll miss me bus," said old Miss Gilhooley, and came to her feet, picking up her ancient haversack. "It'll come to you, don't worry." And with a smile she was through the door.

Seventy-four, Muldoon mused as he walked slowly toward the small house he now shared with his mother-in-law. You'd think old Miss Gilhooley might have been a little more lavish with her clues. She'd never been that cryptic before. Seventy-four! Suddenly Muldoon stopped dead in his tracks. There was only one logical solution, and the more he thought about it, the better it looked. Old Miss Gilhooley and Vera Callahan had been lifelong enemies. And his mother-in-law had certainly mentioned her life insurance policy often enough when she first used it ten years before as her passport into the relative security of the Muldoon ménage. And, after all, seventy-four was a ripe old age, four years past the biblical threescore and ten, not to mention being even further beyond the actuarial probabilities.

Muldoon smiled at his own brilliance in solving the enigma so quickly. Doing away with his mother-in-law would be no chore. By Muldoon's figuring, she had to weigh in at about a hundred pounds dripping wet and carrying an anvil in each hand. Nor, he conceded, would her passing be much of a loss. She did little except creep between bed and kitchen and seemed to live on tea. Actually, since the poor soul suffered such a wide variety of voiced ailments, the oblivion offered by the grave would undoubtedly prove welcome.

He thought for a moment of checking with the insurance company as to the exact dollar value of his anticipated inheritance, but then concluded it might smack of greediness. It might also look a bit peculiar when the old lady suffered a fatal attack of something-or-other so soon after the inquiry. Still, he felt sure it would be a substantial amount; old Miss Gilhooley had never failed him before.

When he entered the house, the old lady was stretched out on the couch, taking her afternoon nap (she slept more than a cat, Muldoon thought) and all he had to do was to put one of the small embroidered pillows over her face and lean his two hundred pounds on it for a matter of several minutes, and that was that. She barely wriggled during the process. Muldoon straightened up, removed the pillow, and gazed down. He had been right; he was sure he detected a grateful expression on the dead face. He fluffed the pillow up again, placed it in its accustomed location, and went to call the undertaker.

It was only after all decent arrangements had been made, all hard bargaining concluded, and all the proper papers signed, that Muldoon called the insurance company—and got more than a slight shock. His mother-in-law's insurance was for four hundred dollars, doubtless a princely sum when her doting parents had taken it out a matter of sixty years before, but rather inadequate in this inflationary age. Muldoon tried to cancel the funeral, but the undertaker threatened suit, not to mention a visit from his nephew, acknowledged dirty-fight champion of all South Boston. The additional amount of money Muldoon had to get up, to finally get Vera Callahan underground, completely wiped out his meager savings.

So that, obviously, was not what old Miss Gilhooley had been hinting at, Muldoon figured. He was not bitter, nor was his faith impaired; the fault had to be his own. So there he was with the numbers again. Seventy-four . . . seventy-four. . . . Could they refer to the mathematical possibilities? Four from seven left three—but three what? Three little pigs? Three blind mice? Three blind pigs? He gave it up. On the other hand, four plus seven equaled . . .

He smote himself on the head for his previous stupidity and

quickly rubbed the injured spot, for Muldoon was a strong man with a hand like the bumper on a gravel truck. Of course! *Seven and four added up to eleven. ELEVEN!* And—Muldoon told himself with authority—if that wasn't a hint to get into the floating crap game that took place daily, then his grandfather came from Warsaw.

So Muldoon took out a second mortgage on his small house, which netted him eight hundred dollars plus change, added to that the two hundred he got for his three-and-a-half-year-old, secondhand-to-begin-with car, and with the thousand dollars in big bills in his pocket, made his way to Casey's Bar & Grill.

"Casey!" he asked in his ringing voice, "Where's the floating game today?"

"Callahan Hotel," Casey said, rinsing glasses. "Been there all week. Room Seventy-Four."

Muldoon barely refrained from smiting himself on the head again. How dumb could one guy be? If only he'd asked before, he would not have had to deal with that thief of an undertaker, not to mention the savings he'd squandered—although in truth he had to admit the small house was less crowded with the old lady gone.

"Thanks," he said to Casey, and hurried from the bar.

The group standing around the large dismountable regulation crap table in Room Seventy-Four of the Callahan Hotel, was big and tough, but Muldoon was far from intimidated. With one thousand dollars in his pocket and his fortune about to be made, Muldoon felt confidence flowing through him like a fourth beer. He nodded to one of the gamblers he knew there and turned to the man next to him, tapping him on the shoulder.

"Got room for one more?" he asked.

"Hunnert dollars minimum," the man said without looking up from the table. "No credit."

Muldoon nodded. It was precisely the game he wanted. "Who's the last man?" he asked.

"Me," the man said, and clamped his lips shut.

Muldoon took the money from his pocket and folded the bills lengthwise gambler-fashion, wrapping them around one finger, awaiting his turn. When at last the dice finally made their way to him, Muldoon laid a hundred-dollar bill on the table, picked up the dice, and shook them next to one ear. They made a pleasant, ivory sound. A large smile appeared on Muldoon's face.

"Seven and four are me lucky numbers," he announced. "Same as them that's on the door of this room, here. Now, if a guy could only roll an eleven *that* way!"

"He'd end up in a ditch," the back man said expressionlessly.

"You're faded—roll them dice. Don't wear 'em out."

Muldoon did not wear out the dice. In fact, he had his hands on them exactly ten times, managing to throw ten consecutive craps, equally divided between snake-eyes and boxcars. They still speak of it at the floating crap game; it seems the previous record was only five and the man who held it took the elevator to the roof—they were playing at some hotel up in Copley Square that day—and jumped off. Muldoon turned the dice over to the man to his right and wandered disconsolately out of the hotel.

Out in the street Muldoon ambled along a bit aimlessly, scuffing his heavy work brogans against anything that managed to get in his way; a tin can, a broken piece of brick he considered with affectionate memory before he kicked it violently; a crushed cigarette pack. He tried for an empty candy wrapper but with his luck missed. Seventy-four! *Seventy-four!* What in the bleary name of Eustice Q. Peabody could the blaggety numbers mean? (The Sisters had raised Muldoon strictly; no obscenity passed his lips.) He tried to consider the matter logically, forcing his temper under control. Old Miss Gilhooley had never failed him, nor would she this time. He was simply missing the boat.

Seventy-four? *Seventy-four?* The figures began to take on a certain rhythm, like the *Punch, brother, punch with care* of Mark Twain. Muldoon found himself trying to march to it. Sev-en-ty-four! Seven*ty*-four! He shook his head; it lacked beat. Seventy-four-hup! NO. Seven-*ty*-four-*hup!* Better but still not it. The old lady had been seventy-four and now she was zero. He tried that. Seventy-four-zero! Seventy-four-zero-hup! Almost it but not quite. Seven-four-zero-hup! Seven-four-zero, *hup!* Got it! Muldoon said to himself, deriving what little satisfaction he could from the cadence, and marched along swinging. Seven-four-zero, *hup!*

And found himself in front of Casey's Bar & Grill, so he went inside and pulled a stool up to the deserted bar.

"Beer," he said.

"How'd you do in the game?" Casey asked.

"Better give me a shot with that beer," Muldoon said by way of an answer. He slugged the shot down, took about half his beer for a chaser, and considered Casey as he wiped his mouth. "Casey," he said earnestly, really wanting to know, "what do the numbers seven and four mean to you?"

"Nothing," Casey said.

"How about seven, four, and zero?"

"Nothing," Casey said. "Maybe even less."

"How about backwards?" Muldoon asked in desperation, but Casey had gone to the small kitchen in the rear to make himself a sandwich during the slack time, and Muldoon found himself addressing thin air. He tossed the proper amount of change on the counter and started for the door. Where he ran into a small man named O'Leary, who ran numbers for the mob. It wasn't what he preferred, but it was a living.

"Wanna number today, Mr. Muldoon?" O'Leary asked.

Muldoon was about to pass on with a shake of his head, when he suddenly stopped. A thrill went through him from head to foot. Had he been in a cartoon a light bulb would have lit up in a small circle over his head. Not being in a cartoon, he kicked himself, his heavy brogan leaving a bruise that caused him to limp painfully for the next three weeks.

Good Geoffrey T. Soppingham! He must have been blind! Blind! Insane! What possible meaning could numbers have, if not *that they were numbers?* Just thinking about it made Muldoon groan. If he hadn't killed the old lady and gotten into that stupid crap game, at this moment he could be putting down roughly fifteen hundred bucks on Seven-Four-Zero. Fifteen-hundred dollars at five-hundred-to-one odds! Still, if he hadn't smothered the old lady, he'd never have come up with the zero, so it wasn't a total loss. But the floating game had been completely unnecessary.

Because now Muldoon didn't have the slightest doubt as to what the numbers meant.

"Somethin' wrong, Mr. Muldoon?" O'Leary asked, concerned with the expression on Muldoon's face.

"No!" Muldoon said, and grasped the runner by the arm, drawing him back into Casey's Bar & Grill, his hand like the clamshell bucket of a steam shovel on the smaller man's bicep. He raised his voice, bellowing, *"Casey!"*

Casey appeared from the kitchen, wiping mayonnaise from his chin. "Don't shout," he said. "What do you want?"

Muldoon was prying his wedding ring from his finger. He laid it down on the bar. "What'll you give me for this?"

Casey looked at Muldoon as if the other man had suddenly gone made. "This ain't no hockshop, Muldoon," he said.

But Muldoon was paying no attention. He was slipping his wristwatch and its accompanying stretch band over his thick fingers. He placed the watch down on the bar next to the ring.

"One hundred bucks for the lot," he said simply. "A loan, is all. I'll pay it back tonight." As Casey continued to look at him with fishy eyes, Muldoon added in a quiet, desperate voice, "I paid sixty bucks each for them rings; me and Kathleen had matching ones. And that watch set me back better than a bill-and-a half all by itself, not to mention the band, which is pure Speidel. How about it?" A touch of pleading entered his voice. "Come on; we been friends a long time."

"Acquaintances," Casey said, differentiating, and continued to eye Muldoon coldly. "I ain't got that much cash in the cash register right now."

"Jefferson J. Billingsly the cash register," Muldoon said, irked. "You got that much and more in your pants pocket."

Casey studied the other a moment longer and then casually swept the ring and the watch from the counter into his palm, and pocketed them. From another pocket he brought out a wallet that looked like it was suffering from mumps. He began counting out bills.

"Ninety-five bucks," he said. "Five percent off the top, just like the Morris Plan."

Muldoon was about to object, but time was running out.

"Someday we'll discuss this transaction in greater detail, Casey," he said. "Out in the alley," and he turned to O'Leary, grasping both of the smaller man's arms for emphasis. "O'Leary I want ninety-five bucks on number seven-four-zero. Got it? *Seven-Four-Zero!* Today!"

"Ninety-five bucks?" O'Leary was stunned. "I never wrote no slip bigger than a deuce in my life, Mr. Muldoon," he said. He thought a moment. "No, a fin," he said brightly, but then his face fell. "No a deuce. I remember now, the fin was counterfeit. . . ."

"You're wasting time," Muldoon said in a dangerous voice. He suddenly realized he was holding the smaller man several inches from the floor, and lowered him. "Will they pay off? That's the question," he said in a quieter voice, prepared for hesitation.

"Sure they pay off, Mr. Muldoon," O'Leary said, straightening his sleeves into a semblance of their former shape. "How long you figure they stay alive, they start welching?"

"So long as they know it," Muldoon said, and handed over the ninety-five bucks. He took his receipt in return, checked the number carefully to make sure O'Leary had made no mistake, and slipped the paper into his pocket. Then he turned to Casey.

"A beer," he said in a voice that indicated their friendship had suffered damage. "And take it out of that five bucks you just stole!"

Muldoon was waiting in a booth at Casey's Bar & Grill at seven o'clock P.M., which was the time the runners normally had the final three figures of the national treasury balance—which was the Gospel by St. Carlo Gambino that week. Muldoon knew that straight cash in hand would not be forthcoming; after all, he was due a matter of over forty-seven-thousand dollars. Still he'd take a check. If he hadn't gotten into that crap game, he'd have been rich—or, more probably, in a ditch like the man had mentioned this afternoon. Who was going to pay off that kind of loot? The mob in Boston, that was sure. Better this way, Muldoon thought. Forty-seven grand was big enough to be the year's best advertisement for the racket, but still it was enough by their standards for the mob to loosen up.

It was a nice feeling being financially secure after the problems of the past few years, and he certainly had no intention of splurging. All honest debts would be cleared up, of course, and he'd have to buy himself some wheels—a compact, nothing fancy—but the rest would go into the bank. At five percent it wouldn't earn no fortune, he knew, but it would still be better than a fall off a high scaffold onto a low sidewalk.

He reached for his beer and saw old Miss Gilhooley walking through the door. Had a week passed so quickly? He supposed it must have; what with the funeral, and one thing and another, the time had flown. He waved her over and called out to Casey to bring old Miss Gilhooley anything her heart desired.

Old Miss Gilhooley settled herself in the booth across from him and noted the expression on his face. "So you figured it out, Muldoon," she said.

"Not right off," Muldoon admitted. "To be honest, it just come to me this afternoon. But better late than never; at least it come." He leaned over the table confidentially. "It was the numbers, see? The seven and the four of her age, plus the zero at the end, because whether you heard or not, that's what the poor soul is now."

Old Miss Gilhooley sipped the beer Casey had brought, and nodded. "That's what I figured," she said, "especially after seeing O'Leary in me dreams three nights running, and me old enough to be his mother."

"And I can't thank you enough—" Muldoon started to say, and then paused, for O'Leary had just burst through the door of the bar like a Roman candle, and was hurrying over to them, brushing people aside. His eyes were shining.

"Mr. Muldoon! Mr. Muldoon!" O'Leary cried excitedly. "I never seen nothin' like it in all me born days! And on a ninety-five dollar bet!"

Muldoon grinned happily.

"Only one number away!" O'Leary cried, still impressed by his close brush with fame. "Tough you had Seven-Four-Zero. Seven-Five-Zero wins!"

O'Leary sighed, and then put the matter from his mind. After all, life had to go on. "Wanna number for tomorrow, Mr. Muldoon?"

"No," Muldoon said in a dazed tone, and turned to old Miss Gilhooley who was making strange noises. But they were not lamentations for Muldoon; to Muldoon's surprise the old lady was cackling like a fiend.

"That Vera Callahan!" she said triumphantly. "I always *knew* she lied about her age!"

NEVER SHAKE
A FAMILY TREE

DONALD E. WESTLAKE

Actually, I have never been so shocked in all my born days, and I seventy-three my last birthday and eleven times a grandmother and twice a great-grandmother. But never in all my born days did I see the like, and that's the truth.

Actually, it all began with my interest in genealogy, which I got from Mrs. Ernestine Simpson, a lady I met at Bay Arbor, in Florida, when I went there three summers ago. I certainly didn't like Florida— far too expensive, if you ask me, and far too bright, and with just too many mosquitoes and other insects to be believed—but I wouldn't say the trip was a total loss, since it did interest me in genealogical research, which is certainly a wonderful hobby, as well as being very valuable, what with one thing and another.

Actually, my genealogical researches had been valuable in more ways than one, since they have also been instrumental in my meeting some very pleasant ladies and gentlemen, although some of them only by postal, and of course it was through this hobby that I met Mr. Gerald Fowlkes in the first place.

But I'm getting far ahead of my story, and ought to begin at the beginning, except that I'm blessed if I know where the beginning actually is. In one way of looking at things, the beginning is my introduction to genealogy through Mrs. Ernestine Simpson, who has since passed on, but in another way the beginning is really almost two hundred years ago, and in still another way the story doesn't really begin until the first time I came across the name of Euphemia Barber.

Well. Actually, I suppose, I really ought to begin by explaining just what genealogical research is. It is the study of one's family tree. One checks marriage and birth and death records, searches old family Bibles and talks to various members of one's family, and one gradually builds up a family tree, showing who fathered whom and what year, and when so-and-so died, and so on. It's really a fascinating work, and there are any number of amateur genealogical societies throughout the country, and when one has one's family tree built up for as far as one wants— seven generations, or nine generations, or however long one wants— then it is possible to write this all up in a folder and bequeath it to the local library, and then there is a *record* of one's family for all time to come, and I for one think that's important and valuable to have even if my youngest boy Tom does laugh at it and say it's just a silly hobby. Well, it *isn't* a silly hobby. After all, I found evidence of murder that way, didn't I?

So, actually, I suppose the whole thing really begins when I first came across the name of Euphemia Barber. Euphemia Barber was John Anderson's second wife. John Anderson was born in Goochland County, Virginia, in 1754. He married Ethel Rita Mary Rayborn in 1777, just around the time of the Revolution, and they had seven children, which wasn't at all strange for that time, though large families have, I notice, gone out of style today, and I for one think it's a shame.

At any rate, it was John and Ethel Anderson's third child, a girl named Prudence, who is in my direct line on my mother's father's side, so of course I had them in my family tree. But then, in going through Appomattox County records—Goochland County being now a part of Appomattox, and no longer a separate county of its own—I came across the name of Euphemia Barber. It seems that Ethel Anderson died in 1793, in giving birth to her eighth child—who also died—and three years later, 1796, John Anderson remarried, this time marrying a widow named Euphemia Barber. At that time, he was forty-two years of age, and her age was given as thirty-nine.

Of course, Euphemia Barber was not at all in my direct line, being John Anderson's second wife, but I was interested to some extent in her pedigree as well, wanting to add her parents' names and her place of birth to my family chart, and also because there were some Barbers fairly distantly related on my father's mother's side, and I was wondering if this Euphemia might be kin to them. But the records were very incomplete, and all I could learn was that Euphemia Barber was not a native of Virginia, and had apparently only been in the area for a year or two when she had married John Anderson. Shortly after John's death in 1798, two years after their marriage, she had sold the Anderson farm, which was apparently a somewhat prosperous location, and had moved away again. So that I had neither birth nor death records on her, nor any record of her first husband, whose last name had apparently been Barber, but only the one lone record of her marriage to my great-great-great-great-great-grandfather on my mother's father's side.

Actually, there was no reason for me to pursue the question further, since Euphemia Barber wasn't in my direct line anyway, but I had worked diligently and, I think, well, on my family tree, and had it almost complete back nine generations, and there was really very little left to do with it, so I was glad to do some tracking down.

Which is why I included Euphemia Barber in my next entry in the Genealogical Exchange. Now, I suppose I ought to explain what the Genealogical Exchange is. There are any number of people throughout the country who are amateur genealogists, concerned primarily with their own family trees, but of course family trees do interlock, and any one of these people is liable to know about just the one record which has been eluding some other searcher for months. And so there are magazines devoted to the exchanging of some information, for nominal fees. In the last few years, I had picked up all sorts of valuable leads in this way. And so my entry in the summer issue of the Genealogical Exchange read:

> BUCKLEY, Mrs. Henrietta Rhodes, 119A Newbury St., Boston, Mass. Xch data on *Rhodes, Anderson, Richards, Pryor, Marshall, Lord*. Want any info Euphemia *Barber*, m. John Anderson, Va. 1796.

Well. The Genealogical Exchange had been helpful to me in the past, but I never received anywhere near the response caused by Euphemia Barber. And the first response of all came from Mr. Gerald Fowlkes.

It was a scant two days after I received my own copy of the

summer issue of the Exchange. I was still poring over it myself, looking for people who might be linked to various branches of my family tree, when the telephone rang. Actually, I suppose I was somewhat irked at being taken from my studies, and perhaps I sounded a bit impatient when I answered.

If so, the gentleman at the other end gave no sign of it. His voice was most pleasant, quite deep and masculine, and he said, "May I speak, please, with Mrs. Henrietta Buckley?"

"This is Mrs. Buckley," I told him.

"Ah," he said. "Forgive my telephoning, please, Mrs. Buckley. We have never met. But I noticed your entry in the current issue of the Genealogical Exchange—"

"Oh?"

I was immediately excited, all thought of impatience gone. This was surely the fastest reply I'd ever had to date!

"Yes," he said. "I noticed the reference to Euphemia Barber. I do believe that may be the Euphemia Stover who married Jason Barber in Savannah, Georgia, in 1791. Jason Barber is in my direct line, on my mother's side. Jason and Euphemia had only the one child, Abner, and I am descended from him."

"Well," I said. "You certainly do seem to have complete information."

"Oh, yes," he said. "My own family chart is almost complete. For twelve generations, that is. I'm not sure whether I'll try to go back farther than that or not. The English records before 1600 are so incomplete, you know."

"Yes, of course," I said. I was, I admit, taken aback. Twelve generations! Surely that was the most ambitious family tree I had ever heard of, though I had read sometimes of people who had carried particular branches back as many as fifteen generations. But to actually be speaking to a person who had traced his entire family back twelve generations!

"Perhaps," he said, "it would be possible for us to meet, and I could give you the information I have on Euphemia Barber. There are also some Marshalls in one branch of my family; perhaps I can be of help to you there, as well." He laughed, a deep and pleasant sound, which reminded me of my late husband, Edward, when he was most particularly pleased. "And, of course," he said, "there is always the

chance that you may have some information on the Marshalls which can
help me."

"I think that would be very nice," I said, and so I invited him to
come to the apartment the very next afternoon.

At one point the next day, perhaps half an hour before Gerald
Fowlkes was to arrive, I stopped my fluttering around to take stock of
myself and to realize that if ever there were an indication of second
childhood taking over, my thoughts and actions preparatory to Mr.
Fowlkes' arrival were certainly it. I had been rushing hither and thither,
dusting, rearranging, polishing, pausing incessantly to look in the
mirror and touch my hair with fluttering fingers, all as though I were a
flighty teen-ager before her very first date. "Henrietta," I told myself
sharply, "you are seventy-three years old, and all that nonsense is well
behind you now. Eleven times a grandmother, and just look at how you
carry on!"

But poor Edward had been dead and gone these past nine years, my
brothers and sisters were all in their graves, and as for my children, all
but Tom, the youngest, were thousands of miles away, living their own
lives—as of course they should—and only occasionally remembering to
write a duty letter to Mother. And I am much too aware of the dangers
of the clinging mother to force my presence too often upon Tom and his
family. So I am very much alone, except of course for my friends in the
various church activities and for those I have met, albeit only by postal,
through my genealogical research.

So it *was* pleasant to be visited by a charming gentleman caller,
and particularly so when that gentleman shared my own particular
interests.

And Mr. Gerald Fowlkes, on his arrival, was surely no disappointment. He looked to be no more than fifty-five years of age, though he
swore to sixty-two, and had a fine shock of gray hair above a strong and
kindly face. He dressed very well, with that combination of expense and
breeding so little found these days, when the well-bred seem invariably
to be poor and the well-to-do seem invariably to be horribly plebeian.
His manner was refined and gentlemanly, what we used to call courtly,
and he had some very nice things to say about the appearance of my
living room.

Actually, I make no unusual claims as a housekeeper. Living alone,
and with quite a comfortable income having been left me by Edward, it

is no problem at all to choose tasteful furnishings and keep them neat. (Besides, I had scrubbed the apartment from top to bottom in preparation for Mr. Fowlkes' visit.)

He had brought his pedigree along, and what a really beautiful job he had done. Pedigree charts, photostats of all sorts of records, a running history typed very neatly on bond paper and inserted in a loose-leaf notebook—all in all, the kind of careful, planned, well-thought-out perfection so unsuccessfully striven for by all amateur genealogists.

From Mr. Fowlkes, I got the missing information on Euphemia Barber. She was born in 1765, in Salem, Massachusetts, the fourth child of seven born to John and Alicia Stover. She married Jason Barber in Savannah in 1791. Jason, a well-to-do merchant, passed on in 1794, shortly after the birth of their first child, Abner. Abner was brought up by his paternal grandparents, and Euphemia moved away from Savannah. As I already knew, she had then gone to Virginia, where she had married John Anderson. After that, Mr. Fowlkes had no record of her, until her death in Cincinnati, Ohio, in 1852. She was buried as Euphemia Stover Barber, apparently not having used the Anderson name after John Anderson's death.

This done, we went on to compare family histories and discover an Alan Marshall of Liverpool, England, around 1680, common to both trees. I was able to give Mr. Fowlkes Alan Marshall's birth date. And then the specific purpose of our meeting was finished. I offered tea and cakes, it then being four-thirty in the afternoon, and Mr. Fowlkes graciously accepted my offering.

And so began the strangest three months of my entire life. Before leaving, Mr. Fowlkes asked me to accompany him to a concert on Friday evening, and I very readily agreed. Then, and afterward, he was a perfect gentleman.

It didn't take me long to realize that I was being courted. Actually, I couldn't believe it at first. After all, at *my* age! But I myself did know some very nice couples who had married late in life—a widow and a widower, both lonely, sharing interests, and deciding to lighten their remaining years together—and looked at in that light it wasn't at all as ridiculous as it might appear at first.

Actually, I had expected my son Tom to laugh at the idea, and to dislike Mr. Fowlkes instantly upon meeting him. I suppose various fictional works that I have read had given me this expectation. So I was most pleasantly surprised when Tom and Mr. Fowlkes got along famously together from their very first meeting, and even more surprised when Tom came to me and told me Mr. Fowlkes had asked him if he would have any objection to his, Mr. Fowlkes', asking for my hand in matrimony. Tom said he had no objection at all, but actually thought it a wonderful idea, for he knew that both Mr. Fowlkes and myself were rather lonely, with nothing but our genealogical hobbies to occupy our minds.

As to Mr. Fowlkes' background, he very early gave me his entire history. He came from a fairly well-to-do family in upstate New York, and was himself now retired from his business, which had been a stock brokerage in Albany. He was a widower these last six years, and his first marriage had not been blessed with any children, so that he was completely alone in the world.

The next three months were certainly active ones. Mr. Fowlkes—Gerald—squired me everywhere, to concerts and to museums and even, after we had come to know one another well enough, to the theater. He was at all times most polite and thoughtful, and there was scarcely a day went by but what we were together.

During this entire time, of course, my own genealogical researches came to an absolute standstill. I was much too busy, and my mind was much too full of Gerald, for me to concern myself with family members who were long since gone to their rewards. Promising leads from the Genealogical Exchange were not followed up, for I didn't write a single letter. And though I did receive many in the Exchange, they all went unopened into a cubbyhole in my desk. And so the matter stayed, while the courtship progressed.

After three months, Gerald at last proposed. "I am not a young man, Henrietta," he said. "Nor a particularly handsome man"—though he most certainly was very handsome, indeed—"nor even a very rich man, although I do have sufficient for my declining years. And I have little to offer you, Henrietta, save my own self, whatever poor companionship I can give you, and the assurance that I will be ever at your side."

What a beautiful proposal! After being nine years a widow, and never expecting even in fanciful daydreams to be once more a wife, what a beautiful proposal and from what a charming gentleman!

I agreed at once, of course, and telephoned Tom the good news that very minute. Tom and his wife, Estelle, had a dinner party for us, and then we made our plans. We would be married three weeks hence. A short time? Yes, of course, it was, but there was really no reason to wait. And we would honeymoon in Washington, D.C., where my oldest boy, Roger, has quite a responsible position with the State Department. After which, we would return to Boston and take up our residence in a lovely old home on Beacon Hill, which was then for sale and which we would jointly purchase.

Ah, the plans! The preparations! How newly filled were my so-recently empty days!

I spent most of the last week closing my apartment on Newbury Street. The furnishings would be moved to our new home by Tom, while Gerald and I were in Washington. But, of course, there was ever so much packing to be done, and I got at it with a will.

And so at last I came to my desk, and my genealogical researches lying as I had left them. I sat down at the desk, somewhat weary, for it was late afternoon and I had been hard at work since sun-up, and I decided to spend a short while getting my papers into order before packing them away. And so I opened the mail which had accumulated over the last three months.

There were twenty-three letters. Twelve asked for information on various family names mentioned in my entry in the Exchange, five offered to give me information, and six concerned Euphemia Barber. It was, after all, Euphemia Barber who had brought Gerald and me together in the first place, and so I took time out to read these letters.

And so came the shock. I read the six letters, and then I simply sat limp at the desk, staring into space, and watched the monstrous pattern as it grew in my mind. For there was no question of the truth, no question at all.

Consider: Before starting the letters, this is what I knew of Euphemia Barber: She had been born Euphemia Stover in Salem, Massachusetts, in 1765. In 1791, she married Jason Barber, a widower of Savannah, Georgia. Jason died two years later, in 1793, of a stomach upset. Three years later, Euphemia appeared in Virginia and married John Anderson, also a widower. John died two years thereafter, in 1798, of stomach upset. In both cases, Euphemia sold her late husband's property and moved on.

And here is what the letters added to that, in chronological order:

From Mrs. Winnie Mae Cuthbert, Dallas, Texas: Euphemia Barber, in 1800, two years after John Anderson's death, appeared in Harrisburg, Pennsylvania, and married one Andrew Cuthbert, a widower and a prosperous feed merchant. Andrew died in 1801, of a stomach upset. The widow sold his store, and moved on.

From Miss Ethel Sutton, Louisville, Kentucky: Euphemia Barber, in 1804, married Samuel Nicholson of Louisville, a widower and a well-to-do tobacco farmer. Samuel Nicholson passed on in 1807, of a stomach upset. The widow sold his farm, and moved on.

From Mrs. Isabelle Padgett, Concord, California: in 1808, Euphemia Barber married Thomas Norton, then Mayor of Dover, New Jersey, and a widower. In 1809, Thomas Norton died of a stomach upset.

From Mrs. Luella Miller, Bicknell, Utah: Euphemia Barber married Jonas Miller, a wealthy shipowner of Portsmouth, New Hampshire, a widower, in 1811. The same year, Jonas Miller died of a stomach upset. The widow sold his property and moved on.

From Mrs. Lola Hopkins, Vancouver, Washington: In 1813, in southern Indiana, Euphemia Barber married Edward Hopkins, a widower and a farmer. Edward Hopkins died in 1816, of a stomach upset. The widow sold the farm, and moved on.

From Mr. Roy Cumbie, Kansas City, Missouri: In 1819, Euphemia Barber married Stanley Thatcher of Kansas City, Missouri, a river barge owner and a widower. Stanley Thatcher died, of a stomach upset, in 1821. The widow sold his property, and moved on.

The evidence was clear, and complete. The intervals of time without dates could mean that there had been other widowers who had succumbed to Euphemia Barber's fatal charms, and whose descendants did not number among themselves an amateur genealogist. Who could tell just how many husbands Euphemia had murdered? For murder it quite clearly was, brutal murder, for profit. I had evidence of eight murders, and who knew but what there were eight more, or eighteen more? Who could tell, at this late date, just how many times Euphemia Barber had murdered for profit, and had never been caught?

Such a woman is inconceivable. Her husbands were always widowers, sure to be lonely, sure to be susceptible to a wily woman. She preyed on widowers, and left them all a widow.

Gerald.

The thought came to me, and I pushed it firmly away. It couldn't possibly be true; it couldn't possibly have a single grain of truth.

But what did I know of Gerald Fowlkes, other than what he had told me? And wasn't I a widow, lonely and susceptible? And wasn't I financially well off?

Like father, like son, they say. Could it be also, like great-great-great-great-great-grandmother, like great-great-great-great-great-grandson?

What a thought! It came to me that there must be any number of widows in the country, like myself, who were interested in tracing their family trees. Women who had a bit of money and leisure, whose children were grown and gone out into the world to live their own lives, and who filled some of the empty hours with the hobby of genealogy. An unscrupulous man, preying on well-to-do widows, could find no better introduction than a common interest in genealogy.

What a terrible thought to have about Gerald! And yet, I couldn't push it from my mind, and at last I decided that the only thing I could possibly do was try to substantiate the autobiography he had given me, for if he had told the truth about himself, then he could surely not be a beast of the type I was imagining.

A stockbroker, he had claimed to have been, in Albany, New York. I at once telephoned an old friend of my first husband's, who was himself a Boston stockbroker, and asked him if it would be possible for him to find out if there had been, at any time in the last fifteen or twenty years, an Albany stockbroker named Gerald Fowlkes. He said he could do so with ease, using some sort of directory he had, and would call me back. He did so, with the shattering news that no such individual was listed!

Still I refused to believe. Donning my coat and hat, I left the apartment at once and went directly to the telephone company, where, after an incredible number of white lies concerning genealogical research, I at last persuaded someone to search for an old Albany, New York telephone book. I knew that the main office of the company kept books for other major cities, as a convenience for the public, but I wasn't sure they would have any from past years. Nor was the clerk I talked to, but at last she did go and search, and came back finally with the 1946 telephone book from Albany, dusty and somewhat ripped, but still intact, with both the normal listings and the yellow pages.

No Gerald Fowlkes was listed in the white pages, or in the yellow pages under Stocks & Bonds.

So. It was true. And I could see exactly what Gerald's method was. Whenever he was ready to find another victim, he searched one or another of the genealogical magazines until he found someone who shared one of his own past relations. He then proceeded to effect a meeting with that person, found out quickly enough whether or not the intended victim was a widow, of the proper age range, and with the properly large bank account, and then the courtship began.

I imagined that this was the first time he had made the mistake of using Euphemia Barber as the go-between. And I doubted that he even realized he was following in Euphemia's footsteps. Certainly, none of the six people who had written to me about Euphemia could possibly guess, knowing only of one marriage and death, what Euphemia's role in life had actually been.

And what was I to do now? In the taxi, on the way back to my apartment, I sat huddled in a corner, and tried to think.

For this *was* a severe shock, and a terrible disappointment. And could I face Tom, or my other children, or any one of my friends, to whom I had already written the glad news of my impending marriage? And how could I return to the drabness of my days before Gerald had come to bring gaiety and companionship and courtly grace to my days?

Could I even call the police? I was sufficiently convinced myself, but could I possibly convince anyone else?

All at once, I made my decision. And, having made it, I immediately felt ten years younger, ten pounds lighter, and quite a bit less foolish. For, I might as well admit, in addition to everything else, this had been a terrible blow to my pride.

But the decision was made, and I returned to my apartment cheerful and happy.

And so we were married.

Married? Of course. Why not?

Because he will try to murder me? Well, of course he *will* try to murder me. As a matter of fact, he has already tried, half a dozen times.

But Gerald is working at a terrible disadvantage. For he cannot murder me in any way that looks like murder. It must appear to be a natural death, or, at the very worst, an accident. Which means that he must be devious, and he must plot and plan, and never come at me openly to do me in.

And there is the source of his disadvantage. For I am forewarned, and forewarned is forearmed.

But what, really, do I have to lose? At seventy-three, how many days on this earth do I have left? And how *rich* life is these days! How rich compared to my life before Gerald came into it! Spiced with the thrill of danger, the excitement of cat and mouse, the intricate moves and countermoves of the most fascinating game of all.

And, of course, a pleasant and charming husband. Gerald *has* to be pleasant and charming. He can never disagree with me, at least not very forcefully, for he can't afford the danger of my leaving him. Nor can he afford to believe that I suspect him. I have never spoken of the matter to him, and so far as he is concerned I know nothing. We go to concerts and museums and the theater together. Gerald is attentive and gentlemanly, quite the best sort of companion at all times.

Of course, I can't allow him to feed me breakfast in bed, as he would so love to do. No, I told him I was an old-fashioned woman, and believed that cooking was a woman's job, and so I won't let him near the kitchen. Poor Gerald!

And we don't take trips, no matter how much he suggests them.

And we've closed off the second story of our home, since I pointed out that the first floor was certainly spacious enough for just the two of us, and I felt I was getting a little old for climbing stairs. He could do nothing, of course, but agree.

And, in the meantime, I have found another hobby, though of course Gerald knows nothing of it. Through discreet inquiries, and careful perusal of past issues of the various genealogical magazines, the use of the family names in Gerald's family tree, I am gradually compiling another sort of tree. Not a family tree, no. One might facetiously call it a hanging tree. It is a list of Gerald's wives. It is in with my genealogical files, which I have willed to the Boston library. Should Gerald manage to catch me after all, what a surprise is in store for the librarian who sorts out those files of mine! Not as big as surprise as the one in store for Gerald, of course.

Ah, here comes Gerald now, in the automobile he bought last week. He's going to ask me again to go for a ride with him.

But I shan't go.

THE SCARLET THREAD

JACQUES FUTRELLE

The Thinking Machine—Professor Augustus S. F. X. Van Dusen, Ph.
D., LL.D., F.R.S., M.D., etc., scientist and logician—listened intently
and without comment to a weird, seemingly inexplicable story.
Hutchinson Hatch, reporter, was telling it. The bowed figure of the
savant lay at ease in a large chair. The enormous head with its bushy
yellow hair was thrown back, the thin, white fingers were pressed tip to
tip and the blue eyes, narrowed to mere slits, squinted aggressively
upward. The scientist was in a receptive mood.

"From the beginning, every fact you know," he had requested.

"It's all out in the Back Bay," the reporter explained. "There is a
big apartment house there, a fashionable establishment, in a side street,
just off Commonwealth Avenue. It is five stories in all, and is cut up into
small suites, of two and three rooms with bath. These suites are
handsomely, even luxuriously furnished, and are occupied by people
who can afford to pay big rents. Generally these are young unmarried
men, although in several cases they are husband and wife. It is a house
of every modern improvement, elevator service, hall boys, liveried door
men, spacious corridors and all that. It has both the gas and electric
systems of lighting. Tenants are at liberty to use either or both.

"A young broker, Weldon Henley, occupies one of the handsomest
of these suites, being on the second floor, in front. He has met with
considerable success in the Street. He is a bachelor and lives there

alone. There is no personal servant. He dabbles in photography as a hobby, and is said to be remarkably expert.

"Recently there was a report that he was to be married this Winter to a beautiful Virginia girl who has been visiting Boston from time to time, a Miss Lipscomb—Charlotte Lipscomb, of Richmond. Henley has never denied or affirmed this rumor, although he has been asked about it often. Miss Lipscomb is impossible of access even when she visits Boston. Now she is in Virginia, I understand, but will return to Boston later in the season."

The reporter paused, lighted a cigarette and leaned forward in his chair, gazing steadily into the inscrutable eyes of the scientist.

"When Henley took the suite he requested that all the electric lighting appliances be removed from his apartments," he went on. "He had taken a long lease of the place, and this was done. Therefore he uses only gas for lighting purposes, and he usually keeps one of his gas jets burning low all night."

"Bad, bad for his health," commented the scientist.

"Now comes the mystery of the affair," the reporter went on. "It was five weeks or so ago Henley retired as usual—about midnight. He locked his door on the inside—he is positive of that—and awoke about four o'clock in the morning nearly asphyxiated by gas. He was barely able to get up and open the window to let in the fresh air. The gas jet he had left burning was out, and the suite was full of gas."

"Accident, possibly," said The Thinking Machine. "A draught through the apartments; a slight diminution of gas pressure; a hundred possibilities."

"So it was presumed," said the reporter. "Of course it would have been impossible for——"

"Nothing is impossible," said the other, tartly. "Don't say that. It annoys me exceedingly."

"Well, then, it seems highly improbable that the door had been opened or that anyone came into the room and did this deliberately," the newspaper man went on, with a slight smile. "So Henley said nothing about this; attributed it to accident. The next night he lighted his gas as usual, but he left it burning a little brighter. The same thing happened again."

"Ah," and The Thinking Machine changed his position a little. "The second time."

* * *

"And again he awoke just in time to save himself," said Hatch. Still he attributed the affair to accident, and determined to avoid a recurrence of the affair by doing away with the gas at night. Then he got a small night lamp and used this for a week or more."

"Why does he have a light at all?" asked the scientist, testily.

"I can hardly answer that," replied Hatch. "I may say, however, that he is of a very nervous temperament, and gets up frequently during the night. He reads occasionally when he can't sleep. In addition to that he has slept with a light going all his life; it's a habit."

"Go on."

"One night he looked for the night lamp, but it had disappeared—at least he couldn't find it—so he lighted the gas again. The fact of the gas having twice before gone out had been dismissed as a serious possibility. Next morning at five o'clock a bell boy, passing through the hall, smelled gas and made a quick investigation. He decided it came from Henley's place, and rapped on the door. There was no answer. It ultimately developed that it was necessary to smash in the door. There on the bed they found Henley unconscious with the gas pouring into the room from the jet which he had left lighted. He was revived in the air, but for several hours was deathly sick."

"Why was the door smashed in?" asked The Thinking Machine. "Why not unlocked?"

"It was done because Henley had firmly barred it," Hatch explained. "He had become suspicious, I suppose, and after the second time he always barred his door and fastened every window before he went to sleep. There may have been a fear that some one used a key to enter."

"Well?" asked the scientist. "After that?"

"Three weeks or so elapsed, bringing the affair down to this morning," Hatch went on. "Then the same thing happened a little differently. For instance, after the third time the gas went out Henley decided to find out for himself what caused it, and so expressed himself to a few friends who knew of the mystery. Then, night after night, he lighted the gas as usual and kept watch. It was never disturbed during all the time, burning steadily all night. What sleep he got was in daytime.

"Last night Henley lay awake for a time; then, exhausted and tired, fell asleep. This morning early he awoke; the room was filled with gas again. In some way my city editor heard of it and asked me to look into the mystery."

That was all. The two men were silent for a long time, and finally The Thinking Machine turned to the reporter.

"Does anyone else in the house keep gas going all night?" he asked.

"I don't know," was the reply. "Most of them, I know, use electricity."

"Nobody else has been overcome as he has been?"

"No. Plumbers have minutely examined the lighting system all over the house and found nothing wrong."

"Does the gas in the house all come through the same meter?"

"Yes, so the manager told me. This meter, a big one, is just off the engine room. I supposed it possible that some one shut it off there on these nights long enough to extinguish the lights all over the house, and then turned it on again. That is, presuming that it was done purposely. Do you think it was an attempt to kill Henley?"

"It might be," was the reply. "Find out for me just who in the house uses gas; also if anyone else leaves a light burning all night; also what opportunity anyone would have to get at the meter, and then something about Henley's love affair with Miss Lipscomb. Is there anyone else? If so, who? Where does he live? When you find out these things come back here."

That afternoon at one o'clock Hatch returned to the apartments of The Thinking Machine, with excitement plainly apparent on his face.

"Well?" asked the scientist.

"A French girl, Louise Regnier, employed as a maid by Mrs. Standing in the house, was found dead in her room on the third floor to-day at noon," Hatch explained quickly. "It looks like suicide."

"How?" asked The Thinking Machine.

"The people who employed her—husband and wife—have been away for a couple of days," Hatch rushed on. "She was in the suite alone. This noon she had not appeared, there was an odor of gas and the door was broken in. Then she was found dead."

"With the gas turned on?"

"With the gas turned on. She was asphyxiated."

"Dear me, dear me," exclaimed the scientist. He arose and took up his hat. "Let's go see what this is all about."

II

When Professor Van Dusen and Hatch arrived at the apartment house they had been preceded by the Medical Examiner and the police. Detective Mallory, whom both knew, was moving about in the apartment where the girl had been found dead. The body had been removed and a telegram sent to her employers in New York.

"Too late," said Mallory, as they entered.

"What was it, Mr. Mallory?" asked the scientist.

"Suicide," was the reply. "No question of it. It happened in this room," and he led the way into the third room of the suite. "The maid, Miss Regnier, occupied this, and was here alone last night. Mr. and Mrs. Standing, her employers, have gone to New York for a few days. She was left alone, and killed herself."

Without further questioning The Thinking Machine went over to the bed, from which the girl's body had been taken, and, stooping beside it, picked up a book. It was a novel by "The Duchess." He examined this critically, then, standing on a chair, he examined the gas jet. This done, he stepped down and went to the window of the little room. Finally The Thinking Machine turned to the detective.

"Just how much was the gas turned on?" he asked.

"Turned on full," was the reply.

"Were both the doors of the room closed?"

"Both, yes."

"Any cotton, or cloth, or anything of the sort stuffed in the cracks of the window?"

"No. It's a tight-fitting window, anyway. Are you trying to make a mystery out of this?"

"Cracks in the doors stuffed?" The Thinking Machine went on.

"No." There was a smile about the detective's lips.

The Thinking Machine, on his knees, examined the bottom of one of the doors, that which led into the hall. The lock of this door had been broken when employees burst into the room. Having satisfied himself here and at the bottom of the other door, which connected with the bedroom adjoining, The Thinking Machine again climbed on a chair and examined the doors at the top.

"Both transoms closed, I suppose?" he asked.

"Yes," was the reply. "You can't make anything but suicide out of it," explained the detective. "The Medical Examiner has given that as his opinion—and everything I find indicates it."

"All right," broke in The Thinking Machine abruptly. "Don't let us keep you."

After a while Detective Mallory went away. Hatch and the scientist went down to the office floor, where they saw the manager. He seemed to be greatly distressed, but was willing to do anything he could in the matter.

"Is your night engineer perfectly trustworthy?" asked The Thinking Machine.

"Perfectly," was the reply. "One of the best and most reliable men I ever met. Alert and wide-awake."

"Can I see him a moment? The night man, I mean?"

"Certainly," was the reply. "He's downstairs. He sleeps there. He's probably up by this time. He sleeps usually till one o'clock in the daytime, being up all night."

"Do you supply gas for your tenants?"

"Both gas and electricity are included in the rent of the suites. Tenants may use one or both."

"And the gas all comes through one meter?"

"Yes, one meter. It's just off the engine room."

"I suppose there's no way of telling just who in the house uses gas?"

"No. Some do and some don't. I don't know."

This was what Hatch had told the scientist. Now together they went to the basement, and there met the night engineer, Charles Burlingame, a tall, powerful, clean-cut man, of alert manner and positive speech. He gazed with a little amusement at the slender, almost childish figure of The Thinking Machine and the grotesquely large head.

"You are in the engine room or near it all night every night?" began The Thinking Machine.

"I haven't missed a night in four years," was the reply.

"Anybody ever come here to see you at night?"

"Never. It's against the rules."

"The manager or a hall boy?"

"Never."

"In the last two months?" The Thinking Machine persisted.

"Not in the last two years," was the positive reply. "I go on duty every night at seven o'clock, and I am on duty until seven in the morning. I don't believe I've seen anybody in the basement here with me between those hours for a year at least."

The Thinking Machine was squinting steadily into the eyes of the engineer, and for a time both were silent. Hatch moved about the scrupulously clean engine room and nodded to the day engineer, who sat leaning back against the wall. Directly in front of them was the steam gauge.

"Have you a fireman?" was The Thinking Machine's next question.

"No. I fire myself," said the night man. "Here's the coal," and he indicated a bin within half a dozen feet of the mouth of the boiler.

"I don't suppose you ever had occasion to handle the gas meter?" insisted The Thinking Machine.

"Never touched it in my life," said the other. "I don't know anything about meters, anyway."

"And you never drop off to sleep at night for a few minutes when you get lonely? Doze, I mean?"

The engineer grinned good-naturedly.

"Never had any desire to, and besides I wouldn't have the chance," he explained. "There's a time check here,"—and he indicated it. "I have to punch that every half hour all night to prove that I have been awake."

"Dear me, dear me," exclaimed The Thinking Machine, irritably. He went over and examined the time check—a revolving paper disk with hours marked on it, made to move by the action of a clock, the face of which showed in the middle.

"Besides there's the steam gauge to watch," went on the engineer. "No engineer would dare go to sleep. There might be an explosion."

"Do you know Mr. Weldon Henley?" suddenly asked The Thinking Machine.

"Who?" asked Burlingame.

"Weldon Henley?"

"No-o," was the slow response. "Never heard of him. Who is he?"

"One of the tenants, on the second floor, I think."

"Lord, I don't know any of the tenants. What about him?"

"When does the inspector come here to read the meter?"

"I never saw him. I presume in daytime, eh Bill?" and he turned to the day engineer.

"Always in daytime—usually about noon," said Bill from his corner.

"Any other entrance to the basement except this way—and you could see anyone coming here this way I suppose?"

"Sure I could see 'em. There's no other entrance to the cellar except the coal hole in the sidewalk in front."

"Two big electric lights in front of the building, aren't there?"

"Yes. They go all night."

A slightly puzzled expression crept into the eyes of The Thinking Machine. Hatch knew from the persistency of the questions that he was not satisfied; yet he was not able to fathom or to understand all the queries. In some way they had to do with the possibility of some one having access to the meter.

"Where do you usually sit at night here?" was the next question.

"Over there where Bill's sitting. I always sit there."

The Thinking Machine crossed the room to Bill, a typical, grimy-handed man of his class.

"May I sit there a moment?" he asked.

Bill arose lazily, and The Thinking Machine sank down into the chair. From this point he could see plainly through the opening into the basement proper—there was no door—the gas meter of enormous proportions through which all the gas in the house passed. An electric light in the door made it bright as daylight. The Thinking Machine noted these things, arose, nodded his thanks to the two men and, still with the puzzled expression on his face, led the way upstairs. There the manager was still in his office.

"I presume you examine and know that the time check in the engineer's room is properly punched every half-hour during the night?" he asked.

"Yes. I examine the dial every day—have them here, in fact, each with the date on it."

"May I see them?"

Now the manager was puzzled. He produced the cards, one for each day, and for half an hour The Thinking Machine studied them minutely. At the end of that time, when he arose and Hatch looked at him inquiringly, he saw still the perplexed expression.

After urgent solicitation, the manager admitted them to the apartments of Weldon Henley. Mr. Henley himself had gone to his office in State Street. Here The Thinking Machine did several things which aroused the curiosity of the manager, one of which was to minutely study the gas jets. Then The Thinking Machine opened one of the front windows and glanced out into the street. Below fifteen feet was the sidewalk; above was the solid front of the building, broken only by a flagpole which, properly roped, extended from the hall window of the next floor above out over the sidewalk a distance of twelve feet or so.

"Ever use that flagpole?" he asked the manager.

"Rarely," said the manager. "On holidays sometimes—Fourth of July and such times. We have a big flag for it."

From the apartments The Thinking Machine led the way to the hall, up the stairs and to the flagpole. Leaning out of the window, he looked down toward the window of the apartments he had just left. Then he inspected the rope of the flagpole, drawing it through his slender hands slowly and carefully. At last he picked off a slender thread of scarlet and examined it.

"Ah," he exclaimed. Then to Hatch: "Let's go, Mr. Hatch. Thank you," this last to the manager, who had been a puzzled witness.

Once on the street, side by side with The Thinking Machine, Hatch was bursting with questions, but he didn't ask them. He knew it would be useless. At last The Thinking Machine broke the silence.

"That girl, Miss Regnier, *was murdered*," he said suddenly, positively. "There have been four attempts to murder Henley."

"How?" asked Hatch, startled.

"By a scheme so simple that neither you nor I nor the police have ever heard of it being employed." was the astonishing reply. *"It is perfectly horrible in its simplicity."*

"What was it?" Hatch insisted, eagerly.

"It would be futile to discuss that now," was the rejoinder. "There has been murder. We know how. Now the question is—who? What person would have a motive to kill Henley?"

III

There was a pause as they walked on.

"Where are we going?" asked Hatch finally.

"Come up to my place and let's consider this matter a bit further," replied The Thinking Machine.

Not another word was spoken by either until half an hour later, in the small laboratory. For a long time the scientist was thoughtful— deeply thoughtful. Once he took down a volume from a shelf and Hatch glanced at the title. It was *Gases: Their Properties*. After a while he returned this to the shelf and took down another, on which the reporter caught the title, *Anatomy*.

"Now, Mr. Hatch," said The Thinking Machine in his perpetually crabbed voice, "we have a most remarkable riddle. It gains this remarkable aspect from its very simplicity. It is not, however, necessary to go into that now. I will make it clear to you when we know the motives.

"As a general rule, the greatest crimes never come to light because the greatest criminals, their perpetrators, are too clever to be caught. Here we have what I might call a great crime committed with a subtle simplicity that is wholly disarming, and a greater crime even than this was planned. This was to murder Weldon Henley. The first thing for you to do is to see Mr. Henley and warn him of his danger. Asphyxiation will not be attempted again, but there is a possibility of poison, a pistol shot, a knife, anything almost. As a matter of fact, he is in great peril.

"Superficially, the death of Miss Regnier, the maid, looks to be suicide. Instead it is the fruition of a plan which has been tried time and again against Henley. There is a possibility that Miss Regnier was not an intentional victim of the plot, but the fact remains that she was murdered. Why? Find the motive for the plot to murder Mr. Henley and you will know why."

The Thinking Machine reached over to the shelf, took a book, looked at it a moment, then went on:

"The first question to determine positively is: Who hated Weldon Henley sufficiently to desire his death? You say he is a successful man in the Street. Therefore there is a possibility that some enemy there is at the bottom of the affair, yet it seems hardly probable. If by his operations Mr. Henley ever happened to wreck another man's fortune, find this man and find out all about him. He may be the man. There will be innumerable questions arising from this line of inquiry to a man of your resources. Leave none of them unanswered.

"On the other hand there is Henley's love affair. Had he a rival who might desire his death? Had he any rival? If so, find out all about him. He may be the man who planned all this. Here, too, there will be questions arising which demand answers. Answer them—all of them— fully and clearly before you see me again.

"Was Henley ever a party to a liaison of any kind? Find that out, too. A vengeful woman or a discarded sweetheart of a vengeful woman, you know, will go to any extreme. The rumor of his engagement to Miss—Miss——"

"Miss Lipscomb," Hatch supplied.

"The rumor of his engagement to Miss Lipscomb might have caused a woman whom he had once been interested in or who was once interested in him to attempt his life. The subtler murders—that is, the ones which are most attractive as problems—are nearly always the work of a cunning woman. I know nothing about women myself," he hastened to explain; "but Lombroso has taken that attitude. Therefore, see if there is a woman."

Most of these points Hatch had previously seen—seen with the unerring eye of a clever newspaper reporter—yet there were several which had not occurred to him. He nodded his understanding.

"Now the center of the affair, of course," The Thinking Machine continued, "is the apartment house where Henley lives. The person who attempted his life either lives there or has ready access to the place, and frequently spends the night there. This is a vital question for you to answer. I am leaving all this to you because you know better how to do these things than I do. That's all, I think. When these things are all learned come back to me."

The Thinking Machine arose as if the interview were at an end, and Hatch also arose, reluctantly. An idea was beginning to dawn in his mind.

"Does it occur to you that there is any connection whatever between Henley and Miss Regnier?" he asked.

"It is possible," was the reply. "I had thought of that. If there is a connection it is not apparent yet."

"Then how—how was it she—she was killed, or killed herself, whichever may be true, and——"

"The attempt to kill Henley killed her. That's all I can say now."

"That all?" asked Hatch, after a pause.

"No. Warn Mr. Henley immediately that he is in grave danger. Remember the person who has planned this will probably go to any extreme. I don't know Mr. Henley, of course, but from the fact that he always had a light at night I gather that he is a timid sort of man—not necessarily a coward, but a man lacking in stamina—therefore, one who might better disappear for a week or so until the mystery is cleared up. Above all, impress upon him the importance of the warning."

The Thinking Machine opened his pocketbook and took from it the scarlet thread which he had picked from the rope of the flagpole.

"Here, I believe, is the real clue to the problem," he explained to Hatch. "What does it seem to be?"

Hatch examined it closely.

"I should say a strand from a Turkish bath robe," was his final judgment.

"Possibly. Ask some cloth expert what he makes of it, then if it sounds promising look into it. Find out if by any possibility it can be any part of any garment worn by any person in the apartment house."

"But it's so slight——" Hatch began.

"I know," the other interrupted, tartly. "It's slight, but I believe it is a part of the wearing apparel of the person, man or woman, who has four times attempted to kill Mr. Henley and who did kill the girl. Therefore, it is important."

Hatch looked at him quickly.

"Well, how—in what manner—did it come where you found it?"

"Simple enough," said the scientist. "It is a wonder that there were not more pieces of it—that's all."

Perplexed by his instructions, but confident of results, Hatch left The Thinking Machine. What possible connection could this tiny bit of scarlet thread, found on a flagpole, have with some one shutting off the gas in Henley's rooms? How did any one go into Henley's rooms to shut off the gas? How was it Miss Regnier was dead? What was the manner of her death?

A cloth expert in a great department store turned his knowledge on the tiny bit of scarlet for the illumination of Hatch, but he could go no further than to say that it seemed to be part of a Turkish bath robe.

"Man's or woman's?" asked Hatch.

"The material from which bath robes are made is the same for both men and women," was the reply. "I can say nothing else. Of course there's not enough of it to even guess at the pattern of the robe."

Then Hatch went to the financial district and was ushered into the office of Weldon Henley, a slender, handsome man of thirty-two or three years, pallid of face and nervous in manner. He still showed the effect of the gas poisoning, and there was even a trace of a furtive fear—fear of something, he himself didn't know what—in his actions.

Henley talked freely to the newspaper man of certain things, but of other things was resentfully reticent. He admitted his engagement to Miss Lipscomb, and finally even admitted that Miss Lipscomb's hand had been sought by another man, Regnault Cabell, formerly of Virginia.

"Could you give me his address?" asked Hatch.

"He lives in the same apartment house with me—two floors above," was the reply.

Hatch was starled; startled more than he would have cared to admit.

"Are you on friendly terms with him?" he asked.

"Certainly," said Henley. "I won't say anything further about this matter. It would be unwise for obvious reasons."

"I suppose you consider that this turning on of the gas was an attempt on your life?"

"I can't suppose anything else."

Hatch studied the pallid face closely as he asked the next question.

"Do you know Miss Regnier was found dead to-day?"

"Dead?" exclaimed the other, and he arose. "Who—what—who is she?"

It seemed a distinct effort for him to regain control of himself.

The reporter detailed then the circumstances of the finding of the girl's body, and the broker listened without comment. From that time forward all the reporter's questions were either parried or else met with a flat refusal to answer. Finally Hatch repeated to him the warning which he had from The Thinking Machine, and feeling that he had accomplished little, went away.

At eight o'clock that night— a night of complete darkness— Henley was found unconscious, lying in a little used walk in the Common. There was a bullet hole through his left shoulder, and he was bleeding profusely. He was removed to the hospital, where he regained consciousness for just a moment.

"Who shot you?" he was aksed.

"None of your business," he replied, and lapsed into unconsciousness.

IV

Entirely unaware of this latest attempt on the life of the broker, Hutchinson Hatch steadily pursued his investigations. They finally led him to an intimate friend of Regnault Cabell. The young Southerner had apartments on the fourth floor of the big house off Commonwealth Avenue, directly over those Henley occupied, but two flights higher up. This friend was a figure in the social set of the Back Bay. He talked to Hatch freely of Cabell.

"He's a good fellow," he explained, "one of the best I ever met, and comes of one of the best families Virginia ever had—a true F.F.V. He's pretty quick tempered and all that, but an excellent chap, and everywhere he has gone here he has made friends."

"He used to be in love with Miss Lipscomb of Virginia, didn't he?" asked Hatch, casually.

"Used to be?" the other repeated with a laugh. "He *is* in love with her. But recently he understood that she was engaged to Weldon Henley, a broker—you may have heard of him?—and that, I suppose, has dampened his ardor considerably. As a matter of fact, Cabell took the thing to heart. He used to know Miss Lipscomb in Virginia—she comes from another famous family there—and he seemed to think he had a prior claim on her."

Hatch heard all these things as any man might listen to gossip, but each additional fact was sinking into his mind, and each additional fact led his suspicions on deeper into the channel they had chosen.

"Cabell is pretty well to do," his informant went on, "not rich as we count riches in the North, but pretty well to do, and I believe he came to Boston because Miss Lipscomb spent so much of her time here. She is a beautiful young woman of twenty-two and extremely popular in the social world everywhere, particularly in Boston. Then there was the additional fact that Henley was here."

"No chance at all for Cabell?" Hatch suggested.

"Not the slightest," was the reply. "Yet despite the heartbreak he had, he was the first to congratulate Henley on winning her love. And he meant it, too."

"What's his attitude toward Henley now?" asked Hatch. His voice was calm, but there was an underlying tense note imperceptible to the other.

"They meet and speak and move in the same set. There's no love lost on either side, I don't suppose, but there is no trace of any ill feeling.''

"Cabell doesn't happen to be a vindictive sort of man?"

"Vindictive?" and the other laughed. "No. He's like a big boy, forgiving, and all that; hot-tempered, though. I could imagine him in a fit of anger making a personal matter of it with Henley, but I don't think he ever did."

The mind of the newspaper man was rapidly focusing on one point; the rush of thoughts, questions and doubts silenced him for a moment. Then:

"How long has Cabell been in Boston?"

"Seven or eight months—that is, he has had apartments here for that long—but he has made several visits South. I suppose it's South. He has a trick of dropping out of sight occasionally. I understand that he intends to go South for good very soon. If I'm not mistaken, he is trying now to rent his suite."

Hatch looked suddenly at his informant; an idea of seeing Cabell and having a legitimate excuse for talking to him had occurred to him.

"I'm looking for a suite," he volunteered at last. "I wonder if you would give me a card of introduction to him? We might get together on it."

Thus it happened that half an hour later, about ten minutes past nine o'clock, Hatch was on his way to the big apartment house. In the office he saw the manager.

"Heard the news?" asked the manager.

"No," Hatch replied. "What is it?"

"Somebody's shot Mr. Henley as he was passing through the Common early to-night."

Hatch whistled his amazement.

"Is he dead?"

"No, but he is unconscious. The hospital doctors say it is a nasty wound, but not necessarily dangerous."

"Who shot him? Do they know?"

"He knows, but he won't say."

Amazed and alarmed by this latest development, an accurate fulfillment of The Thinking Machine's prophecy, Hatch stood thoughtful for a moment, then recovering his composure a little asked for Cabell.

"I don't think there's much chance of seeing him," said the manager. "He's going away on the midnight train—going South, to Virginia."

"Going away to-night?" Hatch gasped.

"Yes; it seems to have been rather a sudden determination. He was talking to me here half an hour or so ago, and said something about going away. While he was here the telephone boy told me that Henley had been shot; they had 'phoned from the hospital to inform us. Then Cabell seemed greatly agitated. He said he was going away to-night, if he could catch the midnight train, and now he's packing."

"I suppose the shooting of Henley upset him considerably?" the reporter suggested.

"Yes, I guess it did," was the reply. "They moved in the same set and belonged to the same clubs."

The manager sent Hatch's card of introduction to Cabell's apartments. Hatch went up and was ushered into a suite identical with that of Henley's in every respect save in minor details of furnishings. Cabell stood in the middle of the floor, with his personal belongings scattered about the room; his valet, evidently a Frenchman, was busily engaged in packing.

Cabell's greeting was perfunctorily cordial; he seemed agitated. His face was flushed and from time to time he ran his fingers through his long, brown hair. He stared at Hatch in a preoccupied fashion, then they fell into conversation about the rent of the apartments.

"I'll take almost anything reasonable," Cabell said hurriedly. "You see, I am going away to-night, rather more suddenly than I had intended, and I am anxious to get the lease off my hands. I pay two hundred dollars a month for these just as they are."

"May I look them over?" asked Hatch.

He passed from the front room into the next. Here, on a bed, was piled a huge lot of clothing, and the valet, with deft fingers, was brushing and folding, preparatory to packing. Cabell was directly behind him.

"Quite comfortable, you see," he explained. "There's room enough if you are alone. Are you?"

"Oh, yes," Hatch replied.

"This other room here," Cabell explained, "is not in very tidy shape now. I have been out of the city for several weeks, and—— What's the matter?" he demanded suddenly.

Hatch had turned quickly at the words and stared at him, then recovered himself with a start.

"I beg your pardon," he stammered. "I rather thought I saw you in town here a week or so ago—of course I didn't know you—and I was wondering if I could have been mistaken."

"Must have been," said the other easily. "During the time I was away a Miss——, a friend of my sister's, occupied the suite. I'm afraid some of her things are here. She hasn't sent for them as yet. She occupied this room, I think; when I came back a few days ago she took another place and all her things haven't been removed."

"I see," remarked Hatch, casually. "I don't suppose there's any chance of her returning here unexpectedly if I should happen to take her apartments?"

"Not the slightest. She knows I am back, and thinks I am to remain. She was to send for these things."

Hatch gazed about the room ostentatiously. Across a trunk lay a Turkish bath robe with a scarlet stripe in it. He was anxious to get hold of it, to examine it closely. But he didn't dare to, then. Together they returned to the front room.

"I rather like the place," he said, after a pause, "but the price is——"

"Just a moment," Cabell interrupted. "Jean, before you finish packing that suit case be sure to put my bath robe in it. It's in the far room."

Then one question was settled for Hatch. After a moment the valet returned with the bath robe, which had been in the far room. It was Cabell's bath robe. As Jean passed the reporter an end of the robe caught on a corner of the trunk, and, stopping, the reporter unfastened it. A tiny strand of thread clung to the metal; Hatch detached it and stood idly twirling it in his fingers.

"As I was saying," he resumed. "I rather like the place, but the price is too much. Suppose you leave it in the hands of the manager of the house——"

"I had intended doing that," the Southerner interrupted.

"Well, I'll see him about it later," Hatch added.

With a cordial, albeit pre-occupied, handshake, Cabell ushered him out. Hatch went down in the elevator with a feeling of elation; a feeling that he had accomplished something. The manager was waiting to get into the lift.

"Do you happen to remember the name of the young lady who occupied Mr. Cabell's suite while he was away?" he asked.

"Miss Austin," said the manager, "but she's not young. She was about forty-five years old, I should judge."

"Did Mr. Cabell have his servant Jean with him?"

"Oh, no," said the manager. "The valet gave up the suite to Miss Austin entirely, and until Mr. Cabell returned occupied a room in the quarters we have for our own employees."

"Was Miss Austin ailing any way?" asked Hatch. "I saw a large number of medicine bottles upstairs."

"I don't know what was the matter with her," replied the manager, with a little puzzled frown. "She certainly was not a woman of sound mental balance—that is, she was eccentric, and all that. I think rather it was an act of charity for Mr. Cabell to let her have the suite in his absence. Certainly we didn't want her."

Hatch passed out and burst in eagerly upon The Thinking Machine in his laboratory.

"Here," he said, and triumphantly he extended the tiny scarlet strand which he had received from The Thinking Machine, and the other of the identical color which came from Cabell's bath robe. "Is that the same?"

The Thinking Machine placed them under the microscope and examined them immediately. Later he submitted them to a chemical test.

"It is the same," he said, finally.

"Then the mystery is solved," said Hatch, conclusively.

V

The Thinking Machine stared steadily into the eager, exultant eyes of the newspaper man until Hatch at last began to fear that he had been precipitate. After a while, under close scrutiny, the reporter began to feel convinced that he had made a mistake—he didn't quite see where, but it must be there, and the exultant manner passed. The voice of The Thinking Machine was like a cold shower.

"Remember, Mr. Hatch," he said, critically, "that unless every possible question has been considered one cannot boast of a solution. Is there any possible question lingering yet in your mind?"

The reporter silently considered that for a moment, then:

"Well, I have the main facts, anyway. There may be one or two minor questions left, but the principal ones are answered."

"Then tell me, to the minutest detail, what you have learned, what has happened."

Professor Van Dusen sank back in his old, familiar pose in the large arm chair and Hatch related what he had learned and what he surmised. He related, too, the peculiar circumstances surrounding the wounding of Henley, and right on down to the beginning and end of the interview with Cabell in the latter's apartments. The Thinking Machine was silent for a time, then there came a host of questions.

"Do you know where the woman—Miss Austin—is now?" was the first.

"No," Hatch had to admit.

"Or her precise mental condition?"

"No."

"Or her exact relationship to Cabell?"

"No."

"Do you know, then, what the valet, Jean, knows of the affair?"

"No, not that," said the reporter, and his face flushed under the close questioning. "He was out of the suite every night."

"Therefore might have been the very one who turned on the gas," the other put in testily.

"So far as I can learn, nobody could have gone into that room and turned on the gas," said the reporter, somewhat aggressively. "Henley barred the doors and windows and kept watch, night after night."

"Yet the moment he was exhausted and fell asleep the gas was turned on to kill him," said The Thinking Machine; "thus we see that *he was watched more closely than he watched.*"

"I see what you mean now," said Hatch, after a long pause.

"I should like to know what Henley and Cabell and the valet knew of the girl who was found dead," The Thinking Machine suggested. "Further, I should like to know if there was a good-sized mirror—not one set in a bureau or dresser—either in Henley's room or the apartments where the girl was found. Find out this for me and—never mind. I'll go with you."

The scientist left the room. When he returned he wore his coat and hat. Hatch arose mechanically to follow. For a block or more they walked along, neither speaking. The Thinking Machine was the first to break the silence:

"You believe Cabell is the man who attempted to kill Henley?"

"Frankly, yes," replied the newspaper man.

"Why?"

"Because he had the motive—disappointed love."

"How?"

"I don't know," Hatch confessed. "The doors of the Henley suite were closed. I don't see how anybody passed them."

"And the girl? Who killed her? How? Why?"

Disconsolately Hatch shook his head as he walked on. The Thinking Machine interpreted his silence aright.

"Don't jump at conclusions," he advised sharply. "You are confident Cabell was to blame for this—and he might have been, I don't know yet—but you can suggest nothing to show he did it. I have told you before that imagination is half of logic."

At last the lights of the big apartment house where Henley lived came in sight. Hatch shrugged his shoulders. He had grave doubts—based on what he knew—whether The Thinking Machine would be able to see Cabell. It was nearly eleven o'clock and Cabell was to leave for the South at midnight.

"Is Mr. Cabell here?" asked the scientist of the elevator boy.

"Yes, just about to go, though. He won't see anyone."

"Hand him this note," instructed The Thinking Machine, and he scribbled something on a piece of paper. "He'll see us."

The boy took the paper and the elevator shot up to the fourth floor. After a while he returned.

"He'll see you," he said.

"Is he unpacking?"

"After he read your note twice he told his valet to unpack," the boy replied.

"Ah, I thought so," said The Thinking Machine.

With Hatch, mystified and puzzled, following, The Thinking Machine entered the elevator to step out a second or so later on the fourth floor. As they left the car they saw the door of Cabell's apartment standing open; Cabell was in the door. Hatch traced a glimmer of anxiety in the eyes of the young man.

"Professor Van Dusen?" Cabell inquired.

"Yes," said the scientist. "It was of the utmost importance that I should see you, otherwise I should not have come at this time of night."

With a wave of his hand Cabell passed that detail.

"I was anxious to get away at midnight," he explained, "but, of course, now I shan't go, in view of your note. I have ordered my valet to unpack my things, at least until to-morrow."

The reporter and the scientist passed into the luxuriously furnished apartments. Jean, the valet, was bending over a suit case as they entered, removing some things he had been carefully placing there. He didn't look back or pay the least attention to the visitors.

"This is your valet?" asked The Thinking Machine.

"Yes," said the young man.

"French, isn't he?"

"Yes."

"Speak English at all?"

"Very badly," said Cabell. "I use French when I talk to him."

"Does he know that you are accused of murder?" asked The Thinking Machine, in a quiet, conversational tone.

The effect of the remark on Cabell was startling. He staggered back a step or so as if he had been struck in the face, and a crimson flush overspread his brow. Jean, the valet, straightened up suddenly and looked around. There was a queer expression, too, in his eyes; an expression which Hatch could not fathom.

"Murder?" gasped Cabell, at last.

"Yes, he speaks English all right," remarked The Thinking Machine. "Now Mr. Cabell, will you please tell me just who Miss Austin is, and where she is, and her mental condition? Believe me, it may save you a great deal of trouble. What I said in the note is not exaggerated."

The young man turned suddenly and began to pace back and forth across the room. After a few minutes he paused before The Thinking Machine, who stood impatiently waiting for an answer.

"I'll tell you, yes," said Cabell, firmly. "Miss Austin is a middle-aged woman whom my sister befriended several times—was, in fact, my sister's governess when she was a child. Of late years she has not been wholly right mentally, and has suffered a great deal of privation.

I had about concluded arrangements to put her in a private sanitarium. I permitted her to remain in these rooms in my absence, South. I did not take Jean—he lived in the quarters of the other employees of the place, and gave the apartment entirely to Miss Austin. It was simply an act of charity."

"What was the cause of your sudden determination to go South tonight?" asked the scientist.

"I won't answer that question," was the sullen reply.

There was a long, tense silence. Jean, the valet, came and went several times.

"How long has Miss Austin known Mr. Henley?"

"Presumably since she has been in these apartments," was the reply.

"Are you sure *you* are not Miss Austin?" demanded the scientist.

The question was almost staggering, not only to Cabell, but to Hatch. Suddenly, with flaming face, the young Southerner leaped forward as if to strike down The Thinking Machine.

"That won't do any good," said the scientist, coldly. "Are you sure you are not Miss Austin?" he repeated.

"Certainly I am not Miss Austin," responded Cabell, fiercely.

"Have you a mirror in these apartments about twelve inches by twelve inches?" asked The Thinking Machine, irrelevantly.

"I—I don't know," stammered the young man. "I —have we, Jean?"

"Oui," replied the valet.

"Yes," snapped The Thinking Machine. "Talk English, please. May I see it?"

The valet, without a word but with a sullen glance at the questioner, turned and left the room. He returned after a moment with the mirror. The Thinking Machine carefully examined the frame, top and bottom and on both sides. At last he looked up; again the valet was bending over a suit case.

"Do you use gas in these apartments?" the scientist asked suddenly.

"No," was the bewildered response. "What is all this, anyway?"

Without answering, The Thinking Machine drew a chair up under the chandelier where the gas and electric fixtures were and began to finger the gas tips. After a while he climbed down and passed into the next room, with Hatch and Cabell, both hopelessly mystified, following. There the scientist went through the same process of fingering the gas jets. Finally, one of the gas tips came out in his hand.

"Ah," he exclaimed, suddenly, and Hatch knew the note of triumph in it. The jet from which the tip came was just on a level with his shoulder, set between a dressing table and a window. He leaned over and squinted at the gas pipe closely. Then he returned to the room where the valet was.

"Now, Jean," he began, in an even, calm voice, "please tell me *if you did or did not kill Miss Regnier purposely?*"

"I don't know what you mean," said the servant sullenly, angrily, as he turned on the scientist.

"You speak very good English now," was The Thinking Machine's terse comment. "Mr. Hatch, lock the door and use this 'phone to call the police."

Hatch turned to do as he was bid and saw a flash of steel in young Cabell's hand, which was drawn suddenly from the hip pocket. It was a revolver. The weapon glittered in the light, and Hatch flung himself forward. There was a sharp report, and a bullet was buried in the floor.

VI

Then came a fierce, hard fight for possession of the revolver. It ended with the weapon in Hatch's hand, and both he and Cabell blowing from the effort they had expended. Jean, the valet, had turned at the sound of the shot and started toward the door leading into the hall. The Thinking Machine had stepped in front of him, and now stood there with his back to the door. Physically he would have been a child in the hands of the valet, yet there was a look in his eyes which stopped him.

"Now, Mr. Hatch," said the scientist quietly, a touch of irony in his voice. "hand me the revolver, then 'phone for Detective Mallory to come here immediately. Tell him we have a murderer—and if he can't come at once get some other detective whom you know."

"Murderer!" gasped Cabell.

Uncontrollable rage was blazing in the eyes of the valet, and he made as if to throw The Thinking Machine aside, despite the revolver, when Hatch was at the telephone. As Jean started forward, however,

Cabell stopped him in a quick, stern gesture. Suddenly the young Southerner turned on The Thinking Machine; but it was with a question. "What does it all mean?" he asked, bewildered.

"It means that that man there," and The Thinking Machine indicated the valet by a nod of his head, "is a murderer—that he killed Louise Regnier; that he shot Weldon Henley on Boston Common, and that, with the aid of Miss Regnier, he had four times previously attempted to kill Mr. Henley. Is he coming, Mr. Hatch?"

"Yes," was the reply. "He says he'll be here directly."

"Do you deny it?" demanded The Thinking Machine of the valet.

"I've done nothing," said the valet sullenly. "I'm going out of here."

Like an infuriated animal he rushed forward. Hatch and Cabell seized him and bore him to the floor. There, after a frantic struggle, he was bound and the other three men sat down to wait for Detective Mallory. Cabell sank back in his chair with a perplexed frown on his face. From time to time he glanced at Jean. The flush of anger which had been on the valet's face was gone now; instead there was the pallor of fear.

"Won't you tell us?" pleaded Cabell impatiently.

"When Detective Mallory comes and takes his prisoner," said The Thinking Machine.

Ten minutes later they heard a quick step in the hall outside and Hatch opened the door. Detective Mallory entered and looked from one to another inquiringly.

"That's your prisoner, Mr. Mallory," said the scientist, coldly. "I charge him with the murder of Miss Regnier, whom you were so confident committed suicide; I charge him with five attempts on the life of Weldon Henley, four times by gas poisoning, in which Miss Regnier was his accomplice, and once by shooting. He is the man who shot Mr. Henley."

The Thinking Machine arose and walked over to the prostrate man, handing the revolver to Hatch. He glared down at Jean fiercely.

"Will you tell how you did it or shall I?" he demanded.

His answer was a sullen, defiant glare. He turned and picked up the square mirror which the valet had produced previously.

"That's where the screw was, isn't it?" he asked, as he indicated a small hole in the frame of the mirror. Jean stared at it and his head sank forward hopelessly. "And this is the bath robe you wore, isn't it?" he demanded again, and from the suit case he pulled out the garment with the scarlet stripe.

"I guess you got me all right," was the sullen reply.

"It might be better for you if you told the story then?" suggested The Thinking Machine.

"You know so much about it, tell it yourself."

"Very well," was the calm rejoinder. "I will. If I make any mistake you will correct me."

For a long time no one spoke. The Thinking Machine had dropped back into a chair and was staring through his thick glasses at the ceiling; his finger tips were pressed tightly together. At last he began:

"There are certain trivial gaps which only the imagination can supply until the matter is gone into more fully. I should have supplied these myself, but the arrest of this man, Jean, was precipitated by the attempted hurried departure of Mr. Cabell for the South tonight, and I did not have time to go into the case to the fullest extent.

"Thus, we begin with the fact that there were several clever attempts made to murder Mr. Henley. This was by putting out the gas which he habitually left burning in his room. It happened four times in all; thus proving that it was an attempt to kill him. If it had been only once it might have been accident, even twice it might have been accident, but the same accident does not happen four times at the same time of night.

"Mr. Henley finally grew to regard the strange extinguishing of the gas as an effort to kill him, and carefully locked and barred his door and windows each night. He believed that some one came into his apartments and put out the light, leaving the gas flow. This, of course, was not true. Yet the gas was put out. How? My first idea, a natural one, was that it was turned off for an instant at the meter, when the light would go out, then turned on again. This, I convinced myself, was not true. Therefore still the question—how?"

"It is a fact—I don't know how widely known it is—but it is a fact that every gas light in this house might be extinguished at the same time from this room without leaving it. How? Simply by removing the gas jet tip and blowing into the gas pipe. It would not leave a jet in the building burning. It is due to the fact that the lung power is greater than the pressure of the gas in the pipes, and forces it out.

"Thus we have the method employed to extinguish the light in Mr. Henley's rooms, and all the barred and locked doors and windows would not stop it. At the same time it threatened the life of every other person in the house—that is, every other person who used gas. It was probably for this reason that the attempt was always made late at night, I should say three or four o'clock. That's when it was done, isn't it?" he asked suddenly of the valet.

Staring at The Thinking Machine in open-mouthed astonishment the valet nodded his aquiescence before he was fully aware of it.

"Yes, that's right," The Thinking Machine resumed complacently. "This was easily found out—comparatively. The next question was how was a watch kept on Mr. Henley? It would have done no good to extinguish the gas before he was asleep, or to have turned it on when he was not in his room. It might have led to a speedy discovery of just how the thing was done.

"There's a spring lock on the door of Mr. Henley's apartment. Therefore it would have been impossible for anyone to peep through the keyhole. There are no cracks through which one might see. How was this watch kept? How was the plotter to satisfy himself positively of the time when Mr. Henley was asleep? How was it the gas was put out at no time of the score or more nights Mr. Henley himself kept watch? Obviously he was watched through a window.

"No one could climb out on the window ledge and look into Mr. Henley's apartment. No one could see into that apartment from the street—that is, could see whether Mr. Henley was asleep or even in bed. They could see the light. Watch was kept with the aid offered by a flagpole, supplemented with a mirror—that mirror. A screw was driven into the frame—it has been removed now—it was swung on the flagpole rope and pulled out to the end of the pole, facing the building. To a man standing in the hall window of the third floor it offered precisely the angle necessary to reflect the interior of Mr. Henley's suite, possibly even showed him in bed through the narrow opening in the curtain. There is no shade on the windows of that suite; heavy curtains instead. Is that right?"

Again the prisoner was surprised into a mute acquiescence.

"I saw the possibility of these things, and I saw, too, that at three or four o'clock in the morning it would be perfectly possible for a person to move about the upper halls of this house without being seen.

If he wore a heavy bath robe, with a hood, say, no one would recognize him even if he were seen, and besides the garb would not cause suspicion. This bath robe has a hood.

"Now, in working the mirror back and forth on the flagpole at night a tiny scarlet thread was pulled out of the robe and clung to the rope. I found this thread; later Mr. Hatch found an identical thread in these apartments. Both came from that bath robe. Plain logic shows that the person who blew down the gas pipes worked the mirror trick; the person who worked the mirror trick left the thread; the thread comes back to the bath robe—that bath robe there," he pointed dramatically. "Thus the person who desired Henley's death was in these apartments, or had easy access to them."

He paused a moment and there was a tense silence. A great light was coming to Hatch, slowly but surely. The brain that had followed all this was unlimited in possibilities.

"Even before we traced the origin of the crime to this room," went on the scientist, quietly now, "attention had been attracted here, particularly to you, Mr. Cabell. It was through the love affair, of which Miss Lipscomb was the center. Mr. Hatch learned that you and Henley had been rivals for her hand. It was that, even before this scarlet thread was found, which indicated that you might have some knowledge of the affair, directly or indirectly.

"You are not a malicious or revengeful man, Mr. Cabell. But you are hot-tempered—extremely so. You demonstrated that just now, when, angry and not understanding, but feeling that your honor was at stake, you shot a hole in the floor."

"What?" asked Detective Mallory.

"A little accident," explained The Thinking Machine quickly. "Not being a malicious or revengeful man, you are not the man to deliberately go ahead and make elaborate plans for the murder of Henley. In a moment of passion you might have killed him—but never deliberately as the result of premeditation. Besides you were out of town. Who was then in these apartments? Who had access to these apartments? Who might have used your bath robe? Your valet, possibly Miss Austin. Which? Now, let's see how we reached this conclusion which led to the valet.

"Miss Regnier was found dead. It was not suicide. How did I know? Because she had been reading with the gas light as its full. If she had been reading by the gas light, how was it then that it went out and suffocated her before she could arise and shut it off? Obviously she must have fallen asleep over her book and left the light burning.

"If she was in this plot to kill Henley, why did she light the jet in her room? There might have been some slight defect in the electric bulb in her room which she had just discovered. Therefore she lighted the gas, intending to extinguish it—turn it off entirely—later. But she fell asleep. Therefore when the valet here blew into the pipe, intending to kill Mr. Henley, he unwittingly killed the woman he loved—Miss Regnier. It was perfectly possible, meanwhile, that she did not know of the attempt to be made that particular night, although she had participated in the others, knowing that Henley had night after night sat up to watch the light in his rooms.

"The facts, as I knew them, showed no connection between Miss Regnier and this man at that time—nor any connection between Miss Regnier and Henley. It might have been that the person who blew the gas out of the pipe from these rooms knew nothing whatever of Miss Regnier, just as he didn't know who else he might have killed in the building.

"But I had her death and the manner of it. I had eliminated you, Mr. Cabell. Therefore there remained Miss Austin and the valet. Miss Austin was eccentric—insane, if you will. Would she have any motive for killing Henley? I could imagine none. Love? Probably not. Money? They had nothing in common on that ground. What? Nothing that I could see. Therefore, for the moment, I passed Miss Austin by, after asking you, Mr. Cabell, if you were Miss Austin.

"What remained? The valet. Motive? Several possible ones, one or two probable. He is French, or says he is. Miss Regnier is French. Therefore I had arrived at the conclusion that they knew each other as people of the same nationality will in a house of this sort. And remember, I had passed by Mr. Cabell and Miss Austin, so the valet was the only one left; he could use the bath robe.

"Well, the motive. Frankly that was the only difficult point in the entire problem—difficult because there were so many possibilities. And each possibility that suggested itself suggested also a woman. Jealousy? There must be a woman. Hate? Probably a woman. Attempted extortion? With the aid of a woman. No other motive which would lead to so elaborate a plot of murder would come forward. Who was the woman? Miss Regnier.

"Did Miss Regnier know Henley? Mr. Hatch had reason to believe he knew her because of his actions when informed of her death. Knew her how? People of such relatively different planes of life can know each other—or do know each other—only on one plane. Henley is a typical young man, fast, I dare say, and liberal. Perhaps, then, there had been a liaison. When I saw this possibility I had my motives—all of them—jealousy, hate and possibly attempted extortion as well.

"What was more possible than Mr. Henley and Miss Regnier had been acquainted? All liaisons are secret ones. Suppose she had been cast off because of the engagement to a young woman of Henley's own level? Suppose she had confided in the valet here? Do you see? Motives enough for any crime, however diabolical. The attempts on Henley's life possibly followed an attempted extortion of money. The shot which wounded Henley was fired by this man, Jean. Why? Because the woman who had cause to hate Henley was dead. Then the man? He was alive and vindictive. Henley knew who shot him, and knew why, but he'll never say it publicly. He can't afford to. It would ruin him. I think probably that's all. Do you want to add anything?" he asked of the valet.

"No," was the fierce reply. "I'm sorry I didn't kill him, that's all. It was all about as you said, though God knows how you found it out," he added, desperately.

"Are you a Frenchman?"

"I was born in New York, but lived in France for eleven years. I first knew Louise there."

Silence fell upon the little group. Then Hatch asked a question:

"You told me, Professor, that there would be no other attempt to kill Henley by extinguishing the gas. How did you know that?"

"Because one person—the wrong person—had been killed that way," was the reply. "For this reason it was hardly likely that another attempt of that sort would be made. You had no intention of killing Louise Regnier, had you, Jean?"

"No, God help me, no."

"It was all done in these apartments," The Thinking Machine added, turning to Cabell, "at the gas jet from which I took the tip. It has been only loosely replaced and the metal was tarnished where the lips had dampened it."

"It must take great lung power to do a thing like that," remarked Detective Mallory.

"You would be amazed to know how easily it is done," said the scientist. "Try it some time."

The Thinking Machine arose and picked up his hat; Hatch did the same. Then the reporter turned to Cabell.

"Would you mind telling me why you were so anxious to get away to-night?" he asked.

"Well, no," Cabell explained, and there was a rush of red to his face. "It's because I received a telegram from Virginia—Miss Lipscomb, in fact. Some of Henley's past had come to her knowledge and the telegram told me that the engagement was broken. On top of this came the information that Henley had been shot and—I was considerably agitated."

The Thinking Machine and Hatch were walking along the street.

"What did you write in the note you sent to Cabell that made him start to unpack?" asked the reporter, curiously.

"There are some things that it wouldn't be well for everyone to know," was the enigmatic response. "Perhaps it would be just as well for you to overlook this little omission."

"Of course, of course," replied the reporter, wonderingly.

THE MAN WHO
WENT TO TALTAVUL'S

DAVID ALEXANDER

I suppose there are few men alive who remember Barnaby's Tavern in Boston.

Barnaby's was on Milk Street, near the Old Market, and it was a great, glittering place with blazing gas chandeliers and twinkling tiers of crystal bottles and huge gold-framed mirrors, and a gleaming stretch of ornately carved mahogany that was famed as the longest bar in the world. The bartenders were proper bartenders, too, wide-shouldered beefy men with spit curls, abundant mustaches, starched aprons, and diamond stickpins. To a boy my age—I was a stripling of eleven when I first walked into Barnaby's—all the customers were heroes. John L. Sullivan, the Boston Strong Boy himself, set up drinks for the house at Barnaby's every time he was home from one of his triumphal tours. A waspish little dude of a man who was sports editor of the *Transcript* held court there; he had earned great prestige by picking Spokane to beat the vaunted Proctor Knott in the Kentucky Derby the year before. The bluff, bearded police chief often came in mufti to drink his four-ounce shots of Maryland rye. Pompous politicians from the State House elected governors of Massachusetts in the back room.

It was at Barnaby's that I met The Man Who Always Wept.

I don't wish to give the impression that I was a precocious

alcoholic or a juvenile delinquent when I tell you I frequented a saloon at the tender age of eleven. I went to Barnaby's because of one of the most powerful moral forces of my youth, Horatio Alger. Alger was born in Revere, the beach district near Boston, and in 1890 he was living in nearby Natick. I never saw him, but I felt very close to him in spirit. It seemed to me that all the main characters of *Pluck and Luck* and *Tattered Tom* and *Ragged Dick* had widowed mothers. In this respect, at least, I qualified as an Alger hero. My father had died before I was born. He left my mother a comfortable house, but she went out to families in Louisburg Square to do "day sewing," as dressmaking was called in the nineties. Actually, she was well paid for her genteel work and we lacked none of the comforts of life. But many of Alger's characters had been bootblacks before they stopped a runaway team and saved the banker's daughter, so I bought polish, made myself a crude bootblack stand, and after school I sought customers on the streets and in the more respectable saloons like Barnaby's. I saved the nickels and dimes and, in time, the dollar bills we called "frogskins" in those days, hiding them in a secret cache in my room. I felt sure that some day a villainous character with a waxed mustache would storm into our little home waving a mortgage at my mother, despite the fact that I knew our house was free and clear of such entailment. I was prepared to uncover my hoard when he arrived, pay off the mortgage, and hurl the dastardly villain bodily from the house.

Barnaby's was my lushest source of income. The sporting gentry and politicians there would nearly always pay a dime, and sometimes even a quarter, if they were in their cups. It's true that my special hero, the chief of police, never gave me more than a nickel for his shine, but he would accompany it with good advice. "Industry and thrift, my boy," he'd say. "Industry and thrift—and keep away from bad companions. Remember that and you'll never have business at my place." My great ambition was to black the boots of John L. Sullivan, who had knocked out Jake Kilrain in the 75th round of their bare-knuckle fight at Richburg, Mississippi, the year before. But I was never lucky enough to be in Barnaby's when the champion was present. It was part of the Sullivan legend that he would pay a frogskin to the boys who blacked his boots.

The Man Who Always Wept stood alone at the far end of Barnaby's long bar. He was a spare man and he seemed very old to me, although I suppose he was only in his sixties. I always thought of him as the gray man. He wore an old gray suit and an old gray hat. His hair was gray and so was the stubble of beard on his face. But it was his flesh most of all that gave me the impression of grayness. His skin was the color of death.

He would stand there alone, hour after hour, drinking as long as he had any money in his pocket, speaking to no one, living on a forlorn and desolate little island of his own making. After a while he would begin to weep. He was not noisy or ostentatious in his weeping—there was a peculiar kind of dignity to his grief. The tears would begin to flow down his cheeks and he would stand there staring into his glass, not even bothering to wipe the tears away. I had never seen any person who was so desperately unhappy, and I was drawn to him through sympathy.

"Why does the old man always cry?" I asked a bartender one day.

He shrugged his meaty shoulders. "It's the drink," he said. "It makes some laugh and it makes some fight and it makes some weep. He's the kind that weeps, that's all."

I had seen The Man Who Always Wept several times before I had the courage to approach him. One day I walked up to him and asked him most respectfully if he'd care to have his boots blacked. He shook his head at me sadly. "No, son," he said. "I'm a man who's driven by the Devil. I must spend all the nickels I have on the Devil's poison—I can't waste them on such things as polish for my boots."

Somehow I felt he was desperately in need of help. I longed to show him some kindness, so I offered him the only thing I had to give.

"There's mud on your shoes, sir," I said. "Just let me brush it off for you. There'll be no charge."

Without waiting for his permission I dropped to my knees and began to brush his cracked old boots. When I had finished, I looked up at him. He was weeping silently.

"You should not do that, boy," he said. "I am an evil man. Stay away from evil companions. I've heard the police chief tell you that. It's good advice. I am evil and all who trust me come to harm."

When he stopped talking, his shoulders shook.

I stood there for a moment, tongue-tied and embarrassed. On a sudden impulse I touched his arm. He shrank away. "Don't touch me, boy," he said. "Stay away from me. I am an evil man who spent an evil night in an evil place—and I am damned forever."

The next day I asked my friend, the bartender, "What is the name of the man who is always crying?"

"He calls himself Smith," the barman said. "It is as good a name as any."

"What does he do?" I asked. "Why is he so sad?"

"He drinks, that's all. He drinks until his money's gone and then he staggers off to wherever he lives so he can sleep awhile and then drink again. Also, he broods on his sins."

"Is he a murderer?" I asked.

The bartender tapped his head. "He is a drunk. His sins are in his head."

I have discovered there is a queer affinity between old men and young boys. Perhaps it is because both old men and young boys know a great truth that is hidden from the others. They know that the things that really happen are of no importance; it's only the things that happen in the head which count.

Now that I am old I spend many fine days sitting on a bench in the public gardens of Boston Common and almost always some young sprout of eight to twelve will wander up and regard me speculatively. Just the other day a moppet of nine or ten who wore a Davy Crockett cap came up to me and began a conversation. "You're awful old, aren't you?" he asked.

I agreed that I was pretty old.

"You old enough to remember Davy Crockett?" he inquired.

I smiled and said, "Not quite that old."

"He's alive," my young friend told me. "I saw him just the other day on Commonwealth Avenue. He wears a coonskin cap like mine and he's got a buckskin suit with fringe all around it and now he's got a long, white beard. He don't carry his rifle any more. He's kind of feeble and he carries a long stick that he leans on. He didn't get killed at the Alamo. He was the only one escaped. He *told* me so."

"That's very interesting," I said inadequately.

My young friend's face grew puzzled. "He must be about a hundred-fifty years old by now," he said. "Can anybody really live that long?"

"Sure," I answered. "A man can live that long if he has good dreams inside his head."

"He's got good dreams, I guess," the boy declared, happy to

confirm the existence of his hero. "The Indians and Andy Jackson and the Alamo and all."

The dreams inside the head of The Man Who Always Wept were bad dreams, black nightmare figments of violence and evil so repugnant to him that he dared only to hint at the horror of them. My own dreams in those days were bright ones—Alger dreams of catching a runaway horse and marrying the banker's daughter and buying my mother a castle to live in. Yet a strange kinship grew up between the eleven-year-old bootblack and The Man Who Always Wept. Everyday, after I had served my paying customers in Barnaby's, I would stoop and brush the shoes of the man who drank alone; and at last he accepted my small gesture without protest. In time I not only brushed his shoes, I also polished them. He offered to pay me for this, but I would not take his money. He seemed so old and his clothes were so shabby. I knew he could not afford the luxury of a daily shine.

One afternoon he ordered his glass refilled while I was polishing his cracked old shoes and he discovered he had no more money to pay. A stricken look came into his gaunt face. It was a look of terror, the look of a man deprived of his last defense against nightmare horrors. A two-ounce glass of bar whiskey cost fifteen cents at Barnaby's. I slipped three nickels into my firend's trembling hand.

Not long after that I took him home for the first time.

It was winter and there were snow and ice and slush on Milk Street. The Man Who Always Wept grew more wan and feeble by the day, it seemed. On this occasion he fairly staggered from the saloon after his money had been spent, supporting himself against chairs and tables as he steered his uncertain course toward the door. The men who lined the bar watched his progress with mingled expressions of amusement and disgust. I wanted to take my friend's arm and help support him, but I sensed that this would only embarrass him. As soon as he stepped into the street he slipped and fell heavily. Some of the men at the bar who were watching through the plate-glass window hooted with laughter. An irascible old bluenose from Beacon Hill sniffed disdainfully and told the bartender that sots should not be permitted to drink at the bar with gentlemen who could hold their liquor. No one went out to help the fallen man. He was now attempting to scramble to his feet on the slick sidewalk, threshing about with the frantic futility of a large fish that has been washed up on dry land.

I was the only one who went to his assistance. I was a well-grown boy for my age, but it took all my strength to get the old man to his feet. He had hurt his leg and there was blood on his face. Tears were running down his face, too, but they were not the tears of pain or rage; they were the tears, it seemed to me, of a man who has abandoned hope.

The man who called himself Smith lived in a decaying neighborhood of warren tenements near the Old Market, not far from Barnaby's. Our staggering journey over the slippery streets was a perilous one. Twice I fell and the old man plummeted down on top of me. Once a fat policeman whose face was cherry-red from the cold stopped us. "Is that your grandfather, son?" he asked me.

"No, sir," I replied. "He is a friend."

When the policeman walked away the old man I was supporting broke into peals of drunken laughter. "Friend!" he exclaimed. "No human being has been my friend since that evil night!"

The wooden house he lived in was ancient and rickety and sagged under heavy festoons of icicles suspended from the eaves. He roomed in a dark cubicle on the topmost floor and it took almost a quarter of an hour for me to drag my burden up the groaning stairs. A bed, a washstand, a chair, an old trunk, and a little stove were in the room— that was all. The wide-board floors were bare.

The Man Who Always Wept dropped on the bed without removing his wet, torn overcoat and he fell at once into a fitful sleep. I stood by, not knowing what to do. It was cold. There were a few sticks of wood by the stove; I found some paper and matches and made a fire. A stale piece of bread and a half-filled bottle of milk stood on the window sill. Beside the bed there was another bottle with a very small amount of whiskey in it.

The old man began to mutter in his sleep. "The door," he said. "The white door." Then he would groan and mumble something unintelligible about a box. I looked about the room. There was no box there and I wondered if he were referring to the trunk.

I sat by the stove while the shadows deepened outside the smeared little pane of window. Finally the old man awakened with a cry and jerked upright in the bed. He sat there shaking with a terrible seizure.

"Go away!" he screamed. "You must not stay with me. I am an evil man!"

He groped for the bottle beside the bed and drank the remaining whiskey at a gulp. Faint color came into his pasty face, and the shaking stopped. I lighted a smoky, evil-smelling lamp, poured water from a pitcher, went to the bed, and began to wipe the blood from his face with a wet rag.

He tried to push me off. "Don't!" he begged. "I belong to the Devil, boy. I've lived in hell for twenty-five years now. You mustn't touch me."

I went about my business despite his protests. I got the clothes off his scrawny body, found a frayed nightshirt, and forced him to put it on. Then I covered him with a threadbare blanket.

"I don't think you are evil," I told him. "You are only sick."

"Ha!" he cried. "You don't know me, boy. You don't know my name, do you?"

"The barman told me your name was Smith."

He shook his head and a cunning look came into his eyes.

"My name is not Smith," he said.

"You spoke about a door while you were sleeping," I said. "A white door."

He threw off the blanket and his talon-hand clutched my shoulder. "Don't mention the white door!" he cried.

I was persistent. I was determined to discover what nightmare fancies made the old man weep.

"You spoke about a box, too," I said. "Was that a secret? Where is the box? Do you keep your money in it?"

He laughed bitterly. "Money," he said. "I have no money. Each month there is a tiny sum from an inheritance. I pay my lodging, buy a crust or two, and then I put the rest inside the trunk there. I take out a few coins for my booze each day and when I've spent them I come back here and lie in darkness . . . with my memories. Remember the trunk, boy. Someday they'll find me dead. I haven't got much longer before the Devil takes me. When it happens, open the trunk. If it's early in the month there may be a few coins left. I will them to you. I make you the heir of an evil man."

"Are the coins in the box you mentioned in your sleep?" I asked.

"No, no. The coins are in a little rawhide bag at the bottom of the trunk."

"What was in the box? Treasure? Pirate treasure?"

The sly look had come into his face again. His pale lips twisted into a mocking smile. "Yes, you might say there was treasure in it," he replied.

"Was the box behind the door?"

"Yes," he answered, in a barely audible whisper. "The box was behind the door."

"Did you steal the pirate treasure and did the pirate gang hand you the black spot and mark you to be murdered?"

"There was murder," he said. "There was murder and there was worse that dark night."

"Are *you* a murderer?" I asked, fearful of his answer.

"I am a murderer who never killed," he said.

Suddenly the awful trembling shook him again. The little room was warm now from the stove but his teeth were chattering. When he had controlled the spasm, he said, "I must have whiskey, boy. There's a brass key to the trunk in the pocket of my coat. Get it and find the rawhide bag with the money in it. Then go to the grog shop on the corner and buy me a pint."

"No," I said. "You've had enough to drink already."

"Please, boy," he begged. "I've got to have it to kill the monsters of the past—they won't be long in coming now. Get the booze for me and I will tell you a terrible secret, a secret no one knows."

"About the door and the box?" I asked.

"Better," he said. "I will tell you my name."

"Is it a famous name?"

"It is an infamous name. Hurry, boy."

I got the whiskey for him, wondering what an Alger hero would have done under similar circumstances. I consoled my conscience by telling myself that he looked so sick he might die if he did not get the stimulant he craved. But I knew in my heart it was curiosity that prompted me to run his errand.

When he had drunk from the bottle, he gasped for a moment and I thought he was going to fall asleep.

"You promised me!" I said.

"Yes," he answered. "I will tell you my name, boy. It is an awful secret and you must keep it until I'm dead. My name is John F. Parker."

The name meant nothing at all to me. I cudgeled my brains. "I—I think there was a fellow named Parker who rode with Jesse James," I said.

"No, boy. I never rode with outlaws."

"Then maybe you were a Western marshal, out in the Dakota Territory?"

He smiled at me sadly and took another drink from the bottle. "I've never been West," he said. "I guess you wouldn't know my name. You're too young for that. But it's a name that men and the Devil will never forget. Go away, now. I want to sleep."

He had drunk nearly half the bottle and he fell into a deep, snorting sleep. It was almost supper-time and my mother would be worried about me. I had left my bootblack stand at Barnaby's, but I knew the barman would take care of it. I checked the dying fire in the little stove, snuffed out the lamp, and hurried home.

The next day I went to Barnaby's and saw The Man Who Always Wept—the man with an infamous name I did not recognize—standing in his usual place at the end of the bar. I decided not to approach him until I had blacked the boots of my customers, as usual.

The bearded police chief stood almost the entire length of the long bar away from Smith, or Parker, or whatever his real name might be. I ventured to ask the chief a bold question, despite the fact that the drunken old man had sworn me to secrecy.

"Sir, was there ever a great criminal named Parker?" I inquired.

"Parker?" he said, wrinkling up his brow. "Why, indeed there was, my boy. The South Boston Butcher, he was called. Chopped the heads off three women with his meat axe, he did. We caught him in the end, of course, and stretched his neck on the gallows. Bloody Billy Parker, the Butcher Boy. That's what the papers called him."

"Not Billy Parker," I said. "John Parker. John *F.* Parker. Have you ever heard of him?"

"Plenty of criminals in the world and some of them named Parker, I suppose," the chief answered curtly. He seemed offended that his identification of Bloody Bill had not impressed me. "Can't say I remember any John *F.* Parker, though."

That night, by tacit consent, I walked home again with The Man Who Always Wept. I did not have to support him this time, except to take his elbow when we crossed streets churned to deep slush by the carriages and wagons.

Day after day for months I would walk him home to the bleak building near the Old Market. I would finish blacking my customers' boots in Barnaby's, then I would go down to the end of the bar and stoop at the old man's feet and make his scuffed shoes as presentable as possible with my brush and rags and polish. By that time he had nearly always spent the last coin of the small amount he allowed himself for his daily drinking at the bar. In the late afternoon we would leave the bar together; the other patrons would regard us curiously, but they made no comment. They seemed to sense that there was some bond between us that they could not understand. The old man grew feebler week by week. It took us a long time to walk the short distance, but he never became as drunk as he had been that first day, and he never fell to the sidewalk again. Often we met the beefy cop with the cherry-red face. He would wave his nightstick at me and say, "I see you're taking good care of your friend, young fellow."

The old man and I played a little game. I think that toward the end his interest in the game was all that kept him alive, for he had nothing else in his life except his dismal room, his few hours at Barnaby's, and the memories which he called the monsters of the past. Almost every day he would give me some sly hint about himself and the thing that he had done, and a certain light would come into his dim and reddened eyes as if he were challenging me to solve the riddle. I would question him and sometimes he would not answer me at all except with a sidelong glance, in which there was a sort of bitter amusement. Sometimes he would answer me in meaningless words that only added to my confusion.

"There was the white door," he would say. "And don't forget the box. And John F. Parker was not there." At first my look of puzzlement would amuse him, but then he would begin to think his dark thoughts again and the tears would come.

I made further inquiries—discreetly, I fancied—about the identity of John F. Parker. I asked the sports editor of the *Transcript* if he had ever heard of such a man, because I considered any journalist a brilliant man with a vast store of esoteric knowledge. He pursed his lips and looked wise. "There was a sparring partner of old John L.'s who had a name like that, I think. A clever ringman with a fast left jab, but no match for our Strong Boy, of course."

One day the old man said to me, "Tell me, boy. What will you do when you grow up? It's time to think about it so you won't waste your life as I have."

"I'm going to be a journalist," I answered immediately. "I am going to write pieces under my name for the *Transcript*."

"Do journalists make good money?" he asked.

"Of course," I answered in my innocence, not realizing that members of the Fourth Estate were then the worst paid workers in the world, aside from Chinese coolies.

"Then you will do something for me," said my friend. "I will die soon—the Devil is on his way. They will find me dead one morning and I will go to the real Hell instead of the one I've been living in. They'll toss my carcass into a hole in Potter's Field and there'll be no gravestone to mark the place. When you grow up and make your fortune you must buy a gravestone for me. Promise."

I promised him I would.

"There is an inscription you must have cut upon the stone," he said. We were in his little room that day. He pushed a piece of butcher's paper and a pencil stub before me. "Write it down," he said. "Write it down so the stonecutter will have it right."

I sat with pencil poised.

"No name on the gravestone," he said. "No dates or pretty sentiments. Just a plain, square stone with these words on it: The Man Who Went to Taltavul's."

I asked him how "Taltavul's" was spelled. He spelled it out for me twice, letter by letter.

"I never heard of Taltavul's," I said. "Where is it? Is it a town in Massachusetts?"

"It is the evil place I went to on that evil night," he answered. He was playing the game again.

I began to make inquiries again among the customers at Barnaby's, but none of them had ever heard of Taltavul's. I even got my father's heavy old gazetteer down from the bookshelves and read over all the fine print in the back, searching down the page with a polish-blackened finger. My eyes ached from squinting at the many maps. But I could find no such place as Taltavul's.

That summer Boston sweltered from a heat wave, and the old man seemed to fail and shrink before my eyes. In the fall, on Halloween, my friend and I stood on a curbing and watched the traditional parade of the

Society of Ancients and Horribles. As the masked, grotesque figures passed, he said, "The creatures of my dreams are more frightening."

And then it was winter again and there was early snow in New England.

I had bought the old man a Christmas present with the dimes and nickels from my secret trove. He needed a warm coat. I couldn't afford that, of course, but I had purchased a heavy woolen muffler.

On Christmas Eve I went to Barnaby's. The place was festive with holly and red paper streamers, and the customers were gaily boisterous, toasting the holiday with egg nogs and Tom-and-Jerries and hot buttered rums.

My heart sank when I entered the place. Many customers greeted me and asked me to black their boots. They would have tipped well because of the season, but I dropped my bootblack stand and ran out into the snow, the package I had wrapped in tissue tucked beneath my arm.

I ran all the way to the dingy street near the Old Market. The door of the wooden house was never locked. I went into the hall and my feet clattered up the creaking flights.

I found him on his bed, an empty bottle beside him, and I knew at once that he was dead.

The Devil had come at last for The Man Who Always Wept.

I dropped my Christmas gift on the floor. I did not remember my inheritance in the trunk, and I stumbled down the stairs. Outside I met the beefy policeman with the cherry-red face and I told him what had happened. He patted my shoulder in a kindly fashion and told me he would take care of everything. I trudged home through the swirling snow, tears streaming down my face.

I had left my bootblack stand at Barnaby's, but I never went back for it. It was ten years before I entered the place again.

When I went back to Barnaby's I was old enough to cast my first vote (I would cast it for McKinley and Teddy Roosevelt, of course). I would graduate from Harvard at the June Commencement. I recall the date quite clearly, because it was a milestone in my life—April 14, 1900.

I had been interviewed that afternoon by the august editor of the *Transcript* and had been engaged as a reporter, my duties to begin directly after my graduation. Soon, I thought, I would be able to keep my promise and buy the gravestone for my friend in Potter's Field. I was to be paid the princely sum of ten dollars a week. The *Transcript* started most of its reporters at seven dollars, but the editor was a Harvard trustee and offered bonuses to graduates of the college who joined his staff. I was treading air that fine spring day, because my own life was about to begin with the death of a century. I felt I should celebrate. I drank only moderately, but I decided impulsively that I would toast my luck and the old man's memory at Barnaby's, the place where we had met.

Barnaby's had belonged to the nineteenth century and it was dying with it. The electric bulbs that had replaced the shimmering gaslight shone nakedly on the dust and desolation. The silence was an oppressive pall in this place where convivial men had laughed and roistered. The bartenders were no longer sleek and plump and mustached, and the aprons they wore were spotted. Half the long bar had been fenced off, and I fancied that ghosts drank in the shadowy reaches that had been closed. It was there that The Man Who Always Wept had stood day after day fighting the monsters of the past.

There were pitifully few customers and, like Barnaby's itself, all of them seemed to belong to the past. I recognized two aging gentlemen with white beards who wore frock coats and flat-topped bowler hats, and I placed myself beside them to order my drink. Each had served his state in the Congress. Of course they did not know that the tall young man next to them was the same lad who had once blacked their boots. Suddenly one of the bearded men made a startling remark. He said, "Yes, it is a memorable day indeed."

Could they have heard of my great fortune? I wondered. I grinned at my own foolishness.

The other old man was saying, "Yes, it was just thirty-five years ago today that it happened. And the tragic part is that it needn't have happened at all if that policeman had only remained to guard the door. The box would have been safe then. What was his name? Parks? Parkman? Parker? Something like that, I think."

The other old man said, "I recall him. He went to Taltavul's that night."

I could restrain myself no longer. I fairly shouted, "Please, sir! You mentioned Taltavul's! What was it? Where was it?"

The two old men were Proper Bostonians. They glared at me to put me in my place. But one of them answered.

"You are an impetuous young man, sir," he said. "It is not good manners to raise your voice and interrupt the conversation of your elders. I have noted that the younger generation is lacking in respect and courtesy. Nevertheless, I will oblige you with the information you request. Taltavul's was a drinking establishment much like this one. It was on Tenth Street in the city of Washington.

"It was, in fact, next door to Ford's Theater."

AUTHOR'S NOTES: John F. Parker, who could have prevented the murder of Abraham Lincoln, is a hazy figure of history, seldom mentioned by name in the chronicles of the event. He was one of the six members of Washington's Metropolitan Police Force assigned as the President's bodyguards. He had served briefly in the Union Army and had joined the Force to avoid further service. When he was about to be drafted, Mrs. Lincoln interceded for him. He was a chronic alcoholic. On April 14, 1865 (the day Booth shot Lincoln and a date important to this story) he was drunk and was three hours late reporting for duty. He was supposed to report at 4 P.M., but he did not arrive until 7. Had he been just a little later, or had he not reported at all, Lincoln's life would have been saved, because Cook, the man he relieved, was a conscientious officer.

The white-painted door of Box 7 in Ford's Theater which Lincoln occupied on the fatal night had a broken lock. The key had been mislaid and a few days previously a theater employee had broken off the lock. It had not been replaced. Parker must have seen the lock was broken, but he did not remain at his post outside the closed door. Once Lincoln and his party were in the box, he went next door to Peter Taltavul's Tavern and began a drinking spree with several coachmen who were waiting to drive their employers home. Some time between 9 and 10 P.M., Parker was actually standing only a few feet from John Wilkes Booth, who came into Taltavul's and ordered a bottle of whiskey at the bar before going up to the box to assassinate the President.

THE RUNNING MAN

DAVID ELY

It was at the shore that Mr. Golding first saw the running man. Each morning Mr. Golding and his wife crossed the dunes to their favorite spot, well back from the beach. Mrs. Golding rubbed herself with lotion, and lay down in the sun. Mr. Golding, having established himself in his camp chair, opened his book to read. From time to time his attention would stray to the water, where children played and bathers plunged into the surf.

With the slow passage of the lazy days of his vacation he came to recognize the families who spread their towels in the same places at the same hours, and the couples who regularly walked along the shore—and so it was that he became accustomed to the sight of the runner, who appeared every morning at about ten o'clock, speeding along at the water's edge with long swift strides.

Watching the young man race by, Mr. Golding was reminded of a summer some 40 years before, when he too had run along the beach each day, to stay in condition for his college track team. When had it been—1934? 1935? He recalled how vigorously he had sprinted across the hard-packed sand with all the force and energy of his young manhood. He might have been elected captain, but he had quit the team that fall, after reading somewhere that running could enlarge the heart and cut years off one's life—a prudent decision, he now reflected, for

164

otherwise he might not be sitting here in the sun, breathing the fresh salt air.

Mr. Golding was not a nostalgic man, but his memories had been stirred, and he mentioned the young runner to his wife. She took no interest in the subject, however, so he returned to his book. Still, he kept thinking about the runner, and found himself glancing along the beach each morning as the hour of ten approached.

"Here he comes, that young fellow I told you about," he remarked to his wife one day. "See?"

Mrs. Golding, annoyed at having her sunning interrupted, raised herself unwillingly on her elbows to look. "Where?" she asked, squinting.

Mr. Golding pointed along the beach. "Over there. You're looking the wrong way. Well, it's too late now. He's gone."

The next morning Mr. Golding alerted her as soon as he saw the running figure in the distance, but by the time she had turned over and sat up and put on her sunglasses, the runner had raced by. On the third morning, after Mrs. Golding had once more missed her opportunity to see the runner, Mr. Golding suggested rather tartly that she might profit from a visit to an eye specialist, and made no further reference to the running man.

It occurred to him that he might take a closer look at the young runner. This would have meant a break in his schedule, however—he never went down to the water for his swim before eleven—and he was above all a man of habit and precision. He always wore a tie and jacket to supper at the hotel for example, and his tips were calculated to the penny. At the beach he carefully picked up any pebbles that happened to be in his path, and made a neat little pile of them near his chair—for what reason, he couldn't have said, except that he had done it on the first day and had kept on doing it since.

In any case, it was improbable that a man like Mr. Golding would alter his routine by going down to the water at ten o'clock simply to peer at some unknown young fellow running by there; and yet one morning, somewhat to his surprise, he did go down early. He didn't realize it until he was actually there, and took a look at his watch. Why, he must have misread it. He was an hour ahead of time! And he should have left the watch on top of his book, as he always did. Now he'd have to take it back up to his chair.

Still, Mr. Golding did not turn back. He remained at the water's edge, waiting.

It was hot that day. The breeze had died, and the sea lay flat. Its glassy surface fired light into his eyes, and the heat constricted his breathing. Oddly enough, he heard what sounded like surf faintly booming far away—and yet there was no surf that day. He turned his head—and saw the running man appear in the distance.

Squinting that way, Mr. Golding experienced a visual distortion for the heated air rising from the sand made the runner look much larger than he should have seemed. The mirage effect diminished as the young man sped closer, so that, to Mr. Golding, the runner remained the same size, appearing to be suspended in space.

This trick of light gave Mr. Golding a sensation of displacement, as though he himself might be somewhere he was not. He realized that he could re-establish his perspective by looking elsewhere; yet he kept watching the runner, even though he no longer really wanted to, for there was rising in him a disturbing awareness of some disarray in the natural order of things that counseled him to leave.

Still, he remained where he was, the sand sucking at his feet and his eyes unwillingly fixed on the apparently hovering runner.

Despite the heat of the sun Mr. Golding felt a strange, premonitory chill. It seemed to him that something unpleasant was about to happen. He sought to move; he could not. Nor could he tear his gaze away from the running man. Everything else seemed to fade away. It was as if the beach had emptied of people, and he and the young runner were the only ones there, as if the sky, the sand, and the water, too, all had vanished, stranding him in some unknown world.

In those few but seemingly endless moments Mr. Golding stood numbed and helpless, his heart pounding as though he, not the other, were the runner, and it was then that he saw clearly for the first time the expression on the young man's face—a look of such piercing sorrow and reproach that Mr. Golding, in his astonishment, felt himself seized by an answering surge of anguish.

Then the runner flashed by, and was gone. Mr. Golding swayed, momentarily dizzied. The beach bloomed once more before his eyes; he heard the cries of children, and saw the swimmers in the water. He noticed that he had sunk to his ankles in the wet sand. With an effort he pulled his feet free and plodded back up the dunes, shaken and bewildered.

"What's wrong?" his wife inquired, looking up at him from her towel.

Mr. Golding shook his head, and eased himself down into his chair. "I must have gotten too much sun," he muttered.

He sat staring out at the horizon for a while. Then, his voice stronger, he remarked as casually as he was able, "You know, Sheila, I think I've had enough of the beach for this summer. Let's go back home."

The Goldings lived in Boston, in the house they had bought when they were married. It was too large for their needs—they had hoped to have children, but Mrs. Golding had always miscarried; yet they had remained there for convenience, since it was just across the Common from Mr. Golding's law office—and it was there, in the park, that Mr. Golding again saw the running man.

Mr. Golding rose early in the summer in order to arrive at work while the air was still fresh. He liked the Common then, for few people were about, and the birds sang undisturbed. At that hour it wasn't unusual to see men jogging on the paths for exercise. One of the residents of Mr. Golding's block, in fact, donned a sweatshirt every morning for a pre-breakfast trot.

When Mr. Golding glimpsed a running figure in the distance on one particular August morning, his first impression was that it was his middle-aged neighbor. But this runner was young and lithe, and moved with swift strides. Mr. Golding, having taken a second look, hastened his own pace. He tried to persuade himself that it was some other young man, although he knew instinctively who it had to be.

He had no intention of stopping and turning, but he found himself doing so all the same. The young man raced toward him across the brown and dusty grass. His sweatshirt had something lettered on it—the name of a college, perhaps—but Mr. Golding hardly noticed that. It was the runner's face that commanded his attention. Again there was that look of sorrow and reproach, and it wrung from Mr. Golding the same inexplicable distress he'd felt before.

And then the running man sped by, and Mr. Golding was left confounded, in the clutch of a causeless remorse. He sat on the nearest bench, trying to compose himself. In the name of God who was it? He hadn't the faintest recollection of ever having seen the fellow before, although he couldn't be absolutely sure; but in any event there was nothing to justify that rending glance of sadness, or his own puzzling reaction.

It must be sheer coincidence, thought Mr. Golding. He had seen the young man at the beach; now he had seen him on the Common. There was nothing extraordinary in that. As for the runner's peculiar expression, it was in all likelihood the grimace of physical effort. Nothing to worry about, Mr. Golding told himself firmly.

But he no longer went to work at that early hour, and he chose a roundabout route to his office, avoiding the Common.

The next time it happened was in a restaurant a few days later, when Mr. Golding was lunching with Judge Barnes. The young man wasn't running, but he was moving quickly. He seemed to be a busboy hurrying past with a tray of dishes just as Mr. Golding glanced up, but in the confusion of the moment Mr. Golding couldn't be sure. All he knew was that it was the same young man, for he caught that unmistakable piteous look, and felt again the pang in his own heart.

Mr. Golding fiddled with his food and kept glancing about uneasily. He didn't see the mysterious busboy again, but after he and Judge Barnes had paid their bill and left, he noticed the young man across the street.

"Look over there," said Mr. Golding sharply. "See that young fellow—?"

But Judge Barnes was too slow, and near-sighted besides. "What young fellow?" he asked, peering about in vain, for the young man had vanished into the midday crowd. "Never mind," said Mr. Golding.

As Mr. Golding was leaving his office building the next day, he saw the running man rush by in the crowd. The following morning, as he was buying a newspaper on Tremont Street, he noticed him striding past. The day after, Mr. Golding saw him racing for a bus on State Street. On each occasion he caught from him, if only for an instant, that same mystifying look of tormented reproof. Could all this be coincidence? Mr. Golding began to fear it was not.

The running man's appearances came with increasing frequency, at unexpected moments of the day. Mr. Golding could hardly walk a block without at least a fleeting glimpse of that mournful face. The young man hurried out of elevators that Mr. Golding was waiting to use, and he was among the movie-goers streaming out of theaters that Mr. Golding was about to enter. If Mr. Golding took a taxi, he would see him crossing a street, or rounding a corner.

One afternoon, looking up from his desk, Mr. Golding saw him glance in at the open office door, and then pass quickly on. Mr. Golding rushed out to the corridor. It was empty. He questioned his secretary, but she had been busy at the file cabinet, and hadn't see anyone.

"It must have been a messenger," she said. "I'll speak to him if he comes in again. What does he look like?"

But Mr. Golding really didn't know what the young man looked like.

This episode disturbed Mr. Golding. It was bad enough to keep encountering that ubiquitous young man in public places, but it was intolerable to have his own premises invaded. Who the devil was the man? What did he want? If he had some grievance, why didn't he speak out plainly about it instead of casting those hurt and agonized looks? Mr. Golding tried to think of someone who might conceivably have a grudge against him, but there was no one he had wronged, no one.

He began working with his door closed, although that made the room stuffy. When he stepped out of his office, he glanced around suspiciously for his unknown pursuer. At home he became sulky and subdued; at work he grew snappish. He had always been physically lean, but now he was becoming drawn and wasted. He was losing sleep and eating poorly. His nerves were ragged too. One afternoon as he was passing the Parker House, the young man swung around the corner and hurried toward him.

"Now see here," Mr. Golding rapped out sharply. He tried to block the way, but the young man sidestepped him and passed on. "You'll pay for this!" cried out Mr. Golding.

He set off in pursuit, but collided with someone, and paused to apologize. In the meantime the young man had vanished, leaving Mr. Golding peering all about and muttering under his breath.

"You all right, Pop?" a passerby asked, taking him by the elbow. Mr. Golding angrily shook off the hand, and went on his way, humiliated.

"I've got to put an end to this," he kept thinking. He considered going to the police. But what complaint could he make? That some young fellow was going about giving him reproachful glances? Why, they'd think *he* was the crazy one!

He finally decided to seek advice from an old friend, George Sloan, a tax specialist who had his office on the floor above, and whose experience and judgment were frequently sought by Mr. Golding on professional problems.

At the conclusion of one of these discussions Mr. Golding broached the matter in an off-hand manner. "I've got a little personal difficulty, George," he said. "There's some young fellow who keeps showing up wherever I go. I don't know whether he's followng me or not, but it's a peculiar situation."

As he recounted the story of the running man, Mr. Golding felt calmer. Mr. Sloan's office had a soothing regularity of décor, and the tax lawyer, a portly and confident man, was listening with sober attention. ". . . the whole thing is very annoying to me," Mr. Golding concluded, "and I simply don't know how to handle it."

"It may be a case of mistaken identity," suggested Mr. Sloan. "You may resemble someone who's treated this fellow badly."

"I thought of that," said Mr. Golding. "If it had happened once or twice, I might agree—but it's been going on for weeks, several times a day. No, he knows me, all right. He knows where I work, and the places I go for lunch. He pops up everywhere!"

"You're sure you've never met him?"

"Oh, I couldn't swear to it. Everybody under the age of thirty looks more or less the same to me now," said Mr. Golding, "and besides, the fellow goes by so quickly I don't get more than a glimpse of him. But whether I've met him or not in the past, I certainly don't remember him, and there's no justification for the way he looks at me— as if I'd done him some injury."

"Well, just to cover all possibilities," said Mr. Sloan, "let me ask you if you've ever caused injury to anyone—unintentionally, of course. An automobile accident, for example."

"Never," replied Mr. Golding. "I've never had an accident of any kind."

"What about neighbors? Have you had any trouble with neighbors—or relatives?"

"No, no trouble whatever," said Mr. Golding firmly. "You know me, George. I'm not the sort of man who looks for trouble. I never have been. I don't know whether I've ever mentioned this to you, but back in the Thirties, when I was a law student, several of us volunteered for the Loyalist side of the Spanish civil war—oh, I was quite a firebrand in those days—but at the last minute I didn't go. I couldn't stand the idea that I might kill someone, even for a cause I believed in." He sighed, and shook his head. "I've never hurt a soul, George. Not only that, I've always gone out of my way to avoid getting into a position where I might inadvertently injure others. In fact, I gave up criminal practice for just that reason."

"I didn't know you'd ever practiced criminal law."

"It wasn't for long. Just for a few months, when I was fresh out of law school. I had a vision of myself defending penniless clients—you know how idealistic young men are. But I was very much aware of my youth and inexperience. I was worried about making a mistake that might send some poor devil to prison. I didn't want that kind of responsibility—and that's why I decided to switch over to corporate law."

Mr. Golding smiled a wry little smile. "It hasn't been the sort of career I once imagined—but it's had its own rewards—and I've done my level best, George. I've played fair with everybody—everybody!"

He frowned down at his clasped hands then, for he remembered an exception, but he decided not to mention it. He'd betrayed his wife once with a secretary. It must have been 20 years ago. He'd got worried about it after a few weeks, though, and persuaded the girl to break off the affair. She'd taken a job elsewhere. But his wife hadn't known about it, of that he was sure.

No harm done, thought Mr. Golding. He glanced up at his friend. "Well, George, what do you think about all this?"

"It seems obvious that this young man is some sort of crank," said Mr. Sloan. "Still, he may be harmless. He hasn't threatened you, has he?"

"Well, no," admitted Mr. Golding. "He hasn't—not yet, anyway. But the fact remains that it's a damned impertinent intrusion into my life, and I'd like to find some way of putting an end to it."

"I don't blame you," remarked Mr. Sloan, with a glance at his watch. "You say you see him every day? What about my taking a look at him, then, just to size him up?"

"Well, that would be very kind of you, George," said Mr. Golding. For some reason, however, he found that he was not eager to accept Mr. Sloan's friendly offer. "But I've already taken up enough of your time as it is—"

"Not at all," interrupted Mr. Sloan, rising to his feet. "Let's go out right now and see if he shows his face."

Mr. Golding rose too. "Really, I can't ask you to go to so much trouble," he said uncertainly, greatly puzzled by his mounting reluctance. "Perhaps some other day, when you're not as busy."

"Nonsense," said Mr. Sloan heartily, conducting Mr. Golding to the door. "We'll just stop at your office for your hat, and then we'll go out and see what happens."

The two men walked along Washington Street, and it was in front of Filene's that Mr. Golding saw the running man. "There he is," he exclaimed, but the fellow vanished in the crowd of shoppers before Mr. Sloan could pick him out. A few minutes later Mr. Golding spotted his quarry entering a drug store, but by the time he and Mr. Sloan had gone inside, the runner was no longer there, presumably having left by another door.

"He's like lightning," complained Mr. Golding. "That's the problem. I catch a glimpse of him, and then he's gone."

He and Mr. Sloan made a similar tour the following day, at Sloan's insistence, and although Mr. Golding saw the running man on four separate occasions, his friend wasn't quick enough to spot him. They headed back toward the office.

"It would help if you could give me a clearer description," Mr. Sloan remarked.

Mr. Golding sighed. "It's a look he has, that's all," he said defensively. Then he stopped short. "There he is—right across the street. See? In the brown jacket!"

Mr. Sloan took a look. "Well, I see a man in a brown jacket," he said, "but didn't you say he was wearing a gray suit before?"

Mr. Golding was puzzled. "Why, yes, that's true," he said. "He *was* in gray—at least I think he was." He stared intently across the street, but the young man in the brown jacket was gone. "Perhaps I made a mistake," Mr. Golding muttered. Mr. Sloan made no comment. "It may have been someone who resembled him," Mr. Golding added. He suddenly felt terribly tired and old.

As they continued along the street, he saw the running man again, hurrying into a camera store, but he couldn't tell whether he was wearing brown or gray, and said nothing about it to Sloan. When they entered the lobby of the office building, Mr. Golding thought he saw the young man once more—just a flash of his face among the office workers crowded into an elevator whose doors were closing—but he couldn't be sure.

"We'll give it another try tomorrow," said Mr. Sloan, but without enthusiasm. He wasn't looking at Mr. Golding.

"I don't think I'll be coming to the office tomorrow," said Mr. Golding. . . .

He stayed home the next day. At noon he stepped outside, intending to go to the corner to buy a newspaper, but when he saw someone a block away running his way along the sidewalk, he went back inside, and remained there the rest of the day and the day after that. On the third day, irritated by having him around the house, his wife announced that she was going up to Marblehead to visit her sister for a few days. Mr. Golding thought of going, too, but he could tell that his wife didn't want his company.

That evening he heard footsteps outside, the rapid steps of someone running, steps that beat up swiftly, drummed by, and sank in the distance. Mr. Golding went to the telephone in the front hall. "This must stop," he said under his breath.

The police number was on an emergency list tucked in at one corner of the hall mirror. Mr. Golding dialed, his hands trembling. But he immediately replaced the receiver. By the time the police arrived, the running man would be far away.

He went back to the living room and turned on the television, with the volume high. Now he couldn't hear the steps outside. But then he wondered: suppose the runner came right up to the house? He turned off the television and went to the window, pulling the curtain aside to peer out. No, the street was empty. He looked through the peephole in the front door to be sure no one was on the stoop. Then he opened the door.

It was a misty evening, with a touch of fall in the air. The street lamps cast a damp, smeared glow. When he heard the steps in the distance, he fought the impulse to leap back in and slam the door. His breath quickened and his heart pounded. Where the devil was the runner? Ah, there he came, a dark figure swiftly striding.

"Who's that?" called out Mr. Golding, his voice cracking. He
cleared his throat. "Who's that?" he called again. The runner sped
along the sidewalk, drawing closer. "Stop," shouted Mr. Golding from
his doorway. "You there—stop! Who are you? What do you want?" But
the runner raced by and was gone.

Mr. Golding returned to the telephone and dialed Mr. Sloan's
number. "It's happening all the time, George," he said, trying to keep
his voice steady. "That fellow, he's after me day and night. Just a
minute ago he ran right by the house."

"Try not to think about it," Mr. Sloan advised him. "Do
something to take your mind off the subject. Play a game of cards with
your wife, or get her to read to you."

"Well, my wife's not here. She's gone up to her sister's for a few
days."

"You shouldn't be alone," said Mr. Sloan.

"You're right, George. I realize that. Look, I'll just get in the car
and drive up there—"

"I wouldn't drive, if I were you."

"Nonsense. I'm perfectly all right."

"Isn't there a neighbor who would come in and stay with you?"

Mr. Golding made no reply. He was straining his attention,
listening for the running man. "Wait a minute," he whispered. He
thought he could hear him now, his steps echoing faintly in the distance.
"He's coming back." He laid the receiver down and rushed to the door,
pulling it open. "Can you hear them, George?" he puffed, having
snatched up the phone again. But there was silence outside. "No, I was
wrong. He's not coming, not now. But he'll be along any minute now.
He never leaves me alone—"

"You'd better get a neighbor to come over," Mr. Sloan repeated.

"If I'd ever done anything to deserve it—but I haven't. My God,
I've never done anything," said Mr. Golding, his voice shaking. He
was staring through the open door at the misty street. "I could have
been a runner, too, but—" He broke off, squinting intently, his head
tilted as he listened. "No . . . not yet. He's waiting."

Mr. Sloan was continuing to urge him to get someone to stay with
him, but Mr. Golding paid no attention. "I've lived a careful life,
George," he said, keeping his voice low so he could hear the running
man when he came. "I've avoided risks of any kind, to myself and

others. That's why this is so—so intolerable. If I'd gone to Spain—but I *didn't* go!"

He stiffened. "Here he comes," he whispered. There was no doubt about it now. The footsteps were far away, but coming closer. "Can you understand my feelings, George? To be persecuted for what I haven't done? It's so damned unfair—after I quit trial work, after I gave up the only woman who ever gave me any real tenderness and—"

He hurried to the door. The running man was sprinting along the street. "Stop—stop!" shouted Mr. Golding. His eyes were teary from the strain. He could barely see the figure hurtling through the mist. "Stop—in the name of God, stop!"

Mr. Golding's throat burned from the force of his outcry, and he was choked with sobs. "Please . . . please . . ." He was gasping; his tears blinded him. He could hear the steps, but saw nothing. He turned and fumbled his way back inside, wiping his eyes on his sleeve. From the telephone receiver he heard Sloan calling his name. Mr. Golding stood panting in the hall. His heart was slamming in his chest.

He lifted the receiver. "Did you hear the steps, George?" he whispered, and then he saw something in the mirror. "Oh, my God, he's inside. He's in the house now!"

He whirled about. The hall was empty. He could see into the living room, and it was empty too. "No," whispered Mr. Golding. "I made a mistake. He didn't come in. He—"

He raised his eyes slowly to the mirror. He knew now what he had seen there, and what he would see again—that terrible gaze of sorrow and accusation. He stared at it, anguish storming within him.

When he spoke, his voice was dry and clear. "I'm sorry, George," he said. "There was something I didn't mention. I'd forgotten." He seemed to see before him, as in a dream, the sunlit beach, and someone running. "There was a young man once," said Mr. Golding softly. "Many years ago . . ."

He replaced the receiver, and stood gazing at the memory of what he had killed until it blurred in his tears, and he could no longer make it out.

A CASE OF
CHIVAS REGAL

GEORGE V. HIGGINS

Panda Feeney, fifty-three, was employed as a court officer. He escorted juries between the courtrooms and the rooms where they deliberated, and he made hotel and restaurant accommodations for them when they were sequestered. He fetched sandwiches and coffee for them when they were deliberating, and he delivered messages between them and the judges on their cases when they thought of silly questions during their deliberations. "But basically," Panda would say, "my job is to take care of the judges and do what they want, all right? What the judges want."

Panda did not like all of the judges that he served. Those he disliked made his back hurt, so he would disappear. He would stay somewhere around the second civil session, technically on duty but a little hard to find. It was not that he feared detection, loafing; he still remembered much of what he had learned wrestling, so he was indifferent to detection.

"My back," Panda would say, rubbing it, when some assistant clerk of courts located him bent over morning papers and a cup of coffee in the vacant jury room and said: "Judge wants to see you." Panda would nod painfully, writhing slowly in his chair. "Naturally, he wants to see me. Could've bet on it. Never fails: my back acts up, there's some guy like him in here. What's he want, huh? You know? Can you tell me that? This damp weather, Jesus, I can hardly move."

Clerks would never know what it was that judges wanted, only that they wanted Panda and had not seen him around. Panda would nod, once, when they told him that, and grimace. "Okay," he would say, "then can you do me a favor? Tell the judge: when I fought Casey—he has heard of Crusher Casey, even if he is a moron like he acts like he is—Crusher may've been an old guy, but he still had a body slam that ruined me for life. You can get the Judge's coffee for me, can't you? Do an old, lamed-up guy a favor? Tell him that for me."

One judge that Panda especially disliked was Henry Neelon. Before Judge Neelon was relieved of trying cases so that he could spend all of his time as the administrator of the courts, he had had a run-in with Panda Feeney. Panda after a few drinks would sometimes recall the story. "Hanging Hank'd spent the morning sending guys to Walpole. Handed out about a hundred years and still he wasn't satisfied. Gets back in his chambers and he's still looking to make trouble. Sends Grayson, that pinhead, out to look for me.

"I give Grayson the routine," Panda would say, chuckling. "Grayson'd believe anything you told him. He goes down and gives the word to Hanging Hank.

"Henry blows a gasket," Panda would say, laughing now. "He does not believe what Grayson tells him I said about my back, all right? He is going to check it out.

"I am sitting there, in the jury room. I can hear old Henry coming, stomping up those iron stairs and swearing like a bastard. He is going to take my head off. 'Lazy goddamned officers. Good-for-nothing shirkers.'

"So, I think quick," Panda said. "I don't have much choice. And when old Henry comes in, I am lying on the table. 'Damn you, Feeney,' he says, when he slams the door open, and then he sees me lying there like I am all set to be the guest of honor, my own wake. Except I do not look as good as I will look when old Dave Finnerty finally gets me and lays me out in the front room. I've been holding my breath, so my face is red. And I have got a look on me like we used to use when the guy that's supposed to be the loser in the matches is pretending he is chewing on your leg, or pulling some other dirty trick that only bad guys do. Pain, you know what I mean? *Pain.* I am in agony—one look and you can see it. And Henry's jaw drops down.

"I dunno, Judge,' I say. I have got big tears in my eyes. 'I hate to even think about it, but the pain is awful. It doesn't stop, I'm gonna have to. Even though I don't want to, go on disability and just collect the pension. I may not have any choice.'

"Does he believe me?" Panda said. "At first, I guess he does. and then when he starts to suspect something, maybe I am jerking his chain, right? But he isn't sure. And even to this day, I catch him looking at me, he still thinks I was giving him the business that day I was on the table. And if he ever gets a shot at me again, that guy is gonna take it. I can see it in his eyes."

Panda Feeney liked Judge Boyster, so his back was always fine when Andrew Boyster drew his session. "Now you take someone like Drew Boyster," Panda would tell other judges when he served them the first time. "He is my idea, a judge. Not the kind of guy, you know, where everything is hard and fast and there's no allowances for human nature, you know? Drew Boyster is the kind of guy that I'd want judging me, if I was ever in that spot, which God forbid, I should be. If we had more like Andrew Boyster this would be a better world."

Andrew Boyster always squirmed when Panda's praise got back to him. "Ahh," he'd say, looking embarrassed, "I wish Panda wouldn't do that. Every new judge comes along, Panda gives indoctrination. And all it really means, I guess, is that I am too easy. I let Panda disappear, if I don't really need him—I suppose he's sleeping, but then, Panda needs his rest. Then too, I let Panda pick the hotels when the juries are sequestered, and the ones that Panda picks are always grateful for the business. He selected the restaurants when the juries sit through dinner, and he picks out the delis when they're having sandwiches. He's probably enriching pals, but then, should he pick those who hate him? And they probably show their appreciation in ways that might be worth some money. Nothing against the law, of course—I am not suggesting that. But I bet Panda has some trouble, paying for his dinners out." He did not tell Neelon that.

Panda's explanation differed. "You know why I like Drew Boyster?" He would squint when he said that, studying the novice judge for some sign of inattention. "He thinks I am smart, is why. He does not think I am stupid. Judge Boyster doesn't come in here, like lots of these guys do—and, Christ, you come down to it, some of the broads we get are worse. He doesn't just barge in here and start throwing weight around, acting like he owns the place and everybody in it. Drew

Boyster . . . well, I had one case he was involved in, before he became a judge. And that was all I needed, right? To see what kind of guy he is. This guy, he may be a lawyer and he made a lot of money before he went on the bench, although from what I heard, I guess his first wife made a big dent in that. But he has always had some class. Drew Boyster has got class. I have been here fifteen years. Judge Boyster is the best. I never ate a meal with him, or had a drink with him. It's not like we are buddies, you know? Or anything like that. It's just that, all the years I've been here, he's the best I ever saw."

He made that speech, with variations, to so many judges, that when Drew Boyster dropped dead at the age of fifty-nine, victim of a massive stroke that killed him instantly, Panda's name was mentioned by everyone who saw Judge Neelon on the morning afterward. Henry Neelon was in charge of making the arrangements for the speakers who would say a few words at Boyster's memorial, and as little as he liked the man, Henry Neelon saw the logic of including Panda Feeney.

"Look," he said, "I realize this may be hard for you. I know how you felt about Drew—everybody did."

Panda shook his head and looked down, as though he did not trust his voice to perform reliably.

"The thing of it is," Judge Neelon said to Panda, "you've been to enough of these things so you know what they are like. They are deadly, Panda—they are boring and they're dull. We get a couple lawyers who won recent cases in his court—we do not ask folks who lost. The Chief Justice declares on the record: 'He was not a pederast.' If he has one kid who can talk, we let the kid stand up—and then we all watch carefully to see if he breaks down, or displays any evidence that he's been using harmful drugs. For some reason, we don't ask surviving spouses to address us—it's probably because we're all afraid of what our own might say, if they got full attention, and we weren't there to reply. Then finally, one friend of his, if the dead guy had a friend, takes four or five long minutes to say nobody else knew him.

"You see what I mean, Panda?" Judge Neelon said pleadingly. "The last guy who gets up at those things is the only one who's right— none of the other speakers is a friend of the departed, someone who just *knew* him and enjoyed his company. No one that just *liked* him, unless he's another lawyer, ever gets a chance to speak. And we thought, since you did know Drew, and really did like him, maybe you would say a few words and do everyone a favor."

Panda looked up and he shook his head once more. "I couldn't do it, Your Honor," he said, and cracked his voice. "I would not know what to say. I'm not used to making speeches, standing up in public like that."

"Panda," Neelon said, "it could be very short. You could say . . . that case you had, the one that impressed you so much, you never forgot it? You could talk about that case, how Drew showed so much class. Look, you know Drew Boyster's history. You went back a ways with him. His family, they're not, you know, extremely happy with him, even now that he is dead. His kids, from everything I hear, they sided with the wife. You'd really help us out a lot if you saw your way clear to do it. Good Lord, Panda, all these years, you have drummed it into us. Just tell everybody once more, what a great guy Drew was."

"Your Honor," Panda said, coughing deeply as he started, "I have got to tell you—I can't talk about that case."

"Of course you can," Judge Neelon said. "It's on the public record. If it's the details that escape you, we can pull the files. We'll take care of that for you. That part will be easy."

"Judge," Panda said, "it wasn't that. It was not a case in court. Well, there *was* a case in court, that Judge Boyster was involved in. But the case I talked about . . . I can't talk about that."

"I don't follow you," the Judge said. He was starting to look grim.

"It was Chivas Regal," Panda said with difficulty. "A case of Chivas Regal, all right? That was what I meant."

"Scotch whiskey?" Neelon said. "A case of booze, you mean?" Panda nodded. "Uh-huh," he said. "That was what it was."

"And this was back when Drew, when Drew was a lawyer?" Panda nodded once again. "Yeah. Before he was a judge."

"Panda," Neelon said severely, "this is serious. Drew is dead now. It can't hurt him, not where he is now. But you're still escorting juries, and you still have access to them. If you influenced some verdict, back when Drew was practicing, and he gave you a case of scotch . . . well, I don't have to tell you just how serious this is. What was it you did for Drew? Tamper with a jury, or do something dumb like that?"

Panda looked indignant. "Judge," he said, "I resent that. In all the years I've been here, I have never told a jury how they should vote in a case."

"Uh-huh," Neelon said, "well, you are the first one, then. But you've raised the suspicion now, and I am forced to deal with that. If you don't tell me the truth, and tell me the truth right now, I'll have to investigate and see what you did for Drew. And until I am satisfied, you will be suspended. Without pay, I might add, until this is all cleared up. Now which will it be, Panda? This is your decision now. You can tell me what went on, or you can leave this building right now and wait to hear from the D.A."

Panda looked more sorrowful than he had looked before. He had to clear his throat again. "This won't go any further?"

"It won't if there is nothing wrong," Judge Neelon said grimly. "If I think there is something wrong, it will go further, Panda. No promises apart from that. You understand me, Panda? And I will be the judge of whether you will be reported."

Panda sighed heavily. "All right," he said, "you got me. But there is nothing wrong with this, with what I did for Drew." Judge Neelon did not comment on that.

"Over twenny years ago, I got hurt in the ring."

"I know that," Neelon said. "Get on with you and Drew."

"I'm coming to that," Panda said. "Just give me a minute, will you? The doctors told me: 'Panda,' they said, 'this is it for grappling. You get hit like that again, you'll go out in a wheelchair. You are still a young man and your heart is pretty strong. You get crippled up for life, it is going to be a long one and you will have trouble working.'

"That scared the hell right out of me," Panda told Judge Neelon. "In wrestling there's no insurance. I did not have money . I was always undercard, a couple hundred bucks. And I didn't have any trade, you know. Something I could do. But I am scared, so what I do, I take what comes along. I get into security. I become a guard.

"The first job that I had," he said, "was in the Coast Apartments. This was before it was condo. This was 1963. And since I am new and all, I am put on nights. So I do not see who goes out—I just see who goes in.

"Now, Judge," he said, "I don't know just how I should put this to you. Because I don't want to shock you, or do anything like that. But lots of the big law firms then had pads in those tall buildings. And on the tour they had me on, I'd see those guys come in. See them come in with their girlfriends? Between six and nine at night. And they would not go out again, 'fore I was through at one.''

"Panda," Neelon said, "Spare me. You mean: 'With their nieces, they came in.' Learned counsel for rich law firms do not get so vulgar as to entertain mere girlfriends in deductible apartments.''

"My mistake, Your Honor," Panda said. "Excuse me. On the tour they had me on, I often saw the lawyers come in with their nieces right behind them. Now, this took me a while, before I got this figured out. I was fairly innocent, when I stopped wrestling. And when I first started in there, I did not know much. So one night, this big honcho lawyer comes   with his briefcase, and it is six o'clock or so and I am pretty stupid. And also with him, right behind him, there is this young lady. A very fine looking young lady, I might add. And she has got her handbag, but that's all she's carrying. So I assume they're visiting someone—they do not live in the building, or else they would tell me. So I ask him: 'Which apartment?' Like I was supposed to do. Coast did not want people coming in there without they had destinations, and the people they were seeing wanted to see them.

"He gets all mad at me, the guy does," Panda said to Neelon. "He tells me he belongs to this firm which keeps an apartment there. Their clients in from out of town stay overnight in it. And sometimes in the evening, if they have a lot of work, they come in with their secretaries and they work late hours themselves. And that is what he's doing, and she is his secretary. 'Gleason, Boyster and Muldoon. That is all you need to know.' And they go on upstairs.

"Well, Your Honor, nothing happened. That I got in trouble for. This guy and his secretary, they go up to work late hours and I don't know who they are, except they work for a law firm that he says he belongs to. He don't say that he is Gleason and he don't claim he is Muldoon. I do not know he is Boyster and the lady had no name. All I knew her by was her looks, and like I told you, those were fine. She also had a nice smile and she always gave it to me.

"I say 'always,' Judge," he said, "and when I say that, I mean this: 'Wednesday nights she smiled at me.' Every Wednesday night. The first night was a Wednesday and then they come back, the next one. And I naturally remember them and I don't ask no questions. And then the Wednesday after that, and the one after that, until I see this is a habit, they got going here. This guy apparently can't get his work done, any Wednesday that you name. Tuesdays he's apparently all right, when they blow the quitting whistle. Thursdays he does not show up. I had Fridays off in those days, Fridays and Saturdays. He don't come in any Sunday. He does not show up on Monday. And by now I've gotten so I know a lot of guys that have problems just like his, except their big nights are different, and their secretaries change, or else they have got whole flocks of nieces like you would not have imagined. So I am wising up a little, and I'm keeping my mouth shut. And also I am putting my name in around the city, because I am getting older and those late hours are killing me.

"Anyway, two years go by, and then things start to change. I notice that this guy has started coming in on Tuesdays. And pretty soon it's Thursdays and I'm seeing him on Mondays, and when I come in on Sunday he's been working all weekend. His secretary, too—she's in there, and they're bringing in groceries. And then this other guy gets sick, so I have to cover for him, and damned if the secretary there and her boss are not working Friday nights and Saturday nights too."

"Thriving private practice," the Judge said, nodding at him. "Envy of every practitioner. Those hours are just brutal."

"They must be," Panda said. "Well, anyway, the days go by, and one day I am sitting there, I open up the paper. And what do I see but his picture and his name is under it. This is Attorney Andrew Boyster, who's been working those long hours. And he is in the paper because his wife's suing him. She is suing him in the back and she's suing his front, too. What she wants is a nice divorce, and every dime he's got. And there's another picture, which is of Andrew Boyster's wife. And she does not look like the lady that I know."

"She looked a little older, maybe?" Henry Neelon said.

"Well, I assumed she was," Panda Feeney said. "I didn't think too much about that, just how old she might've been. What caught my eye was, you know, she alleged adultery. And I thought I might have some idea, of just who she had in mind.

"Well," Feeney said, "the papers had their usual field day. And I have got a dirty mind, so of course I read it all. And I am sitting there one night, the two of them come in, and I am looking at their pictures. They give me the great big grin, and she asks me how I like it.

"I do not know what to say. I figure they are going to tell me, I

should mind my own damned business. So I mumble something at
them, and they start to laugh at me. 'You're going to have to do better
than that, if your name is Thomas Feeney,' Andrew Boyster says to me.
And since we're never introduced, that kind of throws me, right? 'How
come me?' I say to him, and that is when he tells me. I am getting a
subpoena. I am going to testify.

"I say: 'Why me? What do I know?' He says his wife thinks that I
know lots. Like who's been coming in and going out the building I am
guarding, and she wants to ask me that.

"Now, I figure," Panda said, "I am in the glue for fair. So I ask
him: 'What do I say?' And he says: 'Tell the truth.' And they go upstairs
laughing, just as happy as can be. Which at least made me feel better,
that the guy's not mad at me. I just may not lose my job."

"Did you testify?" the Judge said.

"Uh-huh," Panda said.

"And did you tell the truth?" the Judge said, looking grim again.

"Absolutely," Panda said. "Told the Gospel truth. Had on my best
blue suit, you know, clean shirt and everything. And they ask me, his
wife's lawyers, did I work the Coast Apartments and how long did I
work there. I told him those things, truthfully, and all the other junk he
asked me before he comes to the point. And when he does that he
decides he will be dramatic. Swings around and points to Boyster and
says: 'Do you know this man?' And I say: 'Yes, I do know him. That is
Andrew Boyster.' Then he shows me a picture, which is Boyster's
secretary that I guess is now his widow, and he wants to know: do I
know her? And I say: 'Yes, I do.'

" 'Now,' he says, like this is this great big salute he's planned,
'how long have you known these people? Will you tell His Honor that?'
And I say: 'Yessir. Yes, I will.' And I turn and face the Judge there and I
say: 'I have known them for two weeks.' "

"Which of course was the strict truth," Neelon said, laughing with
him. "Did he ask you the next question?"

"You mean: 'When did you first see him?' " Panda asked the
Judge.

"Yeah," Judge Neelon said, "that is exactly what I mean."

"No," Panda said, "he didn't. I think he was flabbergasted. He
just stood there and looked at me like his mouth wouldn't work. And
then when he got it working, all he could think of asking me was

whether I was very sure that was my honest answer. And I said: 'Absolutely, sir.' And then I was excused. And then when Christmas came that year, I got a case of Chivas Regal, and it was from Andrew Boyster and that second wife of his who I still think's a nice lady. And then when Drew got his judgeship, my name came up on the list faster than it ever would've otherwise, and that is how I got this job here. Because Drew thought I was smart. What I said, testifying, it did not make any difference to the way the case come out—at least that is what he told me. 'But,' he told me, 'Panda, it was the one laugh that we had while all that crap was going on, and we just wanted you to know that we appreciated it.' Which is why I thought Drew Boyster was a very classy guy—because of how he treated me."

Judge Neelon studied Panda for about a half a minute. Then he nodded and said: "Okay. You are off the hook. You don't have to speak when we have services for Drew. And I will not report you."

"Thank you, Judge," Panda said.

"There's one thing, though, I'd like to know," the Judge said thoughtfully. "At least, I think I'd like to know it, so I'll tell you what it is. That day when you were on the table, up there in the jury room? The day I burst in on you and you described your back pain to me in such colorful detail?"

"I remember it, Judge," Panda Feeney said.

"If I had asked you, that day, if you had that back pain then, what would you have told me? Do you want to tell me that?"

"To be candid, Judge," Panda Feeney said, "since you're giving me that option: No, I don't think that I do."

Neelon nodded. "Uh-huh," he said. "And if I were to ask you: Have you ever lied to me? You'd tell me that you never have."

Panda Feeney nodded. "Yes. And that would be the truth."

THE SWAN-BOAT MURDER

PHOEBE ATWOOD TAYLOR

The fiery glow of the rising sun practically guaranteed Boston its third sizzler in a row, Asey Mayo thought, as he parked his long, black Porter Sixteen roadster by the Boylston Street curb and looked expectantly toward the Public Garden for the plump form of his housekeeper cousin Jennie.

It was exactly 5:30 a.m., and Jennie should be poised by the subway entrance back of the Channing monument with her suitcase in hand, ready to leap into the car and be driven posthaste back home to Cape Cod. For today, June first, was the official opening of Jennie's annual house-cleaning season, and she wouldn't permit anything to interfere, not even the difficulties involved in her return from a family funeral in Chicago.

Asey grinned as he contemplated the relays of relatives pressed into service to rush Jennie home in time to get her curtains down and into the washtub at the proper moment. But his grin faded when no figure bustled toward the car.

"Golly!" he murmured. "Ain't she *here* yet?"

He was in no mood to hang around Boston. He had his own plans for the day—a sail out Cape Cod Bay for tautog, and then a session with the bass on North Beach. He was already dressed for it, in dungarees and a blue shirt and his oldest yachting cap. His rubber boots were on the car floor, next to a pail of lines and tackle.

"I wonder, now, if I got this wrong." Taking Jennie's letter from his pocket, he scanned the final page.

"*'Lisha will pick me up Sunday night at 7 at Cora's,*" he read. "He says the Salty Codfish Sherlock (he means you) could probably make Boston in 5 hours, the way you drive, but it'll take him 8 or so. Allowing for everything, I'll be there sure by 5:30. You meet me then. Everyone asks me if you done any murder detecting lately. I declare, out here they don't realize you're so busy at the Porter factory making those tanks you don't hardly ever get home! Why, Cora didn't even know you was a director of Porter Motors; she thought you was still Captain Porter's hired man and yacht captain, like you was years ago. She said, why would anyone call you a Lithe Hayseed Sleuth, you don't look like a hayseed! Can you beat it? Now, 5:30 Monday morning, back of the Channing monument. Don't be late. I got to start cleaning."

Asey replaced the letter and mentally gave Jennie just half an hour. If she didn't appear by six, she could take the train home.

Sliding out from behind the roadster's wheel, he walked over into the Garden. Perhaps Jennie might already have come and be wandering around. The Public Garden was her favorite spot in Boston. She loved its statues and prim flower beds, and particularly its swan boats. If it were later in the day and the boats were out paddling their leisurely course about the tiny artificial lake, Asey knew he would have found Jennie perched on the front bench of one, gurgling with pleasure while she fed peanuts to the ducks. Maybe even at this early hour she might have strolled over to the boat landing by the bridge.

Asey shook his head as he started off down the dirt walk. Perhaps, as Jennie claimed, the swan boats took her back to her childhood and made her feel young again. But it still didn't seem right for her to get such a thrill from a flat-bottomed water barge, foot-propelled by a stern paddle hidden in a metal swan, and capable of a top speed of two miles an hour!

"For the love of Pete!"

He stopped short at a turn of the path and stared blankly ahead at Jennie's new tan suitcase with the brown stripes and red initials, sitting forlornly on its side in the middle of the walk. Beyond it lay the brown pocketbook he'd given her for Christmas!

But there was no sign of Jennie herself.

"Jennie!" He opened his mouth and bellowed in his best quarter-deck roar. "Jen-nie May-o!"

His voice echoed across the pond, and two moth-eaten gray squirrels stopped their scampering and looked at him.

But Jennie didn't appear.

Asey picked up the pocketbook, peered inside, and then hastily shut it before the miscellaneous hodgepodge of its contents started to spill over. There was only some small change in the money compartment, but that didn't signify anything. When Jennie traveled, not even the Gestapo could find where she hid her funds.

"Ahoy, Jennie! Ahoy, Jennie Mayo!"

Frowning, he tucked the bag and pocketbook under his arm and walked slowly toward the boat landing. He couldn't imagine any situation that would have prompted her to dash off of her own accord and leave her precious belongings behind. She never would have been duped into rushing off with a stranger. Once away from home, Jennie was inclined to view her fellow men with deep suspicion. And, if anyone had tried to rob her, the chances were that the prospective thief and not her two bags would have been stretched out prone on the path.

Asey's bewilderment increased, halfway around the lake, when he came upon her best brown straw hat on the grass by a clump of trees. "She's *been* here!" he muttered. "Where *is* she?"

Slinging the bags on a bench, Asey shinnied up a near-by maple, braced himself, and made a slow survey of the Garden. But the place was deserted except for the ducks bobbing around the lake and the squirrels romping under the trees, and a flock of pigeons waddling along the footbridge railing.

His gaze automatically followed the line of the rail, and then went down the angle of the steps leading to the swanboat landing. What he saw there sent him sliding down the tree and propelled him at a gallop along the path.

"By gum!" He paused at the edge of the landing's worn planking, looked ahead, and winced.

For the body of the gaunt young man in gray slacks lying there behind a settee was not a pretty sight. Decidedly not.

Someone, Asey decided thoughtfully, had done some very expert shooting. The bullet hole in the fellow's forehead was almost mathematically centered, and the condition of the back of his head, turned slightly sideways, indicated that a considerably powerful weapon had been used. The fellow had gone down like a log without even knowing what hit him.

Scattered around near the body were several small cardboard cartons and leather cases, and almost at the water's edge stood a camera, set up on a tripod and aimed at the little fleet of swan boats moored a few feet from the landing.

Asey opened his eyes wide as he looked at them.

He'd ignored the boats entirely in his haste to convince himself that the crumpled body he'd spotted from the tree was not that of his cousin Jennie. He discovered now that the metal swan on the nearest boat had a framed background of blue velvet propped up behind it. And posed with her arms around the swan's neck was an amazingly lifelike dummy of a girl, scantily and bizarrely clad in red and white striped shorts and a blue, star-spangled bra! Her straight blond hair dangled to her shoulders, and she stared at Asey with the bland, disconcerting disdain of a store-window model.

Obviously, the murdered man had been taking pictures of the dummy and the swan, although why he should choose to take them at all, and particularly at this hour, was a puzzle to Asey.

"Let's see!" he thought out loud. "This fellow turned around from his camera—yup, that's it. He's still got a plateholder gripped in his hand. Maybe he heard or saw somethin' behind him. Anyway, he turned, an' that's what someone was waitin' for, an', bang, that was that! Wonder who he was—"

Asey bent over and read the printing on the metal-edged tag attached to the handle of one of the leather cases:

"RUDI BRANDT, STUDIO 5, ARTS BLDG.,
ARLINGTON STREET, BOSTON, MASS."

Since the initials on the breast pocket of the fellow's shirt were "R. B.," Asey decided he could reasonably assume that the fellow was Rudi Brandt.

He rubbed his chin reflectively as he glanced around. There was no trace of any weapon hurriedly discarded by Brandt's murderer. There were no lipstick-stained cigarette butts or shreds of Harris tweed, or anything a movie detective would have pounced on as a vital clue. The only small, extraneous objects on the landing were peanut shells, left over from the swan boats' customers of the day before. And still, in all the Garden, there was no one but himself, and the ducks and pigeons and squirrels.

There must, Asey thought, have been a good, hefty report from the gun firing that shot, and he wondered why the sound hadn't brought some of Boston's cops running to the scene. Someone must have heard the shot. Probably a lot of people had, and promptly dismissed it from their minds. That was the trouble with city folks. They took it for granted that every loud bang was a car backfiring.

Asey tilted his yachting cap back on his head. He could guess, now, what had probably become of Jennie. Arriving earlier than she'd figured, she'd started over for the landing and then—perhaps the shot had launched her off—she'd seen fit to rush in and mix herself up with this nasty business. Heaven only knew where she might be now. He only hoped she hadn't really dashed off on her own in a wild attempt to catch or track down a murderer who blazed away at people as accurately as this one did. But it wouldn't be the first time his firm-minded cousin had barged into a situation where the average angel would fear to tread!

Asey replaced his cap. He was forgetting himself. He shouldn't be dallying around, brooding like this. This was neither his bailiwick nor his business, and he ought to report the affair to the cops, and trust that Jennie would sooner or later come back to the Garden and her belongings. No one as efficient as the person who shot Brandt would ever let himself be hampered for long with Jennie's meddling.

He tried to figure, as he returned to collect her hat and bag and pocketbook, the location of the nearest phone. He couldn't remember any stores open on Boylston Street. Probably the drugstore on the corner of Beacon and Charles was his best bet.

With the bags under his arm he emerged a few minutes later on Beacon Street, just in time to see a girl in a knee-length red coat streak around the corner opposite him and dart up the side street. It occurred to Asey that she looked strangely familiar. He frowned, and then slapped his thigh.

"The dummy!" he said. "That's it! She had the same color blond hair, wore it the same way, an' had on the same red-heeled pumps— Oh—oh! Oh—oh!"

A cop had loomed in sight on the corner where the girl had first appeared. And he had a typical cop's grip on the arm of Jennie!

Asey rushed across Beacon Street in nothing flat.

"Thank goodness, you've finally come!" Jennie's tone insinuated that if anything out of the ordinary were happening, it was all Asey's fault for not being there sooner. "Asey, tell this cop who I am, and who *you* are—see?" She joggled the cop's arm. "Recognize him, don't you? He's Asey Mayo, and I'm his cousin, and you let me go, you!"

"Listen, lady; I seen you snatch that girl's purse!"

"I did not!" Jennie said hotly. "I—"

"Look," Asey said, "both of you stop breathin' fire an' listen to me. Over in the Garden—"

"He's a director of Porter Motors, too!" Jennie joggled the cop's arm again.

"Yeah?" The cop leaned back against the basement railing of the house before which they stood, and gave Asey's fishing costume a critical once-over. "Yeah? I took him for a millionaire. Now, I seen you grab that purse—"

"I never! I was only trying to grab *her*, and all I got hold of was her bag! . . . Asey, did you see a blond girl in a red coat run past? . . . When? Where'd she go to?"

"Around that corner, about two shakes ago." As Asey pointed to the side street, the cop casually turned his head in that direction.

Instantly, in a single swift gesture, Jennie grabbed the red purse from under the cop's arm and shoved him squarely in the stomach. Then she grabbed Asey's belt and started to run. "Hurry up!"

Asey, as he was yanked along, looked back over his shoulder, to see the cop lose a desperate battle with his balance and disappear in a spectacular tumble down the basement steps.

"Hustle!" Jennie almost dragged him around the corner of the side street, glanced along it briefly, and shook her head. "Oh, dear, I've lost that girl *again!* Well, it won't matter so much, now you're here to help get her. Come along quick, before that fool cop sees us!"

Nonchalantly, as if she'd lived there always, Jennie reached out, shoved open the wooden alley door of one of the low brick houses, pushed Asey into the narrow alley, and closed the door behind them. "There! We'll wait till that fool's gone. . . . Asey, the time I been havin'! I never seen anything like it!"

"Neither did I!" Asey told her severely. "D'you realize what you just done? You assaulted a cop, an' city cops don't like bein' assaulted!"

"I never assaulted anyone!" Jennie protested. "I just accidentally pushed that fellow and he happened to slip. Listen; we've got to find that blond girl, because she's just shot and killed a man on the swanboat landin'! I heard the shot, and saw her and everything, with my own eyes!"

"You seen her? Then why, instead of chasin' around like a hen with her head cut off, didn't you *tell* that cop so?"

"You saw why!" Jennie retorted. "He wouldn't listen. Asey, she shot him and then ran away, so I dropped my bags and ran after her. Now go on and ask me why I didn't call a cop!"

"None around?"

"Not a soul, an' *somebody* had to catch her! I almost did, too. That's why I know about this alley," Jennie added parenthetically. "She hid here, once, but I found her and followed her across these back yards. Finally I was so near that I reached out to grab her, and just then that cop turned a corner on Charles Street and seen us. When I turned to call to him to come, the girl jumped ahead, and so I only got her purse. And then that fool cop grabbed *me* for stealin' it! Asey, we can't stand here like bumps on a log! We got to get her!"

"Seems as if we had," Asey agreed. "Golly, if only you hadn't got yourself in Dutch with that cop!"

"I don't care a fig for him! It—it's—" From the quaver in Jennie's voice, Asey suddenly realized she was on the verge of tears. "It's the *other* one I'm scared of!"

"What other one?"

"The other cop that was standing near the Beacon Street Garden entrance," Jennie said, "when I was chasin' the girl. He'd heard that shot, Asey, and he *seen* me tryin' to catch her, but he never paid a speck of attention to her at all! He thinks *I* killed that fellow! He even shot at me to make me stop!" Jennie said.

"A *cop*," Asey said slowly, "shot at *you,* while you was chasin' the girl out of the Garden? A cop did?"

"Yes, and the bang scared me half to death! I'd have run away from him after that even if I hadn't been chasin' her!"

"Look here; you tell me the whole yarn from the beginnin'," Asey said.

"We haven't time! We got to catch the girl! . . . Asey, what're you lookin' so upset for? After all, it isn't as if he hit me!"

"What'd the cop look like?"

"Like a cop, naturally!" Jennie said with asperity. "Dark blue visored cap, white shirt, dark pants. He was standin' near a car. You think I don't know a cop when I see one? Now, let's go after the girl; if we don't catch her now, we'll lose her forever!"

"I don't think it's that fateful," Asey said. "She's too different-lookin' to lose easy, an', besides, we can give a pretty good description of her. . . . Peek in her bag an' see if there ain't somethin' with her name on it."

"I forgot I had it." Jennie snapped the bag open. "Oh, what a lot of powder an' rouge! That's more than I ever owned in my life—but there's no name card."

"No matter. From all that stuff," Asey said, "I'd guess she's a professional model, an' I think we can get onto her track. Right now I want to clear up this other cop trouble."

"The real trouble," Jennie said, "is time."

Asey sighed. "Honest, ten minutes one way or another ain't goin' to affect the tracin' of that girl!"

"I don't mean that. I mean just time. Time out West is all mixed up, Asey. I couldn't get it straight. I figured it'd be five-thirty when 'Lisha dropped me off, but it was *three*-thirty!"

"An' you been wanderin' about the Garden since then?"

"'Course not!" Jennie said. "I went and sat in a bus station in Park Square. Then I had breakfast and sat some more, but come daybreak, I was so fidgety from waitin', I went over to the Garden and—"

Although he seemed to be listening raptly, Asey was too busy with his own speculations to hear much of Jennie's scenic description of the Public Garden at daybreak. He was sure that the person who potted at Jennie was no cop. If a real cop had heard the shot that killed Brandt, and suspected that the shooting involved a killing, he wouldn't have stood still and contented himself with firing a warning shot across Jennie's bow. A real cop would have rushed after her and the girl, nabbed them, and found Brandt's body long before Asey, himself, arrived.

"You listenin'?" Jennie inqured acidly. "Or detectin', or what?"

"I think," Asey said, "I'm detectin' a strong odor of fish. How near was you to that cop? How good a look did you get at him?"

"I don't know; I didn't stop to examine him! I was busy chasin' the girl!" Jennie said. "I naturally thought he'd chase her, too! If only you'd listen, you'd never ask such silly things! You see, I was lookin' at the flower beds and half watchin' for you—it was ten after five, but you're usually early—and I seen this couple come into the Garden from the corner of Boylston and Arlington. It was the blond girl and the fellow who got shot."

"His name was Rudi Brandt." Asey told her about finding him and reading the tag.

"Well, Brandt and the girl was almost runnin', they was in such a rush. He had his hands full of boxes and cameras, and she was carryin' that dummy. Then this other young fellow in white pants and a blue shirt come runnin' after 'em, and stopped 'em."

"Where was you?" Asey asked. "Didn't they see you?"

"No, I was down by the water's edge, feedin' the ducks with some roll I'd saved from breakfast. I heard 'em and saw 'em, but the bushes hid me from them. Anyway, this fellow—his hair was light brown and awful rumpled, like he hadn't combed it, and he wore a pair of those funny triangular spectacles that make you look slant-eyed—well, wasn't he worked up! Wanted the girl to turn around and come with him. But she wouldn't. Told him to leave her alone, and smacked him in the face. Then the boy shook his fist under Brandt's nose."

"So? What'd Brandt do?" Asey asked.

"Just shrugged, and said somethin' I didn't hear, and the boy slammed off, mad as a hatter. Then Brandt and the girl rushed to the landin'. You know, I guessed when I first saw his camera that he was goin' to take a picture," Jennie added, "but d'you know what it was going to be for?"

"What? I wondered, myself."

"A magazine cover for *Fashion-Allure*. The girl told the boy with spectacles so. You know I always buy that every month. There's a copy home on my sewin' table this minute."

"Uh-huh. I glanced at it," Asey said. "Wa-el, I s'pose a picture of swan boats an' that dummy couldn't be crazier than the cover on that copy. Two purple lions an' a head of lettuce—what was it s'posed to mean?"

"It's modern art, I guess," Jennie said. "They always have covers like that. Anyway, they rushed to the landin', and Brandt set up his camera and draped the dummy over the swan. Then he helped the girl hop to the boat, posed her on the boatman's seat, and started takin' pictures lickety-split.''

"The girl? *She* was in the pictures, too?"

"Sure thing. She was dressed just like the dummy. Didn't you know that?''

"All I noticed was her hair," Asey said, "when she rushed past. Her coat covered the rest. Huh! Brandt's pictures'll settle her bein' there an' who she is, an' all. I don't know why it never dawned on me she might've been in the picture along with the dummy. Jennie, now I see why Brandt was out so early, an' in such a rush. He couldn't do a job like that later in the day, with crowds millin' an' gapin' around. This begins to make more sense. Go on. Then what?''

"Well, Brandt helped her jump back off the boat to the landin' and started to fix her hair different, and she didn't like the results one bit! Slapped his face, and grabbed her coat and put it on, and turned to leave. Brandt called out and started after her, and then, *bang!* Down he went. And I begun to run after her, and as we run out of the Garden that cop shot at me—''

"Uh-huh," Asey said as she paused for breath, "only he wasn't a real cop. Firin' a shot at that point wouldn't've stopped either you or the girl. Not unless one of you was hit. A shot'd only do what it did—scare the two of you into runnin' harder. No, I think he was the feller that shot Brandt!''

Jennie planted her hands on her ample hips and looked at him defiantly. "Oh, you do, do you? Well, let me tell you, the girl got mad with the way Brandt fixed her hair, started to leave, and shot him when he started after her! I seen it!''

"Not likin' the way someone's done your hair ain't much of a motive for murder.''

"I can't help that! She shot him!''

"But where'd she get the gun? Where'd she been keepin' it?'' Asey persisted. "There's no room to cram a gun into that red purse of hers. An' if she was dressed like the dummy—or undressed, as you might say—she hardly had any place to hide a gun on herself. Did you honestly *see* her shoot him?''

"Land's sakes, you can't see what's goin' on when someone's back is *to* you, the way hers was to me! But I seen the next best thing. I seen her throw the gun away afterwards!'' Jennie concluded with triumph.

"Why," Asey asked gently, "didn't you mention that before?"

"With you askin' so many fool questions, I never got to it!" Jennie returned. "Listen; after she shot him, she stood there a second, lookin'. Then she reached down and picked the gun up from the grass. She'd dropped it after she fired; see? Same thing I always did when I tried shootin' with the Women's Defense Corps at home. Anyway, I seen her pick up the gun and heave it out to the pond. Only, she missed the water. I was runnin' along the path toward her, then, and I heard the gun hit the wood of a swan boat. She don't know that, either, because she was already rushin' off. And I followed her, and then that cop shot at me. How *could* that cop have anything to do with this, Asey? He *had* a gun—and remember I already *seen* the murder gun thrown away!"

"There's no law against a body packin' two guns," Asey said.

"Land's sakes, Asey Mayo, this isn't a cowboy movie, it's the Boston Public Garden!" Jennie said indignantly. "I tell you, he was a plain cop, and no murderer about it!"

Asey grinned. "In the light of your amended story," he said, "I'll grant you he ain't the murderer. But I still don't think he was a cop. No cop'd blaze away at you like that, without knowin' anymore of what was goin' on than he did!"

"You can't ever tell what cops'll do," Jennie said. "Give me my hat, Asey. That other fool cop must be gone now. Let's get started after that girl. Haven't you got enough evidence to do somethin' about her?"

"I'd think so. Besides all you seen," Asey said, "there's Brandt's pictures to prove she was there, an' the gun to clinch things. Only, first I want to see if the coast if clear."

He walked down the alley to the back yard, disappeared for a moment, and returned wearing a denim coat and bearing an ash can.

"Where'd you get them things?" Jennie demanded.

"From an ash house. Take my cap while I look around."

He lugged the can out to the street, set it down by the curb, and straightened up, to find two policemen striding down the brick sidewalk toward him.

"Hey!" the taller hailed him. "You seen a fat woman with gray hair and a brown print dress around here anywheres? Or a tall guy with a yachting cap?"

"I just come here," Asey said with perfect truth. "Anything the matter?"

"That bag-snatcher again. Sometimes it seems to me there can't be a bag left in this district! They must've cut back up the hill, Mike. You say Riley's ankle was sprained when he took that tumble down the stairs?"

"Yeah. It's his bad ankle, too. This dame always worked alone before, but Riley says the guy with her had a bag and a pocketbook they'd already got so far this morning. The nerve of her! When dames get so fresh they start shoving us over railings, they ought to get learned a lesson, if you ask me!"

"Me, too. Let's get 'em. Let's try the hill."

Asey's eyes narrowed as he watched the pair stride up the street. No matter how you figured it, Jennie was in hot water. These cops wanted her—as much to avenge their friend's sprained ankle as for being a supposed bagsnatcher. The cop who shot at her, if he was real, would begin wanting her as soon as Brandt's murder became known. If he was a fake cop— "I wonder!" Asey said. "Could he have been in cahoots with the blond girl?"

After all, a waiting car with a man standing near suggested a planned quick getaway. Making up an accomplice to look like a cop was an old trick, but it still worked. Suppose the girl had taken a quick look at the pursuing Jennie and decided that outrunning her was wiser than fleeing under her nose? If something like that were the case, and if Jennie were seen hanging around now, it was possible that the next potshot in her direction wouldn't miss her by any mile!

Clearly, his most pressing problem was to remove Jennie from the scene and keep her away till he sorted out some of this mess. It would be a waste of breath to order her to visit someone and stay put till he called for her. The pursuit and capture of that girl loomed so in Jennie's life now that she'd even forgotten about her annual house cleaning. What he really needed was some seemingly important mission to send her on.

He grinned suddenly, and returned to her. "Jennie," he said gravely, "we're in a jam. They're not huntin' only you. They want me—Don't interrupt. Without my yachtin' cap on an' in this coat, I'm safe for a while. But I got to have other clothes. You got to help. First, I'm goin' to put you in a cab. You go to the South Station ladies' room, change your dress, sit there till nine, an' then go to Blanding's."

"Porter's tailor, the one makes your suits?"

"Just so. You're to stand over 'em an' make 'em finish up my new suit in a rush."

"I didn't know you'd got a new suit! What kind?"

Improvising rapidly, Asey described an entirely imaginary new Palm Beach suit. "So you fetch the suit back to the roadster," he concluded. "It's over by the Channin' monument. I'll watch for you. Remember to get shoes an' socks an' all, too. Got a pencil an' paper? I'll write Blandin' a note."

In a masterly six lines, Asey summed up the situation for his old friend Blanding, and begged him to invent things, anything at all, to keep Jennie busy till noon.

"Now"—he gave her the note—"I'll find a cab—Say, was anyone else around the Garden you forgot to tell me about?"

"Only an old man walkin' some dogs, but he left long before Brandt an' the girl come. Before him, there was a woman in evenin' clothes that hustled across the Garden—You sure you'll be all right?"

For his part, Asey thought ten minutes later, as he watched her sail off in a cab, he was going to worry a lot more about her staying put. But, now she was gone, he could start to work. Stuffing his yachting cap into the pocket of his appropriated jacket, he turned back toward the Public Garden.

People were beginning to appear, now that it was nearly seven, he noted as he came to Beacon Street. A maid was half heartedly sweeping the basement steps down which Riley had tumbled, a boy listlessly trundled a grocery cart along the sidewalk, and half a dozen dogs were being walked by sleepy-looking owners. The only wide-awake person in the group was a bearded man in a white linen suit who was trying to unsnarl the leashes of his two Chows.

Asey slowed down at the sight of that white hair and flowing white beard, which he recognized, although he hadn't seen them in the ten years since their owner, Judge Thatcher Sudbury, sold his shooting box on North Beach and left the Cape. Under less urgent circumstances, Asey would have enjoyed stopping and chatting with him, and he was rather relieved to see that the Judge also appeared to be in a hurry, for he whistled to his dogs and ran with them up the front steps of a brownstone house.

At least, Asey decided, it was comforting to know there was

someone of importance and integrity living in the neighborhood who would probably go to bat for him if the need arose.

Once back in the Garden, he made a beeline over the grass toward the swan boats. The absence of police and the general lack of hubbub confirmed his suspicion that no one had yet discovered Brandt.

He made rapid plans as he strode forward. After another look about the landing he'd visit Brandt's studio. Somehow he could get in. Somewhere he should be able to find a clue to the girl's name and her address.

There was no sense in worrying about any possible problems that might surround his contemplated projects, or any use in trying to locate any of his friends out at the State Police barracks. They couldn't help him in Boston. On this job, Asey thought, he'd have to trust to luck and ingenuity.

An involuntary whistle escaped from his lips as he came to a stop by the swan-boat landing. Even if no one had officially found the body, someone had been there, all right! For Brandt's leather case of plateholders had been opened and tipped over, and the plates them-selves, used and unused, spilled out on the planking under the glare of the sun, were now exposed and worthless.

Nothing else had been moved or touched as far as he could determine. But those ruined plates were sufficient to convince him that the blond girl was no dummy, no matter how much she was made up to look like one. After escaping from Jennie, she must have circled back here and, with a couple of simple gestures, blotted out the ultimate, damning evidence of her presence on the landing. Now the proof of her being here depended solely on Jennie's word, which at the moment wasn't worth two cents, in the estimation of the police.

Stepping past the settee to the water's edge, Asey gazed out steadily at the moored swan boats for some trace of the gun.

At last he caught sight of it, lying on a rear bench in the shadow of a rolled-up awning top. Again he whistled.

He'd guessed right about its being a powerful weapon! That was a model you couldn't mistake, a Smith & Wesson .357 Magnum, famous for shooting the most powerful revolver cartridge in the world. He understood now the condition of Brandt's head, he thought, as he walked slowly off the landing back to the path.

"For a girl like her to pack a gun like that!" he murmured. "I can see how droppin' it would be easier than carryin' it—"

The sudden sound of pounding heels sent him scurrying off the path to the refuge of a clump of low bushes, and a moment later he thanked the impulse that had prompted him. The two men rushing toward the landing were the same two cops who had seen him taking the barrel out of the alley.

Behind him, apparently winded, walked a young man wearing white flannels and a blue shirt. His rumpled mop of light brown hair caused Asey to wonder if this mightn't be the fellow Jennie described as butting in on Brandt and the girl when they first entered the Garden. When the boy put on a pair of spectacles with triangular-shaped lenses, Asey decided his surmise was correct. He was somewhere in his early twenties, Asey judged, and neither the griminess of his mussed flannels nor the grubbiness of his saddle shoes could disguise the fact that both were expensive.

The boy sat down on the grassy slope above the path and watched in a detached manner while the two cops scurried about the landing. the tall cop called out some question Asey couldn't catch. But he saw the boy shrug, and heard his answer:

"I tell you, I just happened to walk past, and I found him, that's all!" His accent was so thoroughly Bostonian, Asey thought, you could cut it with a knife.

"How'd you know who he was? See anyone around here?"

"Everyone knows Rudi. I didn't see a soul. I merely found him," the boy returned. "Er—d'you think you could bring yourselves to do something about it all? Like calling detectives?"

Asey grinned at the expression on the cops' respective faces, and looked with renewed interest at the boy. It was one thing to own a genuine broad "a," and something else to quell cops with it. For all his sloppy appearance and his air of detached weariness, this boy knew what he was doing. That he didn't mention having seen the blond girl with Brandt probably meant that he didn't intend to mention her at all. And, if people questioned him, they were going to smack themselves up against the barrier of that super-nonchalant broad "a."

It wasn't the first time Asey had seen an untidy-looking Boston youth stump people with similarly bland passive resistance. Cap'n Porter's son Bill had the same backfield physique and boyish look—and he ran the Porter factory like a Prussian field marshal. Later on, Asey decided, he'd seek out this young man and have a chat with him. Within an hour, a phone call to any Boston newspaper office would elicit the name and address of the discoverer of Brandt's body. That part wouldn't be hard, and the boy would be something to fall back on in case he drew a blank at Brandt's studio.

But right now, he thought, as he quietly retreated from the clump of bushes, he ought to tackle the studio before the place became littered with cops. He'd nothing to gain from hanging around the Garden. The cops could see nothing he hadn't already seen, and he rather doubted that they'd notice that gun right away, either.

Ten minutes later he tried the knob of Studio 5 on the third floor of the Arts Building, found the door unlocked, and entered a small waiting-room whose walls were almost obliterated by framed photographs, most of which looked like *Fashion-Allure* covers.

Asey glanced at them, then crossed the waiting-room's plum-colored broadloom and pushed open the door at the opposite end. That was the studio proper, a barnlike room stuffed with a miscellaneous clutter. There were screenlike backdrops, disjointed arms and legs and plaster heads, a duplicate of the dummy out on the swan boat, and a fat, masculine dummy wearing a green top hat. There were odd chairs and tables, stray bits of bric-à-brac, piles of draperies, and at least a dozen bizarrely decorated screens.

Peering behind one of the latter, Asey came on a stack of prints. Not only was the top picture a study of the blond dummy and the blond girl, but so, he found, were all the rest! They were posed with practically everything under the sun, including a washtub and some dead trees. The longer he looked, the less Asey liked the girl and the harder it was for him to tell her from the dummy.

"If she come here first to change to that costume," he said aloud, "her own clothes ought to be around somewheres. They might lead to— By gum!"

He almost crowed as he spotted an opened magazine on the floor beyond the screen. There, staring up at him, was a full-page photograph of the blond girl in evening dress! Grabbing up the magazine, he eagerly read the caption beneath the picture.

"LISSOME, IMPULSIVE LISS," it was headed. "Virtually unnoticed at the time of her debut, Liss Lathrop has been glamorized into national prominence by the genius of photographic wonder-worker, Rudi Brandt, and now graces magazine covers, tobacco ads, mink coats, beer. A member of one of Boston's oldest families, Liss is newly engaged to the young tycoon Jackson Poor. Wiseacres wonder if Romance will abruptly cut off a career bound to end on Broadway or in Hollywood. Liss says it won't. Next pages show Liss in her younger days, Liss in her delightfully charming Old-World home." (*Pictures by Brandt.*)

Asey flipped over the page, to discover, in a picture headed *Sub-deb at Hunt Club*, that the boy with the rumpled hair and glasses was Liss's older half-brother, Craig Lathrop.

"So!" Asey said.

He glanced at snapshots of *Liss at Seven in Tartan*, and *Liss at Leggy Eleven with Mother*, and memorized the address of her home, where Brandt's pictures showed her. Throughout the series, he noted, she somehow managed to maintain the same slightly petulant expression of a sulky child.

Asey looked back meditatively at the picture of her tousle-headed brother, and then looked up and listened as the outer door of the waiting-room squeaked open. It couldn't be the cops slipping in so quietly, he thought, nor could it be clients, at seven-thirty in the morning. He ducked behind a screen as light footsteps padded toward the studio.

A good-looking black-haired girl entered, made for a tablelike desk he had missed entirely in the studio's confusion, and, with the casual confidence of one familiar with the place, yanked out the top drawer.

Peeking around the screen, Asey watched while she extracted a checkbook and wrote a check. Asey could see the nervous flush in her cheeks and hear her rapid breathing. She knew the place and she knew where things were, he thought, but she was sufficiently excited to make a mistake on her first check, and have to rewrite it. Then she reached down into a lower drawer, drew out a small, red leatherbound volume, thrust both it and the check into her pocketbook, and audibly sighed her relief.

Asey waited until she turned away from the desk before he opened his mouth to speak to her. But his request for fuller explanations of her actions died on his lips as the waiting-room's outer door squeaked open again, and the girl, uttering a startled little cry, darted for the very screen behind which he was hiding!

Never had Asey seen any eyes open as wide as the girl's when she found him there. Her expression reminded him of nothing so much as a close-up of an old-time movie heroine registering intense emotional upheaval.

Asey looked at her speculatively. The instant she started to scream, he was going to be forced to imitate an old movie, himself. It was going to be a Douglas Fairbanks Senior act for him, out the studio's side window and down the antique fire escape into the great unknown below.

But the girl, to his amazement, accepted him as casually as if she'd met him at a dinner party. Entirely at ease, she put her finger to her full red lips, and then pointed toward the door in a gesture which indicated that she thought he ought to take a look and see who was out there.

Cautiously Asey ducked down and peered around the edge of the screen.

A tall, broad-shouldered young man stood uncertainly on the threshold of the studio. He was well tailored and well dressed, and his disapproval as he stared around at the studio's litter was obvious.

"Who is it?" The girl prodded Asey.

He shrugged and motioned for her to look.

"It's Jackson Poor!" She breathed the words in his ear as she straightened up.

"What a pigsty!" Poor's muttered comment sounded as if he were viewing the place for the first time.

"Pompous ass!" the girl whispered indignantly in Asey's ear. "What's the mighty tycoon want?"

"S-sh!" Asey shook his head warningly, and squinted through a crack of the screen's frame in time to see Poor start to inspect the floor beneath a broken armchair.

In the course of the next quarter-hour the girl and Asey took turns watching Poor while he carried on a survey of the floor space under every stick of furniture in that section of the studio. Once he stopped to mop his perspiring face with a handkerchief which he jerked irritably from his coat pocket, and when the contents of the pocket jerked out, too, Poor's annoyance bordered on high dudgeon. Muttering to himself, he crawled around the floor retrieving cigarettes, a length of string, and several stubby pencils.

"How utterly absurd of him! What's he hunting?" The girl penciled her comment on an envelope taken from her pocketbook. "Jack Poor never set foot in here before! He hates Rudi. What do you think the egotistical stuffed shirt *wants* here? Why—"

The rest of her question was cut off in mid-air by Asey's hand descending on the pencil. "Watch out!" he hurriedly scrawled.

Poor was looking directly toward their sheltering screen. Suddenly he strode over to a chest in the corner beyond them, grabbed off its top a crumpled white silk dress, rolled it into a ball, and stuffed it into his coat pocket. It was inevitable that he should see them when he turned around.

"What the—" he paused. "Oh. Peg Whiting. What's the big idea, anyway?" he demanded peremptorily.

"We might," the girl said crisply, "ask the same thing of you! Because, if that's Liss's dress you just picked up, the police aren't going to like it!"

"What're you talking about?" Poor asked. "What've the police got to do with Liss's dress? She phoned and asked me to get it for her, and I did." His critical gaze traveled over Asey's denim jacket and dungarees. "Who's he?"

"As far as I'm concerned," Peg informed him, "he's a bundle straight from heaven. He's probably the only person who can save Liss from the police. You will, won't you, Mr. Mayo?" she added.

Asey looked at her quizzically. "So that's why you didn't scream!" he said. "Recognized me, huh?"

"I spent two summers at the Meweesit Girls' Camp on your road," Peg said, "practically panting every time you roared past in your chrome-plated Porter Bullet. D'you still drive that gorgeous, gleaming thing?"

"In the interests of National Defense," Asey said, "the current model's black, an' looks like a hearse. Miss Whitin', what d'you know about—?"

"Look here," Poor broke in, "I want to know what's going on, and why the two of you hide behind screens. If you were here when I came, why in hell didn't you *say* so?"

"You know," Asey said gently, "anybody listenin' to you might almost think you had more business bein' here than we have. Now, s'pose you put that dress back!"

"I will not! Peg, who is this fellow?"

"He's Asey Mayo, Cape Cod's gift to the detective world," Peg said. "And I don't know how he stumbled into this mess. It's enough for me that he's here. Mr. Mayo—oh, I can't 'mister' you! No one at camp ever did. Asey, you know about Rudi Brandt, don't you?"

Asey nodded. "Uh-huh. But I don't know about you, Miss Whitin'. Or about Mr. Poor. Just when did Liss Lathrop ask you to get her dress? Where was she when she phoned you?"

"What's the matter with you? I don't understand this damn' nonsense!" Poor, Asey thought, was working himself up to a good, lathery mad. "Liss begged me to get her white dress she'd left here, and I rushed off without my breakfast. She claimed it was a matter of life and death!"

"It happens to be a matter of death," Peg said. "Rudi's been killed." She spoke in a forced voice, rather flatly, as if she had drilled herself not to break down.

"Oh. Car accident?"

"He's been shot," Peg said. "Murdered."

"Oh! Too bad," Poor said perfunctorily. "That's a nasty business. But I must say I'm not surprised. That fellow seemed to enjoy making enemies. Who shot him?"

Asey watched Peg's face as she answered. He felt that she was furious with Poor, but she spoke calmly enough. "I don't know. Liss was with him."

"Liss? She *was?* Well, she's got nothing to do with it!" Poor said belligerently. "Liss liked the fellow—frankly, I could never see why! Always stood up for him. Always. *She's* got nothing to do with it!"

"I hope not," Peg said. "But Chub—that's her half-brother, Craig," she added parenthetically to Asey; "Chub said Liss was with Rudi when he was setting out to take pictures this morning in the Garden. I don't know where Liss is, now. But Chub found Rudi's body, and called in the police."

"So *Chub* found the body, eh?" Poor said. "How'd that happen?"

"If you want to know"—Peg was making a valiant effort to keep her temper—"Chub was trying to keep Liss from having her picture taken in red-and-white striped shorts and a blue, star-spangled bra, posed on a swan-boat in the Public Garden. For a cover. And with Brenda, too!''

"With that damned dummy? On a *swan boat?*" The veins in Poor's neck were bulging so that Asey expected the fellow's collar button to pop any second. "Nonsense! I don't believe you! Liss promised me she'd never do any more of that sort of stuff! I explained things to her very carefully, and proved that Brandt'd gone far enough with that duplicate-dummy angle— Why, damn it, he's been making Liss look more and more like—what's Rudi call the dummy?—Brenda. I tell you, Liss promised me all that dummy and cover tripe was out!''

"I know she did," Peg returned. "Chub knew it, too. And he knew how furious you got the last time she posed with Brenda. That's why he rushed into this mess! You see, he got up early because he was going sailing at Marblehead, and on the hall table he saw Rudi's message. Apparently Maggie'd taken the call last night and left the note there for Liss to see when she came in. After Chub read what Rudi wanted her for, he tore over here to the studio, and finally he caught up with her and Rudi as they were going over to the swan boats, and stopped 'em, and begged Liss to drop the idea and come along home. But she wouldn't.''

"I don't understand this!" Poor said. "Liss promised me! She gave me her word! What reason did she give Chub for going through with it?''

"If she gave any, Chub didn't tell me what it was," Peg said. "I only know she told him to mind his own business, and smacked him, and went on with Rudi.''

"It's all Brandt's doing!" Poor said. "Because he took a few pictures of her that attracted attention he thought he could make any demands on her he wanted to! Why, only last week Rudi hounded her about that damn' underwear ad till she finally gave in and posed for him. I *told* Liss she wasn't to let him bully her again. She's got to consider *me*, now! I can't have my future wife running around in underwear ads! Chub should have argued her out of it. He shouldn't have quit so easily!''

"Chub knows Liss well enough to know when argument's useless!" Peg said. "Besides, he didn't quit. He went to a phone and called me, and asked if I'd come and see what I could do with Rudi. So—''

"Wait up a sec," Asey interrupted. "Why'd he call you? How d'you happen to come into this, Miss Whitin'?"

"I work for Rudi," she explained. "I'm a combination secretary-receptionist, printer and photo-finisher, and general soother. I used to be his model. Anyway, Chub wanted me to talk to Rudi, so he phoned me. I still don't see," she added, with a frown, "why he couldn't get me then! I was there in bed, and the phone was beside me on the table, and it never rang! I'm sure he must've called the wrong number, though he swears he didn't. He says the bell rang and rang!"

"How'd he get hold of you?" Asey asked.

"He came after me—I live a few blocks over on Beacon Street, you see. And of course the apartment's outer door was locked, so he couldn't get in the vestibule to ring my bell, and had to ring for the janitor, and the janitor didn't choose to be roused. So Chub finally left and phoned me from a drugstore. That time, he got me. And I dressed and met him downstairs, and we came here."

"Why here?" Poor demanded. "If Rudi was taking pictures in the Garden, why didn't you go there and stop him?"

"Because Chub had wasted an hour trying to get hold of me, and I was sure Rudi'd be through and back here long before six-thirty!" Peg said. "I knew Rudi planned to do his work in a rush at the first crack of dawn, so—"

"You mean that you knew all along he intended taking these pictures?" Poor broke in angrily. "Then why in hell didn't you stop him from using Liss?"

"Rudi never told me he was going to use her!" Peg retorted. "When I helped him run up the costumes last night he gave me to understand they were for Brenda and the other dummy, the new one, Bella! Anyway, by the time Chub reached me, I knew the only sensible thing was to come here to the studio and inveigle Rudi into hustling back to the Garden while he could, take the two dummies, and discard the pictures he'd made of Liss and Brenda. You see, there was so little time!"

"Did you persuade him?" Poor asked.

Peg made a helpless little gesture. "I never had a chance to say anything! When Chub and I finally got here, Liss and Rudi hadn't come back. We waited a while, and then decided to hunt them up. Time was so short! So Chub went over to the Garden to see if they might still be there, and I went around the corner to see if they might be having a cup of coffee at the diner. Chub came back and said Rudi'd been shot over on the landing and Liss was gone! He hadn't called the police, so I told him to. But—"

"But what?" Asey asked as she hesitated.

"Well, Chub said he didn't want to be the fall guy and get involved with the police."

"Thinking of the family name, I suppose!" Poor commented.

"He was thinking of Liss!" Peg said. "He said if he called the cops, they'd want his name and ask if he knew who Rudi was, and he'd have to say yes, and so on and so forth, and ultimately Liss's name would get dragged in by way of his. But I finally persuaded him to get a cop, and I stayed at the diner till I remembered my check— Oh!" She stopped short.

"What's the matter now?" Poor asked.

"I just thought— Asey, what must *you* have thought when you saw me writing that check? But it's really all right. I write all Rudi's checks and handle all his bills and accounts, and I forgot to pay myself yesterday. Over there in the diner it dawned on me I'd have to wait until his lawyer or someone got around to paying me—maybe months from now—and I really needed the money. And—well, I suppose it was wrong; but was it *very* wrong, Asey?"

"Where's Liss now?" Poor spoke up before Asey had a chance to answer.

"Where was she when she phoned you?" Asey returned.

"Home, I suppose. I wonder if she—" Poor was silent for a moment. "Who do the police think shot him?"

"I haven't even seen any police," Peg said. "I *hope* they won't try to drag Liss into it because she was with Rudi, but I'm awfully afraid they will."

"Have you seen 'em?" Poor asked Asey. "D'you know anything about it?"

"I'm not in any position to guess what the cops might be thinkin'," Asey said, "but, accordin' to the person who seen all this business happen, Liss got sore at Brandt while he was rearrangin' her hair-do, an' got mad enough about it to shoot him. I—"

He broke off as his ears caught the sound of heavy footsteps clumping somewhere in the hall beyond the waiting-room. With a grin, he darted across the studio, softly closing the door into the waiting-room, locked it, and pocketed the key. He knew police turmoil when he heard it, even though he had never before happened to be on the receiving end.

"What—?" Poor began.

"Those are cops, Mr. Poor," Asey said, "an' at this point I don't feel like meetin' 'em, so I'm—"

"My God, neither do I! Not *here!* Not *now!* How can we get out? Where's that corner door lead to?"

"That's the darkroom," Peg said, "but it's just a blind closet. Asey, I've nothing to hide, but, if you two are going to leave, I'm not going to stay here and face 'em alone! Only, how can we get out?"

Asey took her arm and steered her over to the side window. "Fire escape," he said, raising the window. "Give her a hand down, Poor. Okay?"

"Aren't you coming?"

"Just a sec. Forgot somethin'." Asey, running nimbly across to the desk, caught up Peg's pocketbook, and smiled at the hubbub out in the waiting-room.

The studio door was being rattled now, and several voices were clamoring for someone named Kenny to get the key. Someone else was all for breaking the door in, and quickly.

As far as he, personally, was concerned, Asey thought, they could blow the door down with trumpets as long as he had half a second more in which to get out of the place. His leg was on a level with the sill when the window suddenly, and of its own accord, slid down with a quiet little thump.

Asey reached out a hand to open it again, and, when it refused to budge, he hitched Peg's pocketbook under his arm and used both hands. Then he knelt precariously on the sill and slammed the palms of his hands under the top frame. Then he tried tugging and shoving, simultaneously, while beads of perspiration broke out on his forehead. He was aware suddenly of the growing heat and of an odd odor which he couldn't quite place.

"Smash it in!" The voice of the impatient door-breaker reached him clearly.

It was advice he'd take himself, Asey thought, if only the window glass weren't wired!

Shoulders thudded against the door, and Asey put every ounce of strength he possessed into one final shove. But the window remained stubbornly and irrevocably shut.

The studio door was all but bending under the force of shoulders battering against it when the crown of Poor's hat appeared at the window, and a second later his anxious face peered in. In response to Asey's urgent gesture, he reached out and shoved the window open without any apparent effort.

Asey heard the inside door go down with a crash as he and Poor jumped from the lowest landing of the fire escape onto the brick areaway below.

"Hurry," Poor said. "They may look out that window. Duck through this alley here. . . . Well, that was a close one! I couldn't imagine what'd happened to you till I noticed the window was closed. What was the matter? Did it jam?"

"There was one period"—Asey wiped his forehead with the sleeve of his denim coat—"when I'd have said it was welded, if I'd had the breath to say anythin'! I don't know *what* happened. It just plumb stuck! It might've been an old side-catch fixture, or maybe an old wedge got stuck in it. Your guess's as good as mine. What become of Peg?"

"She ripped her dress jumping down, and she's gone home to change. Frankly"—Poor fanned himself with his hat—"I just think it's an excuse to get away. I think she's come to the end of her emotional tether. She really feels wretched about Rudi's death. She liked him—although what she and Liss ever saw in the fellow—well, I suppose it doesn't matter now. . . . By George, that was exciting for a moment there, wasn't it?"

"Uh-huh." If the little episode had accomplished nothing else, Asey thought, it had succeeded in altering Poor's point of view.

"Funny thing," Poor continued, "going down the fire escape, I suddenly remembered that you're in Porter Motors, aren't you? I know young Bill Porter slightly."

"Uh-huh," Asey said again, and wondered if that slight acquaintance might account for Poor's changed attitude.

"Brilliant fellow. Mayo, I owe you an apology. I felt pretty silly there in the studio, knowing you'd seen me pawing around for Liss's dress. Besides, I was already upset about Liss. The instant I heard her voice over the phone this morning, I knew she was in some sort of trouble. But she wouldn't tell me what was wrong. Only made me promise to get that damned dress. Believe me, I'm not unmoved about this business of Rudi! I know how serious it is— What's the matter?" he added, as Asey stopped short.

"I just got a horrid feelin'," Asey said slowly, "that the woman in the blue dress who just went into that corner drugstore is someone I know! Golly, I better look! Take this pocketbook of Peg's, will you?"

It couldn't be Jennie, he told himself, as he hurried back to the corner. He'd watched her pack, unpack, and rearrange the contents of her suitcase a dozen times, the night before she left the Cape. He was sure that she owned no dress that color blue. Still and all, it had looked awfully like her!

"See her?" Poor sauntered after him.

"No. Wait a sec. I'm goin' inside."

"Hurry," Poor said. "Peg's going to join us at the diner on the next corner. Then I'll get my attorney, and Chub, and we'll all go see Liss and straighten things out, and get her out of any possible trouble— d'you hear me?"

"Uh-huh." Asey swung open the drugstore's screen door and stepped inside.

The place was empty, without even a clerk in sight.

Asey peered into the two phone booths, then walked around them and surveyed the side door which they partly blocked.

Even if, by some mischance, the woman had been Jennie, and even if she'd popped out this side exit, he still had no business letting himself be sidetracked into following her. He had no time now to worry about Jennie. He had frittered away enough precious minutes listening to Poor and Peg Whiting, in the vain hope that they might drop some hint of the one thing he would have liked to know more about before seeing Miss Lathrop. They'd filled in many little chinks, but they hadn't suggested any possible motive the girl might have had for killing Rudi Brandt.

The thing for him to do now was to get to Liss before the cops or Poor and his cohorts did. If Poor, pacing restlessly up and down in front of the store, thought he had any priority on his services, Asey thought, Poor was sadly mistaken in that highhanded assumption.

"I think," he murmured, "that I'll be leavin' you right now, mister, before I get into any more distractions!"

Without further ado, he slipped out the side door.

Back in the studio he had memorized the Lathrops' address, so now he headed again toward Beacon Hill.

It came to him as a distinct surprise, however, to find that Liss Lathrop's home was the brick house in whose adjoining alley he and Jennie had spent so much time earlier in the morning.

It was just possible that Liss herself might have overheard their conversation in the alley, and that Jennie's insistent pleas to "get the girl" might well have been the inspiration for Liss's phoning Poor to retrieve her dress. Anyway, under the circumstances, it might be wise to call on the girl in a backhand way instead of barging along in any direct, frontal attack.

The plate-glass window of a fruit store caught his eye. He grinned, went in, and when he emerged he was carrying a beribboned, fruit-laden wicker basket.

Five minutes later he was ringing the service bell at the rear of the Lathrop house. "Present for Miss Lathrop," he told the worried-looking maid who came to the door. "She's got to sign for it first."

He started to walk past her, but the maid thrust her foot quickly across the threshold.

"You wait here," she said. "Give me the slip. I'll have her sign it."

She grabbed the slip and closed the door. But she didn't trouble to lock it, and a moment later Asey was in the basement hall.

He glanced around. It was a typical city layout of two large rooms to a floor. Making for the back stairs, he ran quietly up to the living-room-dining-room floor, and ducked behind a portiere as the maid panted back downstairs.

From his hiding place he listened to the sound of her footsteps clumping along the basement hall to the rear door, heard her drag in the heavy basket, and waited while she lugged it to the floor above. "Miss Liss, will you please open the door?"

Asey slid out from behind the portieres, crept to the bottom step, and looked up expectantly. He couldn't hear the girl's words, but only the sound of her voice, high, rather shrill, and imperious.

"Miss Liss, I'm afraid of dropping it— There; see? It's only one of the baskets Mr. Poor's always sending us, like I said. The man left it. I told you he was all right. He'll be coming back for his slip later, after he's delivered over to the Garrisons'. He often does that to save waiting!"

Asey sneaked hurriedly back to the shelter of the portieres while the maid clumped down to the kitchen. He waited until it seemed that she was again busy with her own work, and then he mounted the stairs to the floor above. There was little doubt in his mind now that Liss Lathrop had overheard Jennie and himself. She was on guard, suspicious even of a basket of fruit.

Pausing, Asey considered the four doors leading from the hall, and picked the nearest as being the likeliest. All he could do now was to take the bull by the horns, march in, and bluff her. He swung open the door, and entered a bedroom whose walls and ceiling and furniture appeared to be all the same color of silver-gray. His basket of fruit stood in the center of the deep-piled rug. The girl wasn't to be seen, but his ears caught a rustling sound in the connecting room, whose door was ajar.

Asey tiptoed over to it, thrust it open, stepped in, and then made a valiant effort to duck back and away. His last conscious thought was that he had certainly walked right in and asked for it! . . .

Later—how much later he had no way of telling—he rubbed the throbbing lump on the side of his head and told himself ruefully that he couldn't even have the satisfaction of claiming that he didn't know who or what had hit him. Miss Liss Lathrop had done a bang-up job on him with the heel of a well-swung riding boot, and he hated to consider what the results would have been had she got him before he started to duck away.

He groped tentatively in the darkness. He was in a good-sized closet—without doubt Liss Lathrop's own. Somewhat unsteadily, he got to his feet and reached a hand up over his head in an attempt to find a ceiling light. In a lucky fumble, his fingers closed over a cord. He yanked it, blinked at the sudden glare, and surveyed his quarters.

There were enough dresses to stock a small shop, dozens of hatracks and elaborate stands that seemed to sprout shoes. But it was the closet door which interested him far more than the girl's wardrobe. It was thick, sturdy pine, and he knew even before he tried the knob that he would find it locked.

Asey tapped the wood reflectively. That was not a door you butted out with your shoulder or carved up with your pocketknife.

He thought once again that, for a girl who looked so much like a dummy, Liss Lathrop was far from being one. She'd taken him in as neatly as anyone ever had, and left him in what he could only sum up as a spot. Even if he yelled and someone—say, the maid—heard him, his presence in that closet was nothing he could lightly explain away. If Liss, herself, heard him and chose to let him out—Asey shook his head. You couldn't tell what she might be tempted to do!

Certainly this biffing business had dispelled any lingering doubt he might have had, despite Jennie's eye-witness testimony, that anger over a rearranged hair-do was no fit and reasonable motive for Liss's shooting Brandt. To judge from the force with which she'd wielded that riding boot, Liss was apparently a girl who didn't require such a whale of a lot of motive before resorting to violence.

The ceiling light above him suddenly flickered and went out, and a second later Asey started groping toward one of the shoe stands. Once the light went out, he was able to see the thin streak of daylight along the side crack of the door. There was a latch and, about eighteen inches above the latch, there was a bar about two inches wide. But there wasn't any latch bolt!

He found a shoe, jerked out the flexible metal shoe tree, and wrenched off the wooden toepiece. If luck was with him, that bar above would turn out to be a wooden, slatlike block attached to the doorjamb with an old handmade screw, not unlike those that held fast his own closet doors at home. With the metal strip from the shoe tree he could turn up that block in no time!

Thirty seconds later he was out in the bedroom.

He was astonished to find that it was even hotter there than it had been inside the closet, and downright dumfounded to see the hands of the silver clock on the littered writing desk pointing to noon! No wonder he'd been feeling hungry, he thought, as he reached over to the basket of fruit and helped himself.

He was busily tackling a grapefruit, using a silver letter opener for a knife, when the hall door swung open suddenly, and a short, blond woman wearing a pink cotton housecoat stared blankly at him.

"Why, how perfectly amazing!" Her voice, high and twittery, reminded Asey of a sparrow. "I'd no idea anyone was here; Liss never told me! Now, let me think—I'm *sure* I've seen your face before. But I'm always so terrible with names, Mister—er—"

"Mayo," Asey said. "Asey Mayo, ma'am. Er—who—?"

"No!" The woman came in, perched on the arm of a chair, and clasped her hands delightedly. "My dear man, you'll never believe me,

but I've just this minute finished talking with Judge Thatcher Sudbury—
I simply *had* to ask his advice. And he said the only person he could
think of to help me was a man named Asey Mayo from Cape Cod. But
he didn't know how to get hold of you. However did Liss manage to
locate you and drag you here? Of course, it *was* Liss who got you?"

"Wa-el"—Asey's Cape drawl was drawlier than usual—"I guess
you could probably say she dragged me some. An' she sure got me! See
my lump?"

"Oh, did she hit you, too? Liss is *so* impulsive—her artistic
temperament, of course. She inherited it from me."

"Er—you're her mother?" Asey inquired.

"Why, certainly! Didn't she tell you? I suppose in her excitement
she forgot I was home again. Really, Mr. Mayo, I've been *so* worried!
What did Liss want you to do?"

"I ain't sure," Asey said, "just what her basic thought was,
ma'am."

"Well, of course the poor dear girl *is* in frightful danger, no matter
what she says! You *know* she's in danger!"

"So?" Asey said. "What from?"

"Why, those crackpots! The very minute her picture appeared in a
national magazine last year all those people started writing her, wanting
her autograph, and locks of her hair! I knew then that sooner or later,
someone would try to kidnap her, or do something just as terrible. When
she told me Rudi'd been shot, *I* knew at once that someone had really
intended to kill her, and just accidentally hit him instead. But of course
she told you all about that awful business, I suppose. I *do* think she was
so clever to find you!"

"Uh-huh. What does Liss *really* think, herself?"

"Oh, she's sure someone meant to kill Rudi!" Mrs. Lathrop said.
"But I think she's just saying that to keep me from worrying. Do you
understand about the gun?"

"Frankly," Asey said, "she didn't—uh—take the time to explain.
What about it?"

"It's so very confusing!" Mrs. Lathrop sighed. "She said she got
annoyed with Rudi and was leaving him, and then she heard a shot, and,
the next thing she knew, she was throwing away a revolver!— Did you
say something?"

"No," Asey gulped.

Mrs. Lathrop babbled on. "But Liss thinks *she* knows who did it—Why, you look surprised! Didn't she tell you that, either? How careless of her!"

"Uh—who *does* she think shot him?" Asey inquired.

"Well, you understand that this is Liss's idea," Mrs. Lathrop said, "not mine. I always thought Peg Whiting was indifferent to Rudi. I'm sure she is vastly more interested in Chub than she *ever* was in Rudi. But then she made so much more when she worked as Rudi's model than she does now! And, as Liss said, jealousy is jealousy, and money is money. Oh, dear!" She sighed wearily. "Money *is* such a problem always, isn't it?"

"All this"—Asey indicated the room's silver-gray glitter—"wouldn't seem to show any lack of it."

"My dear man, we're as poor as church mice!" Mrs. Lathrop told him. "When Houghton—my husband—died, he left us this place, and the house in Beverly, and the shack in Maine, and all those awful brick buildings downtown here in Boston. It's just taxes and repairs all the time, and of course Chub won't sell a thing, because the Lathrops don't believe in selling, ever. What *you* have doesn't matter, so long as your great-grandchildren are sure of two per cent. Truly, until Liss took to modeling, I was at my wit's end about money most of the time. . . . Look; *is* there any chance of anyone thinking that Liss shot Rudi?"

"Wa-el," Asey said, "perhaps maybe—"

"Oh, dear!" Mrs. Lathrop was genuinely upset. "That's what Liss thought! Of course, she is a simply marvelous shot, but—"

"Is she," Asey said, "indeed!"

"Oh, yes! See her skeet trophies over on the corner shelf?" Mrs. Lathrop pointed with quiet maternal pride. "Houghton taught her to shoot."

"Say!" Asey suddenly became aware of the bruise on Mrs. Lathrop's wrist and the red, scratchlike streak on the side of her face. "Did Liss do that to you?"

"Well, of course, Liss always has been impulsive," Mrs. Lathrop said apologetically. "It's just her way. And of course she was so upset about this awful business of Rudi. Probably she knows best, but I *didn't* think she ought to go to Rudi's studio, really! I suggested that she just ask Peg over to lunch. So much simpler, I thought, and much better taste. But the idea irritated Liss terribly."

"She's gone to Brandt's studio?" Asey demanded. "To see Peg? Does she think that Peg shot him?"

"I didn't want her to go one bit," Mrs. Lathrop said, "but she was *so* determined—Listen; I hear the hall phone ringing. I'll have to run down and answer. Maggie's out. If it's that strange person calling again," she added, as Asey followed her down the stairs, "should I report him to the police?"

"What strange person?" Asey asked curiously.

"Well, of course he *said* he was a reporter, but he didn't sound like one! In fact, it's the oddest-sounding voice I ever heard. First I thought it was Peg, but then it sounded more like a man. He called twice before I talked with the Judge. He wanted Liss— Oh, stop ringing; I'm coming!

She picked up the phone, said hello, and then covered the mouthpiece with her hand. "It's him again!" she said in a stage whisper. "Hello? . . . Miss Lathrop's not home. Who *is* this calling? . . . What? . . . I said, she's not home! And I'm going to tell the police about you. . . . I said, Miss Lathrop's not here, and the police are going to know all about you—" Mrs. Lathrop suddenly broke off, smiled delightedly, and then continued with unwonted vigor, "All right; if you want to know, you can find her at Rudi Brandt's studio!" Slamming down the receiver, she turned to Asey. "That's the oddest voice I ever heard! It might be either a man or a woman with a mouthful of cereal. Wasn't that a brilliant inspiration I had?"

Without giving Asey any chance to answer, she rattled on, "It came to me in a flash! Now—don't you see?—that person will go to the studio hunting Liss, but *you* will go there too, and find out who it is and what's going on. And, if it's some policeman being tricky, just you explain to him that Liss's being a wonderful shot doesn't *mean anything*—"

The rest of her sentence trickled off into an aggrieved little twitter as she watched the front door of No. 19½ close behind Asey.

Outside on the brick sidewalk, Asey paused for a second. Faced with a one-way street and the snarl of traffic beyond, he could probably reach Brandt's studio as quickly on foot as he could in a cab. Whatever the impulsive Liss might be up to now, he wanted to get hold of her before she met any odd-sounding reporters, or anyone else. Particularly Peg Whiting.

"Mayo!"

Asey felt his arm gripped, heard a dog bark, and turned to look into the beaming face of Judge Thatcher Sudbury. Despite the glaring sun, he wore no hat, and, despite the wilting heat, his linen suit looked crisp and pressed. Asey wondered how the man, in such an informal costume, still managed to convey a distinct impression of judicial dignity.

"Hello, Asey! I thought I saw you earlier on Beacon Street!" He pumped Asey's hand heartily. "Well, well, how are you? Didn't you just come out of the Lathrops' house? I thought so! Been visiting my cousins?"

"Uh-huh, an' I got sort of delayed," Asey said. "I—er—I'm goin' to come back an' see you later, Judge, but I'm in a rush now, so if you'll excuse me—"

"What brings you to Boston?"

"Jennie's house cleanin'." Asey detoured around the Judge. "I'll see you later!"

He dodged past the two Chows, which had been watching him with thinly veiled dislike, and hurried along toward the studio.

As he passed the Public Garden, he noticed that the swan boats were paddling around as usual, and that in spite of the heat there were more people in the Garden than he ever remembered having seen there before. The only policeman in sight was a burly man in shirt sleeves who was giving a ticket to a woman driver.

Asey slowed down to buy a newspaper from a boy, glanced at the headlines, came to an abrupt stop, and wondered if the glaring sun had in some way impaired his eyesight. For under the screaming head of "PUBLIC GARDEN SLAYING" was an explanatory line in smaller type that said, "Notorious Woman Bag-Snatcher and Pal Sought in Brandt Shooting. Robbery Motive, Police Assert."

He shook his head slowly as he scanned the column beneath.

The gist of it, as the reporter pointed out with exquisite simplicity, was that, since Brandt had neither wallet nor money, and his pockets were empty, he had obviously been robbed. The police had at once connected the robbery with the bag-snatcher who had been at work in the vicinity that morning, and both she and her male companion were shortly expected to turn up in the police dragnet. Mr. Craig Lathrop, who found the body, had mentioned seeing a suspicious-looking milkman, and the police intended to track him down, too. There was no mention of the girl, or of the gun!

Asey thrust the paper into his pocket, wiped the perspiration off his face, and continued thoughtfully on his way.

Something was more than screwball about all this business. Surely the cops must have found that Smith & Wesson by now, he thought. If they hadn't located it by themselves, certainly some one of the swan boats' passengers would have found it for them. And a weapon like that would undoubtedly be registered. Once they had the gun, they should—

"Hey, you!"

Asey realized suddenly that he was holding up traffic with his speculations, and, with a red face, he stepped onto the sidewalk and strode along to the Arts Building. He hesitated at the entrance and looked around. There were no cops about nor any police cars.

"Asey!" Jennie emerged from the doorway of the next building and marched up to him. "Where've you been? I've waited here so long!"

"So it *was* you I seen," Asey said reproachfully, "in the blue dress, back there in the drugstore! New one, huh?"

"If you saw me, I certainly wish you'd yelled at me!" Jennie said. "I've waited here so long, and I'm so hot!"

"I'm sore!" Asey said. "Didn't I tell you to go to Blandin's, an' stay there?"

Jennie sniffed. "You think you can shunt me off on a wild-goose chase like that? I knew you never bought any Palm Beach suit! You always said you hated 'em. So I just read that note, and changed my dress at the station—just to be on the safe side—and come right back here. My, my, what excitement! You never seen so many cops!"

"You mean, you went back there to the Garden? To the landin'? Under their very noses? Jennie, d'you know they want you, an' me?" Asey demanded. "Did you see the papers?"

"I read 'em," Jennie said, "but I knew it all, anyway. I heard the cops in the Garden talkin' it over. Honest, they haven't caught on to a single thing! And, Asey, that boy with the rumpled hair that tried to stop the girl from goin' with Brandt, his name's Craig Lathrop, and he never told the cops a thing about the girl bein' with Brandt!"

"He's the girl's half-brother," Asey explained. "Her name's Liss Lathrop— What's the matter?"

"Only her brother!" Jennie sounded disappointed. "I thought he might be her beau, and I made up a triangle—Well, anyway, I listened to the cops, and finally, I got so worried about you, I got Brandt's address from the newspaper and come here, thinkin' you'd go where he lived, sooner or later. D'you know those fools never found the gun?"

Asey nodded. "I don't understand that."

"Neither do I. I watched 'em mill around the landin', but I didn't see 'em find it, so of course I thought they must've got it before I come back to the Garden. But the papers say no gun was found! I think it's awful queer, Asey! I'm sure I heard it hit the wood of a swan boat!"

"You did. I seen it, myself."

"Well, then, where is it? The cops never found it, and neither did anyone else that rode on the boats. *I* couldn't find it," Jennie added, "and I certainly tried to! I rode on every single boat, changin' my seat and peerin' around under the benches till folks thought I was daft. It's not on any of those boats now, and I didn't see anyone take it. D'you suppose that brother did? He went away, and then come back with a pretty dark-haired girl and another big fellow."

Asey shook his head and shrugged. "Could be. Jennie, you been here long? Did you see the Lathrop girl?"

"Now, you know," Jennie said, "I thought I *did* see her just after I come—that was over an hour ago. It looked like her, but her hair was done up. But I saw the brother and that dark girl go in. . . . Asey, where've you been? What you been doin'?"

"Come on," Asey said; "I'll tell you on the way. I want to look into things."

"Is it safe for us?" Jennie asked as they entered the building.

"If nobody's spotted us yet," Asey said, "I doubt if they will. Think of you, sittin' under their noses! Jennie, there's somethin' awful haywire about all this. It don't work out. An', by the way, if we should run into any trouble, try to break away an' call Judge Sudbury. It's three flights up, an', if you'll listen while you climb, I'll sum up my mornin' for you."

His brief summary was punctuated by Jennie's breathless and incredulous exclamations. "I never! . . . I absolutely never! . . . I never heard the like. . . . I never—Is this the place?"

Finding the door of Brandt's waiting-room unlocked, Asey squared his shoulders and strode in, fully expecting a cop to jump up and bar his way. But the room was empty.

"I s'pose," Asey said, while Jennie stared open-mouthed at the photographs on the wall, "these cops know best, but I'd have left someone here, or at least locked up! Seems pretty casual of 'em to walk out an' leave things wide open!"

"Probably they took pictures," Jennie said. "They took millions of pictures over on the landin'. I heard one plainclothes feller say that was their system. Soon's they got through, people prowled around all over the place, and they let the swan boats start up. Is that the studio in there?"

Jennie repeated her question and then crossed over to where Asey stood silently in the doorway, and peered in. "Never wasted time cleanin', did he?" she commented. "Oh, look!" Her voice sank to a whisper and she pointed to a figure on a couch.

·   Asey nodded slowly.

"Asey, that's the blond girl herself! She must be asleep. So it *was* her I seen comin' in— Oh, Asey, look at her head! She's been shot, too, the same way! And look there on the floor! There's a gun! Asey, d'you see it?"

"I see it," Asey said grimly. "That is the Smith an' Wesson Magnum that nobody found!" He stared around the room. "So that," he continued, "is why the door was open. I s'pose she had a key. I wonder—"

"Asey, if—if she killed Brandt with that gun, then who"—Jennie's voice quavered—"*who* killed *her?*"

"Same person who shot Brandt, I think," Asey said.

"But it couldn't be! *She* shot Brandt! I saw her!"

"I know, an' her mother says she's a wonderful shot. Jennie, listen. Back in the Garden you heard a shot, an' started to run when you seen Brandt fall. Right? The girl stood there a moment, then reached down, picked up the gun, an' threw it away. Right? You was runnin' along that curvin' path to the landin'. You seen her pick the gun up, but you honestly didn't see her drop it, did you?"

"If she didn't drop it," Jennie said, "I'd like to know who did! There wasn't a soul anywhere near the landin' but her! I couldn't have helped seein' anyone, if they'd been near enough to throw that gun into the clearin' there, after shootin' Brandt. That's what you're drivin' at, isn't it?"

"Somethin' like that," Asey said. "You see—"

"I seen it!" Jennie retorted. "You're the one that needs to do the seein'! You know it isn't easy to throw a gun! That girl could only heave it as far as the swan boats, not more'n twenty-five feet away! She'd have seen anyone, if there'd been anyone there! So would I, if they was within fifty yards of her; it's all clear, around there! We'd have seen anyone throw it! I told you, the only people I saw in the Garden was a man with two Chows, and a woman in evenin' clothes, lots earlier— What are you mutterin' about?"

"Two Chows! Jennie, d'you remember Judge Sudbury? Was it him with the two Chows?"

"Land's sakes, I'm dumb!" Jennie said. "I'd ought to have recognized that beard! That's just who it was! Why, I haven't seen him for years!"

"Let me figure, now," Asey said. "After Liss Lathrop smacked Chub for buttin' in, an' went on with Brandt, then Chub phoned Peg. She said her phone didn't ring—Oh, Jennie, no wonder I been feelin' there's somethin' screwball about this! It was starin' me in the face, but I never looked beyond the tip of my nose! Golly, I should have caught on quicker!"

"I'm not catchin' on any!" Jennie told him bluntly. "I don't even know what you're talkin' about!"

"Chub said he phoned Peg. Peg said her phone didn't ring. That may mean he never phoned when he claims he did. P'raps he followed Brandt an' Liss to the Garden, whether you seen him or not. On the other hand," Asey added thoughtfully, "maybe he was tellin' the truth, an' the phone rang in Peg's apartment, only she wasn't there; see? Peg knew Brandt planned to take pictures early, in a rush. No reason why she couldn't have sneaked over to the Garden, herself. Jennie, it's a shot in the dark, but what did the woman in evenin' dress look like? Did you notice her at all?"

"I only glanced at her. She was blond, and short—"

"What?" Asey demanded.

"Blond and short, and she moved quick. Like a sparrow. She went past me so fast, I didn't think she saw me. She had on a pink dress with ruffles, and she carried an awful pretty beaded bag. Honest, I hardly noticed her!"

"Uh-huh. You just took a passin' glance," Asey said with irony.

"Just a peep. Huh! You know you just give a fine thumbnail description of Liss's mother? Golly, was they all roamin' around? I wonder if Poor was there, too!"

"But the papers said the Lathrop boy come from a fine old family, and his sister was engaged to a rich tycoon!" Jennie said. "And I'm sure the Judge's important. Would folks like that be mixed up in a thing like this?"

"They may be the best people," Asey said, "but they got some odd habits. The rich tycoon sneaked into the studio an' swiped Liss's dress so's the cops wouldn't find out about her, an' Chub Lathrop lied to the cops with the blandest broad 'a' I ever heard. An' Peg was so innocent—but still she remembered to write her pay check! An', golly, I forgot all about that book she stole out of Brandt's desk. An' that mother's most too good to be true. I swallowed her whole, an' put her down as a twitterer, but, now I look back, I'm wonderin' considerable about her!"

"She lie to you?"

"Wa-el, it's my impression she done a lot of skiddin' around the truth. Liss had smacked her. Liss smacked Chub. Poor was sore with the girl for posin'. Liss got Peg's modelin' job. Yup, Jennie, I'm beginnin' to understand a lot of things!"

"I wish I could understand how that girl could've picked up that gun and thrown it away unless she dropped it in the first place!" Jennie said. "You think it dropped from heaven by itself? Asey, it just come to me—Could someone have been hidin' up in the branches of a tree, maybe?"

Asey shook his head. "That's one thing I'm sure didn't happen. I saw Brandt's wound. That bullet he stopped was travelin' horizontal. Now—"

"What you goin' to do?" Jennie asked as he entered the studio. "Should you go in there?"

"I got to. But you stay put." Asey walked over, picked up the Smith & Wesson by the checkered grips, slid the cylinder catch forward, and allowed the cylinder to swing out on its crane. "Huh! Two cartridges fired," he said. "Jennie, lock that outer waitin'-room door, an' stand by it. If you hear anyone comin', let me know."

"Then what do we do?" Jennie inquired.

"We pull another early Fairbanks down the fire escape," Asey told her. "Right now I'm goin' to find out who owned this gun. It'll take a bit of phonin' to Hanson an' the other state cops, but they can dig out the information for me."

It took twenty minutes, and, when the registered owner's name was finally divulged to him, Asey's long whistle of amazement brought Jennie running to the studio door.

"Did you find out?"

"Yup." Asey replaced the receiver. "It's registered to Judge Sudbury, an' it's never been reported stolen. Say, what do you remember about him?"

"Why, he was always nice to everybody when he come to his shootin' shack," Jennie said. "He liked to shoot."

"Just so, an' he was the whale of a good shot," Asey said. "In fact, it was the Judge who stopped a buck with one shot from a gun just like this. You seen him walkin' his dogs, an' I seen him only just now, walkin' them dogs again. When you think it over, a scorchin' day like this ain't ideal weather for so much dog-walkin', is it? But, if you wanted to roam around an' keep your eye on things without attractin' suspicion, there's no nicer way than walkin' dogs. What else can you remember? I need you to check up on what I been recallin'?"

"Well, he was always lookin' up ancestors in the town records, makin' out family trees an' talkin' about family," Jennie said. "He was so proud of bein' descended from a Bay Colony governor, but he lost interest in his precious family awful quick when he found out two of his ancestors was such scalawags they was hanged, and some others got booted out of the Colony. Not long afterward the Judge left the Cape, and it was common gossip he felt so worked up about his ancestors turnin' out so bad he couldn't stand the place any more."

Asey nodded. "That all come back to me, too. An' the Judge's a relation of the Lathrops. He just said so. I wonder, now, if he got sore seein' his relative Liss Lathrop rompin' around underwear ads, an' posin' with a dead-pan dummy that was her twin. Huh! We'll go call on him, but first I'll see how big a check Peg Whitin' wrote for herself."

"Was it a lot?" Jennie asked a minute later as he stared at the checkbook.

"Only twenty-five dollars. Seems modest enough." Asey returned the checkbook to the drawer and looked thoughtfully around the studio. "Jennie, somethin' in here ain't the way it was when I was here before!"

"How could it be, with her lyin' there, poor thing?"

"I don't mean her. I mean somethin's wrong in all this truck." He indicated the litter of disjointed arms and legs and plaster heads. "Let's see. There's the dummy that Peg called Bella, an' there's the fat-man dummy with the hat. An' the chairs an' tables an' bric-à-brac—"

Jennie sniffed. "Findin' what was different in this mess would be a hundred times worse than findin' a needle in a haystack! Why didn't someone hear the shot that killed her?"

"In the city, a loud bang's a car backfirin'. P'raps people who heard it thought it was the cops makin' more din in here," Asey said. "Or else someone bangin' away makin' scenery in one of the other studios in the buildin'. Golly, I'm usually good about rememberin' things an' how they're laid out, but there's a few million too many items here. I'm stumped."

"What you wigglin' your nose like that for?" Jennie wanted to know. "Smell something?"

"I noticed it here before," Asey said, "while I was tryin' to open that consarned window, an' it's somethin' else that's stumpin' me. It ain't exactly a perfume smell—not Liss Lathrop's kind, anyway. I spent enough time in her closet to know hers by heart. An' d' you know who this reminds me of? Old Cap'n Porter. Oh, well; come on! We'll go chat with the Judge—Oho!" He stopped on the threshold and crossed the studio to the window.

"What *now?*" Jennie demanded.

"I sort of hankered to see just what'd jammed that window before," Asey said. "It's a piece of old wedge. I can see the end of it. Huh. I s'pose Poor just happened to shove it the right way from outside. Well, that's that. Now, let's get goin'!"

Once outside the building, Asey marched along Arlington Street at a rapid pace, ignoring Jennie's breathlessly bitter comments about possible heat prostration, and did he think he was Paul Revere, rushing like that? When he abruptly stopped, Jennie's indignation mounted even higher.

"Why *are* you gapin' like a sight-seer from the country at that statue, as if you never saw it before? George Washington's been up on that horse all your life— Oh, for land's sakes!"

She broke off as Asey turned into the Public Garden and walked quickly past the little potted palm trees to the base of the Washington statue, where a boy with a homemade sling in his hand stood looking disconsolately up toward Washington's horse.

"Asey!" Jennie hurried after him "Sometimes you provoke me so! What's the matter with you?"

He grinned and pointed up. "This youngster's lost his parachute trooper up on the general's epaulette. See the little lead soldier danglin' from the cloth 'chute up there?"

"I'm sure it's too bad he lost it," Jennie returned, "but there's nothin' much can be done. . . . Asey, you mustn't climb that statue! You'll be arrested!"

Practically before the words were out of her mouth, Asey had swung himself up the statue's base to the pedestal, rescued the soldier, swung down, and presented the toy to its small owner, who looked dazed by the whole proceedings.

"Gee, thanks!"

"Thank *you*," Asey said. "Come on, Jennie!"

"I think the heat's got you," Jennie told him as she followed him back to Arlington Street. "One minute you rush me to death, and the next minute you got so much time on your hands, you stop to play Good Samaritan to a dirty-faced boy! What's got into you? What you got that cat-that's-swallowed-a-canary look on your face for? You remembered what was wrong at the studio?"

"Nope, not yet."

"You think," Jennie suggested derisively, "maybe a parachute trooper landed that gun at the girl's feet?"

"Nope. Shush up, Jennie, I'm thinkin'."

The note of finality in his voice caused Jennie to refrain from further comment as she trotted along beside him. When Asey used that tone she gave up.

On the sidewalk opposite Judge Sudbury's Beacon Street house, Asey came to a sudden halt and took her arm. "Look over there, goin' up his front steps! There's the Judge with his dogs, an' Mrs. Lathrop, an' Chub, an' Peg, an' Poor! Going to hold a council of war, I bet! Oh, if I could turn into a fly on the wall an' listen to 'em, I'd find out what I want to know, in one swoop! I wonder—Come over to this bench an' sit down an' get your wind while I figger!"

"Why? You know it was the Judge's gun, and you know he was in the Garden this mornin'," Jennie said. "Why don't you just march in and confront him?"

"What we got," Asey said, "is a lot of suspicious-soundin' odds an' ends. Not proof. If I tried any confrontin' act, the Judge'd hand me over to the cops—an' remember they're already dragnetin' for me!"

"I think you've got proof enough!"

"We know the gun belongs to him, that he's a good shot, an' that he was doin' a powerful lot of wanderin' around, yes. We can guess that, in his mind, Liss might've been tarnishin' the family's good name by posin' for ads an' such. But that ain't near enough," Asey said. "An', if you think, you'll find the Judge ain't the only one with a suspicious aura floatin' around his head."

"But it's *his* gun!" Jennie protested. "And you said the cops hadn't any report of its bein' stolen!"

"P'raps," Asey returned, "he don't know it *has* been stolen. Mrs. Lathrop an' Chub have access to his house. They might've swiped it without his knowledge. P'raps Poor did, or Peg. Now, I sort of gathered that Chub supported his stepmother an' half-sister largely from a sense of duty. Once Liss was married to Poor, you could reasonably assume he wouldn't have to support 'em any longer. P'raps then he could get married, himself—"

"To that dark-haired Whitin' girl, I bet!" Jennie interrupted. "When I saw her lookin' at him over in the Garden, and again comin' into the buildin' there, I guessed she was in love with him! that's where I was figurin' out a triangle, see? Her, and the blond girl, and the rumple-haired boy. That's why I was disappointed when you said he was Liss's brother. I bet he wants to marry Peg Whitin'!"

"Maybe. Anyway, s'pose Rudi Brandt was hornin' in on Poor. Chub sees the rich tycoon bein' eased out of the picture. I can see how Chub might have a motive for shootin' Brandt."

Jennie frowned. "But why'd he kill Liss, then?"

"You got me there!" Asey said. "But it gives him one motive, anyway. Take Peg. It's possible she was good an' sore with Brandt for givin' her modelin' job to Liss, an' jealous of Liss for bein' the one to oust her. Maybe she was in her apartment when Chub phoned, an' maybe she wasn't. 'Course," he added thoughtfully, "killin' both of 'em leaves her without any job at all, but there you are."

"I still say," Jennie insisted stubbornly, "that gun belongs to the Judge!"

"Um." Asey didn't seem to hear her. "Maybe Poor thought Rudi was a rival. Maybe he thought that Liss's continuin' to pose for Rudi when she promised she wouldn't meant that she was in love with him. But, doggone, he certainly wouldn't have shot the girl, too! Now, Mrs. Lathrop likes money, an' wants Liss to marry Poor. She wouldn't like Brandt's cuttin' in. An' she was in the Garden. An' later, Liss strikes her. No love pat, either! You know, Jennie, that phone call about the odd-soundin' reporter was awful fishy! But she sure got rid of me in a hurry. P'raps she wanted me to go to the studio an' find Liss's body. P'raps she'd just come back from shootin' her. An' she'd been talkin' with the Judge on the phone. Let's see, now; how can I do it? I might get into a Cape Cod house pretendin' to be a brush salesman, or somethin', but that'd never work on Beacon Street. Give me your pocketbook, Jennie. I seen a badge in there. I'll be an inspector."

"That's my old Woman's Defense Corps badge!" Jennie said as he removed it. "And my Defense Corps certificate!"

"Uh-huh. I know."

"You got a touch of sun?" Jennie inquired.

Asey chuckled. "Whenever I visited the Porters in Boston, I always remarked on the pile of inspectors prowlin' around that everybody took for granted. Now the Judge an' the others'll be too busy to be bothered by an inspector, an' I think I can convince the help. Nobody ever reads credentials, but, if they ask for some, your badge an' certificate are awful impressive. When I get to the back door, I'll put on my yachtin' cap. It'll make a queer uniform, but it won't be any queerer than some defense outfits I seen. Golly, here's a tape measure, too! Just what I need. Stay here, now, till I come back!"

Fifteen minutes later, Asey was in Judge Sudbury's hall outside the living-room door, measuring the floor with his tape measure, and listening as hard as he could to the conversation inside. Two perspiring maids, whipping up what appeared to be a spur-of-the-moment buffet lunch, had let him into the kitchen at once and without question, only commenting that he was the third inspector they'd had in a month.

"Mayo is unquestionably on her trail." The Judge's anxious voice came to him clearly. "We must find her! She can't be at the studio if the phone's not answered. Are you sure, Monica, that Liss intended going there?"

Asey nodded to himself as Mrs. Lathrop assured the Judge that the studio was the girl's destination. As he'd hoped, no one had as yet found Liss or told this group of her death.

"If Liss shot Rudi," the Judge continued, "Mayo will find out! He's uncanny! He always stumbles on things!"

At the moment, Asey thought, he was stumbling on more than he'd dared anticipate.

"He certainly bowled me over, popping up in the studio!" Peg said. "My eyes nearly popped out!"

"When *I* saw him in Liss's room"—Mrs. Lathrop's voice was nervous and twittery—"I was stunned! It was just after I'd phoned you, Thatcher, when you'd warned me about your seeing him. I tried to find out what he knew! I insinuated Liss had called him in—and, really, he somehow made *me* believe she really had!"

"He can make people believe anything," the Judge said. "The instant I saw him rushing across to the Garden, I felt in my bones he knew about Rudi! And when I watched him from the window here, through the binoculars, and saw him make for the landing, I knew the family was in for it!"

"Why didn't you report the gun, Uncle That?" Chub's broad "a" wasn't nearly so broad as it had been when he talked with the cops earlier, Asey noticed.

"My dear boy, when I saw that Smith & Wesson Magnum on the swan-boat seat, I recognized what it was, but I never suspected it was mine! You see, I'd caught a glimpse of Liss and Rudi running along Arlington Street, and wondered what they were up to at that hour, but I lost track of them before I could round up the dogs to follow. Then, later, I heard the shot, although I thought then that it was only a car backfiring. When, still later, I strolled past the landing and saw Rudi lying there and the camera and the dummy, frankly I was appalled!"

"Was that when you tipped over the case of plateholders?" Poor asked.

"Yes." Out in the hall, Asey found himself blinking. "It was obvious that Liss had broken her promise to you about posing, but I was determined that if Rudi'd actually taken pictures of her, no one should know it, or know she was there. When I returned to the house I saw Mayo, and I give you my word, I felt as guilty as if I'd shot Rudi myself! I scuttled up the steps out of his sight, and rushed for the binoculars. I don't know what impelled me afterward to go to the library and see if my Smith & Wesson was all right. And I found it was gone!''

Mrs. Lathrop broke the ensuing silence. "But who stole it? I still can't understand what happened!"

"It took some unwinding," the Judge said. "You see, both Susie and Jane were out last night. I dined at the club and went on to a concert. Only old Annie was here—"

"She's *so* feeble! Why do you keep her?" Mrs. Lathrop said.

"My dear Monica, you can't discard someone who served your family faithfully for fifty years! Old Annie has nowhere else to live! Anyway, the bell rang about nine last night, and old Annie went to the door, to find a policeman standing there. He told her the police wanted some gun of mine for some kind of test. She couldn't remember what kind, but when I suggested ballistics, she thought that might be it. So old Annie told the fellow to come in and get the gun he wished, and he did!''

"And walked off with it! That's incredible!" Poor said. "D'you believe her? *Was* it a cop? How could she have done such a thing!"

"I was furious at first," the Judge said, "but you know policemen often do come here on business; I'm on their Fund board. Annie's seen them come and go. And, as she tearfully said, she thought it was always all right to let in a cop, and, besides, the dogs liked him. Their approval clinched the matter."

"But wouldn't she know him again?" Chub asked. "Can't she describe him?"

Asey heard the Judge's sigh. "To quote her, a cop is a cop and looks like any other cop. Her description of him would fit any male in Boston. Unquestionably he was a fake. I found out that, before he came, Annie had answered the phone three times—a call for each of the maids as well as one for me, so it seems that the man first found out who was home here."

"Well, *he* took the gun!" Mrs. Lathrop said. "So Liss *couldn't* have had it! That settles everything, doesn't it?"

"Yes," the Judge said hesitantly. "Yes, except that old Annie's story is so shaky! I tremble to think what might happen if she were cross-examined in court. She could so easily be confused into admitting that the person masquerading as a policeman might have been a man, *or* a woman! Of course, it's fantastic to think for a moment that one of us would murder anybody, but Liss is so impetuous! Monica, why were you hunting her this morning? I thought you intended to stay in Portsmouth with Mary all week!"

"I did, but she had to rush to New York on the earliest train, so she drove in and dropped me at the house about five this morning; neither of us had had the time to change, because we got Bob's telegram when we got back from the club. And the first thing I saw was a note on the hall table, a message for Liss from Rudi. Of course, I didn't want any more fuss with Liss and Jack about posing, after those underwear ads! I did *so* hope I might catch up with her and stop her, because I truly didn't think I could stand that bickering again!"

"My reaction exactly!" Chub said. "Oh, if Mayo gets onto us! Your gun, Uncle That, and Monica there, and you there, and me there, and Liss there! Anyway, Peg, you and Jack are safe! And, by the way, Peg, what was the idea behind all this early-morning picture taking? I never got that."

"Yesterday, while I was out, Rudi got a call from *Fashion-Allure* for a patriotic cover, so—"

"How in hell"—Chub echoed Asey's own thoughts—"could Brenda and Liss on a swan boat be called patriotic?"

"Old historic Boston, the swan boats, and red-white-and-blue costumes," Peg said. "It's no crazier than those two lions with a head of lettuce we did—that was Aid to Britain, did you know? Anyway, they offered Rudi such a fabulous price that I wanted to call back and check on it when he told me."

Out in the hallway, Asey's eyes narrowed, and a frown gathered on his forehead.

"The problem," Peg continued, "was that they wanted the picture today. Rudi couldn't work yesterday, with those afternoon thunderstorms, so the only time left was early this morning. If the weather'd been bad, Rudi would have been licked, but there was too much money at stake not to take the chance, so we whipped up some costumes. I suppose that after I went home Rudi decided to use Liss and Brenda instead of the two dummies. Judge, someone else must have been in the Garden! Didn't you notice anyone?"

"I passed a charwoman with a bag." Asey grinned at the Judge's description of Jennie. "And I noticed a gas-station man. Didn't you say you saw a milkman, Chub?"

Stifling the sudden exclamation that came to his lips, Asey pocketed the tape measure, hurried downstairs, thanked the maids, and departed.

He found Jennie on the settee where he had left her, eating an ice-cream cone and fanning herself with a handkerchief.

"Why do people live in this hot, muggy place! Asey, I can tell by your face you found out a lot!"

"Some. Look; you got to help me keep that bunch there at the Judge's—Don't look suspicious. I mean it. I want you to take this watch"—he drew an old silver repeater from his pocket—"an' go ask to see the Judge. If the maids say he's busy, you tell 'em you got a bequest for him."

"What?"

"It's always best to string along with as much of the truth as you can," Asey said. "So you tell him you been to Cousin Ed's funeral in Chicago. Then give him the watch an' say Cousin Ed left it to him as a remembrance of the days they went duck-huntin' together. That won't seem too odd, because Ed was his handyman for years. Then you settle yourself down an' ask if the Judge minds your waitin' there for me, because somehow you've missed connections with me, an' we planned I'd pick you up at the Judge's if anything slipped up. Bein' as how you was kind enough to bring him the watch, he can't very well refuse you, an' considerin' the worried mood that bunch is in, I think they'll be only too willin' to wait an' see what I been up to. Now, hop along!"

Jennie hesitated. "Then what'll I talk about?"

"To the best of my knowledge," Asey told her, with a grin, "you never been at a lost for words in your life. Just don't mention what's gone on here today. Talk about the Cape. It's always a good, safe topic. Sooner or later, I'll get back there."

"Where you goin' now? What you goin' to do?"

"I'm goin' to make some phone calls an' fancy house-breakin'," Asey said.

"I know! You've remembered what was wrong at the studio! Tell me, what was it?"

Asey smiled. "Took me a long time," he said, "but I finally got there. The fat-man dummy didn't have on a green top hat, an' the smell was Honeywell's Dressing."

Jennie looked at him. "An' on the basis of that you think you're goin' to find a murderer?"

"Wa-el," Asey drawled. "I'll throw in a vote of thanks to George Washington, too. So long!"

The atmosphere in the Judge's living-room had been tense enough at two o'clock. By three, Jennie was as uncomfortable as she had ever been in her life, but she went on doggedly talking about Cape Cod. Occasionally Judge Sudbury helped her keep the conversational ball rolling with a politely dutiful query about the health of some former neighbor, and once, when Jennie paused to relieve her parched throat with some iced tea, Peg Whiting roused herself and related several nervous and pointless little anecdotes about her life at the Meweesit Camp. Mrs. Lathrop wiggled in her chair, alternately craning her neck to look at the door and twisting her head to read the thermometer. Chub adjusted and readjusted the swing of the electric fan, while Poor sat and traced the carpet pattern with the toe of his shoe, until Jennie wanted to scream at the pair of them to stop their futile, monotonous motions. Instead, she serenely described her method of making bayberry candles, and her grandmother's recipe for beach-plum jelly.

When the mantel clock tinkled at quarter past three, Poor interrupted her in the middle of a sentence. "Stop gabbling about Cape Cod! Where's this cousin of yours? Where's Mayo?"

"I'm—" Jennie caught herself just in time to keep from telling him hotly that she was tired of the Cape, too, and wanted Asey more than he did. "I suppose," she amended in the pleasantest voice she could muster, "he's trying on a new suit, as he planned. Does that thermometer say ninety-*two?*"

"Ninety-*four*," Mrs. Lathrop told her. "The humidity is ninety . . . . *Is* that the doorbell at last? Is it Liss?"

The Judge rose, but before he could cross the room a maid ushered Asey in. He looked incredibly cool. But, as he smiled a greeting, he took from his pocket a blue bandana handkerchief Jennie had never seen before and mopped his face with it.

"I'm sorry I'm late. I got delayed." Asey twisted the bandana into a roll, held both ends in the fingers of his right hand, and sat down at a mahogany table opposite Poor and Peg Whiting.

Jennie experienced a sharp, let-down sensation. She expected fireworks, maybe even a fight, and here was Asey sitting back, gently swinging his rolled-up handkerchief as if he were rocking a cradle!

"Have you seen Liss?" Mrs. Lathrop asked eagerly. "Did you find her?"

"Yes, I have—Huh, that looks familiar!" Reaching out, Asey took his old silver watch from the table, balanced it in the loop of the handkerchief, whose ends he continued to hold in the fingers of his right hand, and swung it back and forth.

"You'll drop that!" Jennie warned him sharply.

"Where *is* Liss?" Peg asked anxiously. "We've been so worried. We've phoned everywhere, and we can't locate her. Where is she?"

"In Brandt's studio." Asey continued to swing the handkerchief with the watch balanced in its fold, and everyone in the room followed the motion as if fascinated by it. "In the Arts Buildin'."

Jennie pricked up her ears at the purring note in his voice and realized suddenly that, for all his calm expression, Asey was somehow set to spring. He was setting a stage for something, leading up to something.

"Mayo, what's the idea? What are you driving at?" Poor demanded impatiently. "We've stood enough of your drawling, home-spun nonsense! We know that Liss isn't at the studio! We've phoned there. We—"

"Look *out* for that watch!" Jennie interrupted.

"I said she was at the studio." Asey paused, and then added more gently, "An' I'm awful sorry to say that she's been shot."

Mrs. Lathrop's scream pierced Jennie's eardrums. Chub turned from the electric fan and stared at Asey as if he were talking some strange foreign language, and for an instant the Judge's face seemed as white as his hair.

"Shot? You don't mean—" Peg's voice broke.

"I'm sorry, but I'm afraid I do," Asey told her.

"Asey." The Judge swallowed. "Asey, has Liss—has she been killed? Asey, do you know who did it?"

"I came here," Asey said, "to get him, Judge!"

The watch dropped suddenly from the loop of the bandana, and even Jennie, with a perfectly clear conscience, found herself at first terrified and confused by the sound. She half jumped from her chair, and then sat back and stared at the group in amazement. They were like a tableau, she thought. Mrs. Lathrop looked like a marble statue; Peg's face was a mixture of fear and confusion; the Judge was gripping the arm of a Chippendale chair till his knuckles seemed almost to drive through the back of his hands. Chub was dazed and bewildered, and his fingers still hovered over the adjustment screw of the electric fan. Asey, grim-eyed and immobile, still sat at the table, still waiting, still set to spring.

"You'll never get me!" Poor's hoarse cry put an end to the little tableau. "Never!"

Jennie's jaw dropped at the sight of the short-barreled revolver that had appeared in his hand. Automatically she turned to see what Asey would do.

"Now, that"—Asey casually took an end of the handkerchief in either hand and smiled coolly at Poor—"is just what I been waitin' for! I felt sure you had on you the gun you potted at Jennie with, an' I kind of didn't feel like rushin' you till you'd pulled your spare—"

"You'll never rush me! You'll never—"

In a motion so quick that Jennie couldn't follow it, Asey's left wrist jerked, and the end of the bandana he had been holding in his right hand seemed to whip across the mahogany table toward Poor's face.

"Oh, my eye!" Poor cried out. "My eye!"

His right hand, still holding the revolver, involuntarily went to his eye, and before he knew what was happening Asey had wrenched the gun from him.

"There!" Asey said. "That's that! Chub, give me your belt to tie him up with—That's right. Now fish in his coat pocket an' see if that piece of twine's still there. Is it? Good! Judge, you s'pose you could fix things up so that the cops'd be willin' to exchange a batch of parkin' tickets an' an assault charge for a double murderer?"

Half an hour later, the Judge turned from his front window and joined Peg Whiting on the sofa over by the electric fan. "I'm glad you didn't watch Poor's departure!" he said. "The police had to carry him out. He's just gone to pieces. I've seen that sort of thing happen before. His kind wilts very easily—"

He broke off as Asey and Chub entered the room. "Ah, Asey, I'm glad you've come. There's much I want explained. And I've already called my friend, Judge Mason. Thoroughly improper, of course, but I can assure you that Poor will be very effectively thwarted if, when he pulls himself together, he attempts to use his wealth or his position or his lawyers to grasp at any possible loopholes in the law. Chub, how is Monica?"

"Jennie and the maids are looking after her, Uncle That." Chub, Asey thought, still had the look of a halfback who'd been hit over the head but who nevertheless intended to play through the last minute of the fourth quarter. "She's stopped crying, and she's getting hold of herself. By the way, Asey, don't let her find out what I did to Poor, will you?"

"What *did* you do?" Peg demanded.

"Nothin'," Asey told her, "that the cops wouldn't have done to him sooner or later if he tried any of that mad-dog snarlin' on them. It was a good, solid right to the jaw, an' it sort of quieted him right down. I don't think he'd ever had a tooth knocked out before."

"Tell me," the Judge said; "what *did* you do when you flipped that handkerchief at him?"

"It's an old gambler's trick," Asey said. "If you'll look, you'll find I tied a lead sinker in the corner I held in my right hand—I got it from my pail of tackle in the car. I wondered if I couldn't harry him some by danglin' a sling in front of him, what with him bein' hot an' anxious, an', so's I wouldn't be entirely unarmed, I added the sinker; see?"

"No," Peg said, "I don't."

"You hold an end of the handkerchief in either hand; see?" Asey demonstrated. "An' then you let go with the weighted end, flip the other wrist, an' someone gets the lead smack in the face. Poor got hoist with some of his own petard."

"Asey, why *did* he kill them?" the Judge asked.

"He thought Brandt was cuttin' him out with Liss, an' he wanted to get Brandt out of the way for good," Asey said.

"He admitted it, Uncle That!" Chub added, as the Judge shook his head in disbelief. "He couldn't see any other reason why Liss continued to pose for Rudi against his wishes. It never occurred to him that she might want money!"

"D'you mean"—the Judge sounded incredulous—"that Poor was really that jealous of Rudi?"

Chub nodded. "Apparently Rudi had always goaded him, all

along, ever since he got engaged to Liss. All that fuss he made about Liss's posing, and all his bickering and his pettishness, and his ranting about her running around in underwear ads—all those things that we just put down to his vanity were serious business with him. He was insanely jealous."

"I suppose," the Judge said slowly, "that there are people like that. Yes, I think I see how he might have been goaded by Rudi's casual air of sophistication. The fellow did have a certain charm—though I'm sure Poor never would have understood it."

"I don't get the rest, Asey," Chub said. "Poor was in such a gabbling state, I couldn't make head nor tail of it."

"It was sort of a variation on the old dime-novel stunt of a villain makin' a horse run away so's he could rescue the heroine," Asey said. "Poor intended to kill Rudi, implicate Liss, an' then heroically get her out of trouble. Oh, I should've got suspicious when he was so quick about suggestin' he get his lawyer to help get Liss out of possible trouble! Then, see, because he'd be the one to save her, she'd have to do what he wanted—like no more posin'—out of gratitude. That was his plan."

"How horrible!" Peg said.

"Uh-huh. But he got stung. Jennie begun gummin' his plan up when she chased Liss away from the scene. An' Liss heard Jennie an' me talkin' in the alley of Nineteen an' a Half, an' it frightened her so much, I guess she decided to sit tight an' say nothin' at all. She didn't pour out the story to Poor an' ask for help. She only asked him to get her dress. After thinkin' things over, she went out on her own to find the murderer; but, in the meantime, the Judge ruined those plates, so there wasn't any pictures for the cops to find her by."

"I can't believe he meant to involve her!" the Judge said.

"He did. He just confessed it. Liss was a good shot, she was impulsive, she was on the scene. That'd be enough to start the cops questionin' her. When it came to a final showdown, Poor knew she'd get off all right, with his lawyers an' Annie's story. An' Poor thought things was workin' out fine. He was sure of it when he heard Peg tell her story in the studio. But, just before the cops bust in on us, I mentioned that someone had seen the whole business, an' after the hurly-burly of gettin' down the fire escape, Poor was a changed man. He wanted to find out who saw things, an' how much, see? I left him to go after Liss without realizin' that his panic when the cops come was real."

He paused and turned toward the door as Jennie and Mrs. Lathrop came into the living-room. Mrs. Lathrop looked years older than when he had first seen her at No. 19½, Asey thought. She was still white and shaken, but she had calmed down to a state of cold, bitter fury not unlike Chub's when he'd smacked that vicious right to Poor's jaw.

"Jennie didn't want me to get up," Mrs. Lathrop said, "but I've got to understand things. Why did he shoot Liss? *Why?*"

"That's what I want to know, too," the Judge said, as he helped her to a chair. "Why, Asey, if Poor shot Rudi to be sure of Liss, why in the world did he shoot *her?*"

"Because this mornin', after I left him, he went to his apartment," Asey said, "an' got his mornin' mail. An' in it was a letter from Liss, breakin' off their engagement."

"No!" Mrs. Lathrop said. "No!"

"Uh-huh— Look, Mrs. Lathrop; don't you want to go back an' lie down? I mean—"

"I'm perfectly all right!" Mrs. Lathrop said. "It's better that I know about things instead of wondering about them. Why did Liss break it off? Did she get that Hollywood offer she was hoping for?"

"She did," Asey said. "You know, I kept wonderin' why she hadn't told Poor more about the jam she was in. Then I remembered the litter on the desk in her bedroom. All the sheets of stationery crumpled up an' discarded, like she'd had a hard time writin' somethin' the way she wanted it. I wondered if maybe she might have busted things off with Poor. So I broke into your house a while ago, an' those crumpled sheets was the first drafts of her letter to Poor. She'd come to the conclusion that her career was goin' to be more fun than him. Then, when I busted into Poor's apartment, I found the original he got this mornin'—Golly, that reminds me, I got to tell the cops his man's tied up there, an' they better send someone to undo him. Call 'em, will you, Chub? The feller said Poor went wild readin' his mail. An' why shouldn't he? There he'd gone an' shot his supposed rival, an' his girl had jilted him anyway!"

"Was it Poor who phoned in that funny voice?" Mrs. Lathrop sat upright.

"Yes. You were home, which he probably hadn't expected, an' he disguised his voice so's you wouldn't recognize him—" Asey stopped short and mentally kicked himself for bringing up an angle he hadn't intended to mention in front of Mrs. Lathrop.

"Then— Oh, *I* told him where she was! Oh!" Mrs. Lathrop said in anguish. "Oh, it was my fault!"

"I hope you won't reproach yourself about that," Asey said gently, "because I'm sure Poor would have killed her, no matter where he found her. Where she was wouldn't have made any difference. But, you see, you talked quick an' said somethin' to the effect that the cops would know about him. You meant you'd tell them if he didn't stop botherin' you with calls, but Poor heard you wrong. He thought you said that Liss went to the studio, an' the police would know. He thought you was insinuatin' that Liss knew who killed Rudi, an' was goin' to tell the cops, see?"

"I never seen Poor come to the studio buildin'!" Jennie said.

"You wasn't watchin' for him," Asey returned. "Nor did he see you; mercifully, he didn't recognize you in a blue dress any more'n I did. But he saw Peg an' Chub, an' hid till they left. An', when Liss come, he followed her in, an' I gather from what he said that she taunted him into a fury, an' he shot her."

"What I want to know," Jennie said, "is how he got that gun off the swan boat!"

"Chub says that he an' Peg an' Poor went back to the Garden just as the boats was startin' up," Asey said. "You seen 'em then, yourself, Jennie. Chub remembers a boatman warnin' Poor to get out of the way as they hooked a boat up to the landin'. Poor caught his heel, an' slipped, an' fell over the boat—That right, Chub?"

"Yes. It seemed a genuine fall, but that must have been when he spotted the gun and took it."

"I guess," Asey said, "he was realizin' then how haywire his plans had gone, what with the cops not mentionin' Liss, at all, but only worryin' about a bag-snatcher an' her pal."

Jennie sniffed. "Fools!" she said. "Asey, why'd he take that gun if he already had another?"

"Wa-el, by that time, he'd read Liss's letter an' probably was determined to kill her; an' when he spotted that Smith an' Wesson on the swan boat, he was smart enough to grab the opportunity of sneakin' it away. You see, he could use the Smith an' Wesson on Liss, an' leave it behind, an' it'd only be traced back to Judge Sudbury. Probably he figgered that would be a lot smarter an' safer than usin' his own spare gun, that some expert might be able to trace back to him. It ain't easy to pick up guns these days. That's why he had to make such an elaborate plan for swipin' the Judge's."

"Why'd he carry the spare gun anyway?" Jennie interrupted.

Asey shrugged. "Wa-el, he also wore both suspenders an' a belt, if you know what I mean. He planned all along to get rid of the Judge's gun, so I s'pose he wanted to have his own, too, in case he might need it."

"What about that dummy," Jennie demanded, "and Honeywell's Dressing?"

"Honeywell's Dressin' is a hair pomade that old Cap'n Porter used to use," Asey said. "Young Bill Porter sometimes uses it now, unless his wife stops him. It's made by an old barber at the Atlantic Club, an' he loves to sell it. I s'pose Poor figured it give him an air of old Boston. Anyway, when I remembered the smell an' finally placed it, I remembered Chub's tousled hair an' the Judge's flyin' locks, an' how Poor's hair was slicked back, an' how he always wore a hat. He was the only one who'd have used the stuff."

"But the fat-man dummy!" Jennie said.

"Oh, when I seen him first, he wore a green hat, but what was wrong later was that he had a visored cap on—get it? In hot weather, anyone in dark pants, like Poor had on, an' a white shirt an' a black tie an' a visored cap, they're a cop. At least, they are to you, Jennie. To Chub, they're milkmen, an' to the Judge, they're gas-station attendants. An'—"

"And to old Annie," the Judge interrupted, "they're cops, too! I see!"

"Just so. That visored cap was made of cardboard, an' it folds up. Poor left it on the dummy, havin' no further use for it, an' assumin' that people would take it for a studio prop if they noticed it at all. It wasn't anythin' anybody could trace to him, an' even if anyone took the trouble to smell, there wasn't any reason for 'em to trace the smell back to the jar of Honeywell's on Poor's bureau!"

"How," Peg asked, "did you ever start suspecting him?"

"Wa-el, he had the best motive for killin' Brandt. I worried about the Judge for a while"— he grinned at the Judge's look of indignation— "but when I seen him outside the Lathrops' house he didn't act much like a murderer, an' murderers don't usually take their dogs along. Then there was the pomade. An' I knew the feller that got the gun from Annie knew the house layout here, an' the maid arrangements, an', as Annie said, the dogs accepted him, which is more'n they did me! They knew he wasn't a stranger. It all run together—that cop, Jennie's cop, Chub's milkman, the Judge's gas-station man—all somebody with a visored cap."

"Hm!" Jennie said. "Now tell me, smarty, how *did* Liss pick up the gun if she didn't drop it an' no one we could see threw it?"

" 'Member the boy with the David an' Goliath sling at the Washington statue?"

"What's that?" Peg asked. "You mean a forked sling with an elastic?"

"David," Asey told her gently, "didn't have no elastic to toy with in them days. What they called a David an' Goliath sling is two pieces of string with a loop at the end of one, an' a knot at the other, attached to a pouch. The kid we saw hurled his lead soldier an' parachute up into the air by slingin' 'em from a pouch."

"An' that's what Poor used?" Jennie demanded.

"Nope, he used the twine we took from his coat pocket. To think," Asey said, "I *seen* that fall out on the studio floor, when he mopped his face with a handkerchief, back when he was huntin' Liss's dress! But it's the same principle, Jennie. He threaded his twine through the trigger guard of the Smith & Wesson, put both ends of the string in his hand, swung his arm sort of like a pitcher windin' up—only underhand—an' then let go. An' the gun landed just where he meant it to, at her feet, probably fifty-sixty yards away."

"But how could he aim it so it landed at her feet?" Peg demanded.

"With a little practice you can sling pretty accurate," Asey said. "The fellers who used to heave an' haul for bass on North Beach could sling their leaded cod lines out an' hit a chip of driftwood on the nose more'n two hundred feet from shore. I've done it myself. Anyway, Poor shot Brandt—he'd been standin' there waitin' for Brandt to make a good target—an' then he hurled the gun at Liss's feet an' run out to the Garden entrance an' put on his visored cap."

"Why?" Chub asked.

"He was clever enough not to run where folks'd see him runnin'," Asey said. "Standin' there, he was anyone you think of when you see what seems to be a man in uniform. You see, he expected the combination of Brandt's bein' shot an' the gun landin' at her feet would be enough to throw Liss into a panic. He thought she'd run out of the Garden screamin' for the police, or for help—"

"Then why'd he stay there?" Jennie interrupted. "If she'd run screamin' to him, she'd have recognized him right away!"

"Because he naturally expected she'd run toward Boylston Street, the short way out of the Garden, an' not all the way over to Beacon Street; see? Even if she'd taken it into her head to rush home without howlin' for the cops, she'd have cut over toward Arlington Street. You gummed up that part, Jennie. You just plumb chased her out the one entrance Poor never expected her to take. When he seen you larrupin' after her, he fired a shot—he told me he done it on impulse—to scare you off. 'Member I figgered it was somethin' like that? Anyway, then he whipped back to his apartment an' waited for Liss to yell to him for help. If anyone seen him shoot, why it would seem all right, because he was a cop, to all appearances; see?"

"Where'd you go," Jennie asked curiously, "besides the Lathrops', an' Poor's, an' the studio? Where was you the rest of the afternoon?"

"Wa-el," Asey smiled, "I got the red diary Peg took from Rudi's desk."

"*My* diary?" Peg's cheeks flamed. "Did you—you *didn't* read it! You didn't break the lock and read it!"

"Uh-huh. It was very enlightenin'," Asey said, "an' Chub's a very lucky feller. An' maybe it'll be some small consolation to Mrs. Lathrop to know she's goin' to acquire a daughter-in-law—"

"Oh, I am glad!" Mrs. Lathrop brightened. "I'm so glad, Peg dear! Because Liss and I were so worried that Chub would take forever getting around to asking you! He's so conservative about things!"

"Then what else did you do?" Jennie demanded.

"Then," Asey said, "I went an' found out about the really interestin' part of all this. I give Poor credit for that angle. That was good."

"What're you talkin' about?" Jennie demanded.

"Wa-el, all the time everyone kept callin' Poor a tycoon, an' I got to wonderin'," Asey said, "what he was a tycoon of. I found out he owns magazines. Includin' *Fashion-Allure*. But there's no record in the

Fashion-Allure office of any order for any cover like Rudi got that call for yesterday."

"What!" Peg said.

"That was Poor who called. Honest, that was clever of him! Because you'd assume that the editors of *Fashion-Allure* would read about Rudi's death in the papers, an' you wouldn't do anythin' more about that swan-boat cover, would you? I thought not," Asey said as Peg shook her head. "An' you wouldn't think it was funny if you didn't hear from them. In short, no one would do any checkin' up on it. See?"

"No," Peg said. "Frankly, no!"

"Poor called Rudi late yesterday; he knew about the thunderstorms as well as you. He knew the only time Rudi could possibly take any such pictures, in order to get 'em done this afternoon, would be this mornin'; see? So Poor knew that at daybreak today Rudi'd be out there on the landin' by the swan boats in a nice, empty Garden."

"D'you mean that order for that cover was a *fake?*"

"I mean that the cover an' the picture was only the means to the end of placin' Rudi where Poor wanted him. An' Liss, too. Poor admitted that he specified that Liss must be in the picture. That's why he offered such a big price—to make sure Rudi'd do it. Poor told me before they took him away that Rudi first hesitated at the order, an' then said okay. I s'pose Rudi misled you, Peg, knowin' you'd try to talk him out of usin' Liss, like Chub an' Mrs. Lathrop wanted to talk her out of it. Really, it was a smart plot. If it rained, he could call an' set another deadline for the picture. . . . Is that my roadster that cop's drivin' up to the door? Honest," Asey said, "when I went to get that sinker out of my pail, I never seen so many parkin' tags an' tire chalk marks!" Casually, he picked up the silver repeater. "Come on, Jennie. We got to get your bags at the station first."

"You're not going to rush off!" the Judge protested. "The police will need you—"

"They won't need me, Judge," Asey said. "Poor give 'em what amounted to a full confession before they took him off, an' he'll clear up any odds an' ends for 'em, all right! You see, tomorrow the Porter factory gets goin' on new big tanks, an' I got to be there. But I promised myself one last fishin' trip before I go, an', with luck, I can make the tide."

"Land's sakes, my cleanin'!" Jennie said. "I forgot my cleanin'!

Well, if you're goin' to make the tide, I guess I can still get my curtains washed on time! Where's my hat?"

"And why," the Judge said, "are you walking off with my watch, Asey?"

Asey grinned. "Sorry," he said. "That was only a passin' contribution to the Swan-Boat Plot. So long!"

SEED OF SUSPICION

GEORGE HARMON COXE

Kent Murdock had no idea he was being followed. Even later, when he had a chance to think things over, he had no way of knowing whether the man picked him up as he left the office, or stepped out of the shadows as Murdock passed on his way to his Marlborough Street apartment.

It was not late—it had been just ten o'clock when he left the photographic studio at the *Times-Clarion*—and he had been too preoccupied with his thoughts to take notice of those who passed him on the street. To him it was just another night, colder than most, with a damp rawness in the air that promised snow before long, and he walked briskly but unhurriedly, a rangy, moderately tall man, with good shoulders and an erect but easy way of holding himself.

He was between Newbury and Commonwealth when it happened.

There was no warning but a sudden rush of footsteps behind him, and in the instant that he became aware of them, and tried to turn, he saw only darkness in the deserted street and the high brick wall enclosing someone's town house and yard.

Then the arm clamped tight about his neck, yanking him off balance.

A mighty fist clubbed him behind the ear. The arm around his neck was still tight, and he could tell from the size of it and the breadth of chest behind him that the man was big and powerful.

Murdock went limp, purposely, turning a little more as the arm sought a new grip, then hooked viciously with his elbow.

The man grunted and hit him again. The sidewalk tilted, and after that things were a little vague for Murdock. He remembered the series of "muggings" that had occurred during the past week. He heard a hoarse whisper that said, "How do you like it, chump?" and then he was down, a kick in the ribs knocking his breath out before he could roll clear.

"Get up and we'll do it again," the voice said, and hands reached for him. Then Murdock was up, swinging blindly, furiously, but without much strength.

Not that he was any weakling. As the Number One photographer for the *Times-Clarion*, and later as picture chief, he had learned how to handle himself, and he seldom worried about the odds; in this case, however, he'd had no chance to defend himself. Now, already groggy, he went down again under a new blow, but this time the expected kick did not materialize. Somehow, there was light in the street and the man was running.

Murdock got his head up. He heard a car in back of him. A second car swung in from Commonwealth, its headlights sweeping wide, and it was this new brilliance that enabled him to get a fleeting glimpse of his assailant.

He was at the corner now, running hard, yet turning for a last look. Murdock saw only the profile and the size of him, and his head was clear enough now to photograph mentally the underslung jaw and the sharp depression where the bridge of his nose should have been.

Then the fellow was gone, and the cars had stopped and a taxi driver and his fare were running across the street.

They asked him what had happened and was he all right, and then someone spoke his name and he turned, recognizing the tall, spare man who had come from the coupé behind him.

"Oh, hello, Mr. Thatcher," he said. "You were just in time."

"A little late, I'm afraid," Thatcher said.

"Yeah," said the taxi driver and spoke profanely of muggers in general and this one in particular. "A minute earlier and we might have nailed the guy. Sure you're all right, Mac? We could drop you at a doctor's."

"I'll take him, driver," Thatcher said. "He's a friend of mine." He had Murdock by the arm now, turning him toward the coupé, asking him whether he wanted to see a doctor first or go to police headquarters.

Bennett Thatcher was one of the city's finest criminal lawyers. As such, Murdock had photographed him often, and because he still felt a little rocky, he was grateful now for the older man's help.

"I don't need a doctor," he said. "I'd rather raise a row at headquarters."

Bennett Thatcher drove around the block and back along Berkeley Street. "You seem to be getting more than your share of trouble," he said. "I read that paragraph in the *Bulletin* about the business with Lloyd Farnsworth at the Club Flamingo. Last night you had to battle him, and now tonight a thug jumps you."

"It wasn't much of a battle. With Farnsworth, I mean." Murdock had been kidded about the incident several times during the day. "Farnsworth was a little drunk," he said. "He resented my being with his wife."

"A two-punch affair, the *Bulletin* said. Farnsworth missed, and you didn't." Thatcher stopped for a traffic light. "Did this fellow tonight rob you?"

Murdock said no, and now he was thinking of the sequence of action and what the thug had said, and it was then, though he did not realize it at the time, that the first seed of suspicion took root in his consciousness and began slowly to sprout . . .

Lieutenant Bacon had set his feet on his desk and a long black stogie in his mouth when Murdock stepped into the little office on the fourth floor of police headquarters, after having tried in vain to locate a certain captain to whom his complaint should have properly been made.

Bacon, a graying, stiff-backed veteran, glanced up casually, and quickly narrowed his gaze. He swung his feet down and removed the stogie. "Now what?" he said.

Murdock sat down and spoke morosely, "I came in to check on a rumor that's going around that you fellows are collecting the taxpayers' money to protect the public from muggers."

"Not me," said Bacon. "I'm strickly homicide." Then, seeing the slight bruise on the photographer's cheekbone and the resentment in his eyes, he asked, "Who got mugged?"

"Me," said Murdock and told him where and when.

"What did you lose?"

"Nothing."

"Those cars scared him off in time, huh?" Murdock thought it over, and now the suspicion in his mind began to blossom. He heard again the hoarse whisper, "How do you like it, chump? . . . Get up and we'll do it again," and he knew now that these were funny words for a mugger to say.

Furthermore, a man intent on robbery could have knocked him out easily from behind, taken his wallet, and been away in half the time the thug had used. "What?" he said, aware that Bacon had spoken.

"I said if you got any kind of look at him we could go into the Bureau of Records and you could look at pictures."

"Some other time." Murdock stood up. "I've changed my mind. I don't think I was mugged."

"Huh?"

"I think that guy was hired to work me over."

"Yeah? Who by?"

"Lloyd Farnsworth."

Bacon straightened in his chair, his gaze troubled. "Wait a minute. You mean on account of that business at the Flamingo last night? I heard about it but—"

Murdock was no longer listening. For his doubt had become a half certainty. He was sitting again with Rhoda Farnsworth at the Flamingo, seeing Lloyd lurch toward their table, while a pretty, dark-haired girl tried to hold him back. Big, blond, handsome in a soft, decadent way, Lloyd Farnsworth spoke insultingly, and as Murdock rose, he swung hard, missed, and tried to slap his wife. Then Murdock hit him.

Now, remembering it all, recalling the threats and imprecations Farnsworth had mouthed as the waiters hurried him from the room, he found his hunch a sound one. Anger expanded inside him.

Lieutenant Bacon stood up, studying the photographer's stormy dark eyes and the hard, clean line of his jaw, and not liking what he saw. He had known Murdock a long time, had worked with him often and respected him greatly, not only for his honesty and ability as a press-photographer, but for his intelligence and sense of humor.

Murdock was intimidated by no one; he could speak the language of cops and bookies and circulation hustlers, and still be understood by dowagers in drawing rooms. Yet he seldom looked for trouble, and that's what bothered Bacon now. He had never seen Murdock in such a state of suppressed fury and he said so.

"Don't blow your top," he said. "So maybe Farnsworth did hire the guy. Go looking for him now, feeling like you do, and you'll get yourself in a jam."

"If I do I can handle it."

"Maybe—if you wait until tomorrow. Then, if you still feel like it, go ahead and poke him in the nose. Being strictly a rat, he'll probably charge you with assault, and the judge'll slap a fine on you and you'll wish you'd let it ride. But if that's the way you want it—" The Lieutenant put a hand on Murdock's arm. "Come on. I'll drive you home."

"I can walk."

Bacon hesitated, his eyes wise. "Okay. Walk. Maybe that'll cool you off. Maybe, between here and your place, you'll start to think again. If you do, remember what I said. Don't go looking for Lloyd Farnsworth tonight."

Kent Murdock remembered the words as he walked cross-town, striding hard, eyes up but unaware of his surroundings. By the time he had crossed Boylston he had begun to think again, and when he turned into the entrance of the small apartment house his boiling rage had been reduced to the simmering stage and common sense was exerting its steadying hand.

It was still impossible to think of Lloyd Farnsworth without rancor, and his bitterness had deeper roots than the affair at the Flamingo and the beating he had received tonight. It was a resentment of long standing, based on the suffering and humiliation Farnsworth had inflicted on his wife; and only now could Murdock appreciate the soundness of Bacon's advice that his desire to strike back be postponed until another time.

He was crossing the little foyer with this in mind when the woman rose from the settee by the elevator and came to meet him, tall and blonde and bareheaded, her mink coat covering a simple woolen dress.

"I phoned your office," Rhoda Farnsworth said. "They told me you'd left, so I thought I'd wait."

He took her hands in his, surprised that she should come here like this. He regarded her anxiously. "Has he been bothering you again?"

"No, Kent. I haven't seen him since last night."

"Something is. Bothering you, I mean. Come on."

Upstairs he made no further reference to the reason for her visit, but offered a drink, and when she refused, made one for himself. He excused himself and washed up, seeing now that there was no mark on his face except the small, faint bruise on one cheek.

When he had finished he sat down opposite her and said, "Now."

"It isn't anything," she said. "I'm going away for a while. I wanted to say goodbye."

She rose, leaving her coat on the sofa, and paced across the room, a gracefully slender woman, with gray eyes, a wide, mobile mouth, and honey-colored hair drawn tight back at the sides and worn in a low bun. When she stopped to stare out the window, his mind went back and he remembered how it had been in the beginning. She had been nineteen at the time, a gay, vital girl, spoiled, but good inside and genuine.

They had talked of love and marriage then, and it had been Murdock who hesitated. For she had money of her own, and he had been a sixty-a-week press photographer; he had been afraid of what might happen. But they were young and there were no lasting scars, and even with the beaux that followed they had remained friends.

She had been away when he was discharged from the Army. She had come back six months ago and called him, and because the thing that had once been between them had been fine and honest, the basis of their companionship was sound. They had lunch now and then, or cocktails, or occasionally a dinner. And they talked. That was all. Neither, it seemed, wanted or expected more.

It had been that way when Lloyd Farnsworth came back from Mexico City, three months later. He had his apartment and Rhoda had hers, but they remained legally married, and it was his nature to see that she did not forget this. Murdock had seen the bruises on her wrists and arms, and knew there must be other bruises that did not show.

When he asked why she did not get a divorce, she gave him an answer he had to accept, though he felt sure there must be another reason she would not discuss. . . .

"You don't have to leave," Murdock said.

"You don't know him. After last night he won't rest until he gets even."

"I'll take care of that." Murdock went on to tell what had happened during the past hour, seeing her gray eyes widen with disbelief and then with fear.

"Yes," she breathed. "It would be like Lloyd to do a thing like that."

"Physical punishment is a thing he understands." Murdock hesitated, his anger starting to build again. "He's been handing it out quite a while. A dose of the same medicine properly applied might cure him," he said.

The telephone rang, and he picked it up. "Yes," he said, and then stiffened as the familiar voice came to him.

"Hear you had a little trouble tonight," Lloyd Farnsworth said.

Murdock had difficulty talking. The taunting phrase smashed his defenses, and all the bitterness and resentment came surging back. He started to speak, and found he had to swallow first. He said, "Where are you?"

Farnsworth's reply was measured and distinct. "If you want to settle things, come on up."

"I'll be there," Murdock said.

Kent hung up, shaking a little with this new anger he no longer tried to control, the things in his mind written clearly in his hot, dark eyes and the tight lines of his face.

Rhoda Farnsworth saw it all and guessed the answer. She gave a little cry when he confirmed her fears; she pleaded with him, her voice distressed. "No, Kent! Please! I've caused you enough trouble."

Murdock got his coat and hat, and she kept pace with him. "You don't know him," she said. "You don't know how strong he is. Last night he was drunk."

"You mean he's bigger than I am." Murdock held her coat, his smile grim. "Come on, baby. And stop worrying. This is no trouble; this will be a pleasure."

He got her out of the apartment, closing his mind to the things she said, and on the sidewalk she knew further talk was useless and was quiet as he handed her into her car.

He waited until she drove off, and then walked quickly to Beacon Street, looking for a taxi. There was some traffic here, a few cabs, but none that were empty. He kept walking, his rage riding him.

He forgot about the taxi until he started to cross Massachusetts Avenue, and then, aware that he had but three blocks farther to go, decided to do without one. As a result, it took him a good twenty-five minutes to reach the block-long street where Lloyd Farnsworth lived on the top floor of a remodeled three-story brick house.

It was quiet here at the moment, and dark. The little park across the way was deserted. There were a few cars parked in front of the apartments on the east side of the street, but on the park side there was only one, a heavy coupé with a three-digit license number which Murdock noted absently and from long habit, since low numbers often signified owners of some importance.

He noticed, too, that the coupé was empty, and then he turned into Farnsworth's house. He found the lower door unlocked, and climbed swiftly to the top floor.

He knocked loudly on the heavy wooden door. When a muffled voice called from within, he opened the door. He stepped into the entrance hall and saw the lighted room beyond. He took one step, and then, without warning, the lights went out.

Before he could turn, before he could close the door or duck away from the certain peril he now knew was close, something slammed down on his head, and he felt himself falling as the pain exploded inside him . . .

When Kent Murdock opened his eyes he was flat on his back and the room lights were on. It did not mean anything to him, then; nothing meant anything but the ache in his head and the nausea at the pit of his stomach.

He tried to look about, but his neck hurt when he twisted it; so he rolled slowly over and got his knees under him, pushing and turning until he could sit up. His hat was off and he explored his head, finding that the source of pain was a lump over one ear. His face hurt, too, and he wondered about that.

He wanted to lie down again, but he didn't. He moved his hand to brace himself, and it touched metal. When he glanced down he found the object, a heavy brass candlestick he had never seen before. As he stared at it, seeing now the dark stain on the top edge, he remembered how the lights had gone out as he stood in the hall.

But the lights were on again and he was no longer in the hall. He was in an enormous living room, with portraits on the walls and two life-size nudes, one a dark-haired woman sitting at a dressing table, and the other a full-length profile of a girl with a mirror in her hand.

Then, as he began to think again, he glanced back at the brass candlestick, a growing sense of horror pressing in on him.

He got quickly to his feet. That was when he saw Lloyd Farnsworth.

In life a big, well-built man with wavy blond hair and a smooth, tanned skin, he now lay in front of a kneehole desk, face down, one arm crumpled under him. Even from where he stood, Murdock could see the matted darkness of the blond hair, the dark red spots on the rug. And it was then that the answer came to him.

For Murdock had seen and photographed too many dead men to be in any doubt about Farnsworth. In that same instant that he caught his breath and fought against the shock of his discovery, he understood the meaning of the red-tarnished candlestick, and knew with intuitive certainty that his own fingerprints would be on it.

Other things came to him with discouraging finality. He touched his face and found new marks there to explain the soreness he had felt. He looked at his right hand and saw the skinned knuckles. Then he moved quickly to Farnsworth and, kneeling down, found other marks on the man's cheekbone.

The scene was so circumstantially perfect that there was one terrifying moment when he wondered if perhaps he had not done this thing and forgotten it, like fighters he had heard of who, out on their feet, kept punching on instinct alone until consciousness finally returned.

He shook off the thought with an effort and walked quickly through the apartment. In the bathroom he examined his face and saw the cut chin and the new lump on his jaw. He went into the bedroom, not looking for anything, but moving dazedly as he waited for the shock to pass.

A leather-framed portrait of a smiling, dark-haired girl stood on the bureau. Across it was scrawled *All my love, Nancy,* and he knew this was the girl who had been with Farnsworth the night before.

He went back into the living room, trying to think reasonably, wondering what he should do. When he found himself staring again at the candlestick he bent down and polished it clean with his handkerchief, all but the darkened edge.

Yet, even as he put it back, he knew this was not enough. If the killer was as smart as he seemed, there would be other prints on other objects in the room—prints that would match exactly Murdock's own. And now, standing there with his thoughts bogged down in hopelessness and dismay, he remembered his talk with Lieutenant Bacon.

Bacon would recall each detail, once the murder was discovered, and he would amplify and embellish these details with supposition and suspicion. Bacon was his friend, yet Bacon would have no choice but to arrest him, under the circumstances. Therefore, the thing to do was to get out while he could, give himself a chance to think, and make his plans.

This much was clear, and still he did not go. Perhaps it was because he was tired, beaten, and discouraged. Whatever the reason, he dropped down on the desk chair. That was how he happened to see the torn pieces of paper on the floor.

He went to one knee, knowing what they were now, not picking them up but nudging the bits in place, like a puzzle, until he had pieced together two Pullman tickets to Miami, Florida, and a reservation for a stateroom. After staring at them a moment, he scrambled the pieces with his hand and dropped back on the chair. Then, for want of something better to do, he began absently to open the desk drawers.

He saw at once that those at the sides were in order, and he did not disturb the contents. He might have gone away then had he not found the center drawer locked. It challenged him, and hardly aware of what he did, he went to Farnsworth, slid one hand into a trouser pocket until he found a ring of keys.

He straightened, and began moving to the desk as he examined them; then, unaccountably, he stopped. He found himself listening.

In spite of himself, he turned and looked about the room, as though half expecting to find someone lurking in the shadowed corners. The next moment he heard the sound that warned him of danger: the strident whine of tires as a speeding automobile rounded a nearby corner. With it came the throb of the motor, rising briefly, then falling away as the power was cut and the car drew closer.

He was at the window overlooking the street when the small sedan swerved in front of the building and rocked to a stop. He saw the three men jump out below him, one of them in uniform. When they crossed the sidewalk, Murdock wheeled from the window and ran down the hall toward the kitchen.

At the far side of this was a door. He tried it, handkerchief in hand, found it unlocked, opened it, and went out fast, feeling his way down the black stair well. A minute later he was in a narrow alley, its open end silhouetted against the night sky.

Groping his way along, he reached the corner without difficulty. He crossed to the little park, moved thirty feet inside its line of trees, and keeping in the deep shadows, he started back. The police car, he saw, was empty. He glanced up and could see no movement behind the Venetian blinds of Farnsworth's front room.

Then, about to back away, he noticed that the heavy coupé with its low license number was no longer there; instead, a dark sedan was parked diagonally across from the house, and the man behind the wheel seemed intent on it and the police car.

Murdock picked out a tree near the curbing, and stood behind it. The man in the sedan seemed vaguely familiar. As Murdock watched, the dashlight flicked on and the motor started.

Murdock recognized the driver, then. Dr. John Carlton. What made it important was that Carlton, like Murdock, had once been in love with Rhoda Farnsworth . . .

Jack Fenner had an apartment off Hemenway Street, within easy walking distance of Lloyd Farnsworth's place. Murdock thought of it almost at once, not only because it was close, but because Fenner, besides being a friend of long standing, was probably the best private detective in the city.

Luckily, Fenner was in. He was a medium-sized man with a look of sinewy toughness about him and a sharply chiseled face. His quick agate eyes took one look at Murdock's face and expression, and he suppressed the wisecrack he would have normally made.

"You know where the bathroom is," he said. "Clean up. I'll make a drink." He locked the door and went off to the kitchen. When he had the drinks he came into the bathroom and nodded his approval. "You look better already," he said. "Here."

Murdock took the drink, swallowed gratefully while Fenner administered to the cut chin and skinned knuckles. When he had finished, they went into the living room and Fenner made another drink for his guest. Murdock told his story from the beginning, while Fenner slumped in his chair and listened.

"You were smart to come here," he said when Murdock finished.

"I wanted to talk to you before I went home."

"You're not going home," Fenner said. "After what you told Bacon, he's probably got a man there waiting for you now. He's got to arrest you. If I was a dick I'd have to arrest you. And murder is not a bailable offense in this city."

Murdock sighed. He said, "They'll get me, anyway. And when they do, if they find out you put me up, they'll make you an accessory."

"Probably."

"You'll lose your license. And then what'll you do?"

Fenner opened his eyes and grinned. "If we try hard and get to be model prisoners," he said dryly, "they might let us play gin rummy a couple of nights a week." He stood up, his manner abrupt. "Come on, snap out of it! You've cracked jobs like this before. Let's see what we've got."

Fenner started pacing, and Murdock watched him. It made him feel good, knowing how Fenner felt, hearing him talk.

"Farnsworth hired a thug to beat you up," the detective said. "He did it in such a way that you'd probably tumble to what was behind it. You did tumble. You told Bacon. Then Farnsworth got scared you weren't coming up so he could beat the tar out of you, so he phoned and dared you to come. The trouble was, somebody must have been with him when he made that call, and your luck was bad. Probably this guy had been wanting to kill Farnsworth for a long time, and all of a sudden he knows this is the perfect setup. He beats Farnsworth's skull in, lays for you, marks you up, and frames it neat; then he goes out and tips off the cops."

He paused, brow wrinkled. "Either that, or the guy comes in just after Farnsworth made the call and Farnsworth tells him what's cooking—and the guy jumps him. How long did it take you to get there? . . . Twenty-five minutes would have given the killer plenty of time. Now, who'd want to kill him?"

Fenner glanced up, as though just realizing what he'd said. He shrugged and grunted disparagingly.

"That's a silly question," he said. "There must be a dozen guys who would've liked to kill him. Dames, too. He painted enough of them—with and without their clothes. There was something wrong with him, something morbid. He was nuts."

"He was a pretty fair painter."

"Yeah. I understand he could get fifteen hundred a throw."

"He got the women, too," Murdock said, his thoughts sliding off on a tangent.

"Sure. He was big and blond and handsome, and he had the kind of smile that promised women whatever they wanted. I don't know how else you can explain it. They knew the reputation he had, but they kept coming, letting him do portraits of them, figuring this time it would be different."

He glanced up, one lid half shut. "His wife is an old friend of yours, huh? He didn't care anything about her, did he? Then why didn't she divorce him?"

"She had a lot of pride," Murdock said. "She was young, then, and spoiled by too much money and not enough responsibility. Everyone advised her against the marriage, but she went ahead, and afterward, when it blew up, she didn't want to admit it."

"To stick it out as long as she did there must've been another reason."

"I think you're right," Murdock said. "But she says no."

Fenner yawned and got up. "Let's go to bed. Let's sleep on it, and tomorrow I'll nose around and see what the score is."

In the morning Jack Fenner went out for newspapers while Murdock put breakfast on the table. When the detective returned, he pointed to a half-column story in the *Times-Clarion*.

Murdock scanned it but found no mention of his name. Police, summoned by an anonymous tip, said the paper, had gone to Lloyd Farnsworth's apartment shortly before midnight and found him dead of a fractured skull . . . Several clues had been uncovered . . . Pending an arrest, the veil of official silence had been drawn about the case. That was all.

"I'll be in the bulldog edition of the afternoon sheets," Murdock said morosely. "I wonder what they'll use for a picture, if any."

"Cut it out!" Fenner said. "Eat!"

Murdock obeyed and found he was hungry. He felt better when he had finished, and went directly to the telephone. He dialed the *Times-Clarion* and asked for T. A. Wyman, the Managing Editor.

Wyman's reaction to the call was characteristic. "Are you all right?'' he asked first. Then, having satisfied himself on this point, he said, "Are you crazy?"

He wanted to know where Murdock was, and what he thought he was doing by hiding out, and why he didn't come down and thrash things out properly.

Murdock said he had an idea the police were looking for him; that was why he couldn't come in yet. He said he had some things to do first, and once the police caught him they'd probably hold him without bail.

"Not for long, they won't," Wyman said. "You want to bet? . . . I talked to Bennett Thatcher," he said. "He's agreed to handle the case."

Murdock took a breath and felt immeasurably better. Not just because Wyman had hired the best lawyer in town for him, but because Wyman assumed his innocence, unquestioningly.

"All right," he said. "I'll see him. But not downtown. I don't want to get picked up."

"I'll call him," Wyman said. "I'll tell Thatcher to wait for you at his home, and that you'll be there in an hour. Okay?"

Jack Fenner nodded approval when Murdock relayed the information. "If you've got Thatcher you're halfway off the hook already." He rummaged around in the closet and brought out a trench coat and a gray felt hat. "You wore a brown hat and a brown topcoat. Today you wear a gray hat and a trench coat—and these."

He produced a pair of tinted, shell-rimmed glasses, not dark enough to be conspicuous, but with off-white lenses.

"Don't flag any taxis," he added. "You know too many drivers. Get your cabs at the stands after you've looked over the hackies. Come back here and wait for me after you've finished with Thatcher."

"And what'll you be doing?

"The best I can."

Murdock watched Fenner move toward the door, and then stopped him. He remembered John Carlton and his sedan the night before and his interest in Farnsworth's place. He remembered the heavy coupé that had been parked outside when he went in, and had been gone when he came out. He gave the detective the three-digit number, and asked him to check it, and told him why.

Fenner was interested. "Will do," he said. "That's a good place to start."

* * *

Bennett Thatcher lived with two servants in a brick-and-frame Tudor house in the suburbs, and when Murdock rang, Thatcher himself opened the door and led the way across the paneled hall and into the high-ceilinged drawing room. Here Murdock stopped to gaze at the portrait over the mantel, which showed a slim, golden-haired woman in a simple evening gown, a woman of perhaps twenty-eight, delicately made, with a gentle mouth and smiling eyes.

He remembered her now, and the wedding, some six years back, of the successful middle-aged lawyer and this girl not long out of college. Murdock had been in the Army at the time of her death, but he had since heard that it had happened as the result of an accidental overdose of sleeping tablets, and he knew that because of this, Thatcher had taken the lead in advocating state legislation to restrict the sale of barbiturates. Yet it was not these things that held Murdock now, but rather the beauty of the portrait.

Thatcher, following his glance, looked at the picture, too. Thatcher was a neat, well-groomed man with a lean, fit look about him not often seen in men of fifty. A shrewd, implacable adversary in a courtroom, he had a crisp, direct way of talking that fitted perfectly his naturally stern countenance and steady, penetrating gaze. Yet now looking up at the portrait, there was little of the lawyer about him and no sternness at all in his eyes.

"She's beautiful, isn't she?" he said. He hesitated, continued presently, his tone quiet. "She gave it to me for my birthday two years ago, as a surprise. I lost her only two months later, and but for this I would have nothing left but memories . . . She was the only woman I ever loved," he added simply, and then, as though reluctant to display his emotions further, he motioned toward the adjoining study.

"Let's go in here," he said, "and talk about you . . . Did you kill him?" he asked when they were seated.

Murdock's eyes darkened and his voice was as blunt as Thatcher's. "What do you think?"

The lawyer shrugged. "It's a question I always ask. It doesn't make much difference, but I like to know. Suppose you start from the time you entered police headquarters last night. And I want all the details, understand?"

Murdock told the same story he had related to Jack Fenner, and

Thatcher, sitting in his desk chair and staring out the window, came up with much the same reaction.

"It seems obvious enough," he said. "Whoever knew of Farnsworth's phone call to you killed him, then bruised his face and yours to make this hypothetical fight look authentic." He stuck his bony jaw out, massaged it briefly.

"That makes it bad," he said. "You've got a lot of friends around town; the police know you. If Farnsworth was shot to death it would look better, because the police know you're not the sort to go out with a gun to settle a personal grudge. But from things I've heard about you, you might use your fists. As a matter of fact, that is exactly what you started out to do . . . Maybe that's a break for us," he said presently. "Looking at it in the right way, it might work to your advantage."

Murdock grunted softly. "I'm glad something works to my advantage."

"What I mean is, with the physical facts as they are, you could never be convicted of first-degree murder. You went there without a weapon and premeditation could not be proved."

Murdock had a sarcastic answer for that, too, but he kept it to himself.

"I think we could make a deal right now for a manslaughter charge," the lawyer said. "In court I might even get an acquittal on self-defense."

"It's not enough," Murdock cut in. "I'm not interested in an acquittal. If I stand trial, acquitted or not, a lot of people are going to remember. Always I'll be the guy who murdered Lloyd Farnsworth, and I say that's no good. I didn't kill him, and I don't want to stand trial on any charge."

Thatcher's brows came up. "What do you suggest?"

"Ha!" Murdock's laugh was abrupt and unpleasant. "I suggest I go out and find out who *did* kill him."

Thatcher smiled briefly to show he appreciated the sardonic humor of the remark. "That would be the ideal solution, of course, but—" He paused, his fingers drumming the desk top. "What you want is time—right?"

"I want to stay out of jail. I'll surrender on any charge, provided I can get bail."

"All right." Thatcher sat up, his tone brisk. "That makes sense.

The police don't know yet that I'm acting for you. I understand they have certain evidence that points conclusively to your guilt, according to them. I'll find out about it. I'll see the District Attorney and throw my weight around. With your record and the *Times-Clarion* behind you I think we'll make out all right."

He stood up and shook hands. "Call me tonight. And don't worry about it. Also"—he hesitated, smiled again—"try not to get yourself caught until I know where we stand."

When Jack Fenner came back to the apartment shortly after six that evening he brought a newspaper that said the police were looking for Kent Murdock; also some news of his own.

"That coupé you saw last night with the three-figure number belongs to Rudy Yates," he said.

"The gangster?"

"Ex-gangster," Fenner said. "And what do you think? Rudy came to see me this afternoon." He took out a hundred-dollar bill and spread it on the kitchen table. "Retainer."

Murdock peered at him, dark eyes puzzled. "Why?" he asked. "Why should Rudy come to you?"

"On account of my reputation and great ability. Also," Fenner said, "I think he was playing the odds. He knows you're in hiding, and he knows I'm a friend of yours. He wants to see you."

"About what?"

"He didn't say." Fenner folded the bill and pocketed it lovingly. "I sort of made a tentative date for you. At the Club 66."

Murdock greeted the remark with a grunt of derision. "Oh, fine," he said, recalling the club's central location, popularity, and reputation for decorous dancing and good food. "I just walk in and ask for Rudy and wait for the police."

"No," said Fenner. "You go down the alley beside it, coming in from the street behind, and you sneak up to a certain door that I will tell you about, and walk in."

"It'll be all unlocked for me, of course."

"Of course. Because I'll go in first and unlock it." Fenner grinned. "Then you cross the hall to the first door on the left and open it, and that is Rudy's office. He don't know when you're coming, or if you're coming at all, so it ought to be a surprise."

Murdock thought it over and liked the idea.

"Yes," he said. "I can ask Rudy about his coupé. He might even know something about those torn Pullman tickets I found."

Judging by the procession of taxis that stopped to discharge passengers, business at Club 66 was good at 9:40 that night. Out front, the street lamps and a fancy marquee made the entrance a well-lighted and inviting spot; but forty feet back from the sidewalk the alley was dark and windy, and Murdock had to grope his way to find the proper door.

It was unlocked, as Jack Fenner had promised, and with a quick backward glance to make sure he was alone, Murdock stepped into a narrow, dimly lighted hall and crossed diagonally to another door marked: PRIVATE. He moved in without knocking.

It was a squarish room with another door on the left, no windows, modern furniture, and indirect lighting. Opposite the hall door was a white, flat-topped desk and behind it sat a black-eyed man of forty or so, with a pink, freshly massaged face that looked more muscular than soft, and sleek black hair. In that first instant as he glanced up, the mouth was hard, the eyes annoyed; then, as he leaned back, the lips relaxed.

"Hello," Rudy Yates said. "I've been looking for you, Murdock. Sit down."

Murdock turned down his coat collar and leaned back against the door, surveying Yates's stocky, dinner-jacketed figure, the carnation in his buttonhole. He took his time saying hello, and remembered many things.

Rudy Yates had started young, and until recently his business had been rackets, any kind of racket promising generous profits. He had done exceedingly well. He had sufficient resources to enter heavily into early-war black-market activities in tires and nylons and second-hand cars, and though he had been indicted for his activities in such used cars, the case had not come to trial.

More lately he had worn a more legitimate mantle. His Club 66 was a model of propriety, catering neither to gangsters, hepcats, nor swing music. He had extensive real estate holdings, with offices downtown. He dressed expensively and spoke, not out of the side of his mouth, but with suave politeness.

Murdock thought of all these things as he stood there, but his eyes were no longer on Rudy Yates; they were fastened on the photograph of a dark-haired, vivacious-looking girl which stood on the bookcase. It was the same girl who had signed her name *Nancy* on the photograph he had seen last night in Farnsworth's bedroom.

"I heard you did a job on Lloyd Farnsworth last night," Yates said.

"You ought to know," Murdock said. "You were there." He watched something flicker in Yates's narrowed eyes and said, "What did you want to see me about?"

Rudy Yates selected a cigar from a silver humidor, offered it to Murdock, then closed the lid when his offer was refused. He carefully removed one end with a gold cutter, then gestured toward the photograph before inserting the cigar in his mouth.

"I've got a kid sister," he said. "She doesn't like me much right now. She's been chasing around with Farnsworth."

"She was with him the other night at the Flamingo."

"She moved out of my place a month ago." Yates shrugged. "She's twenty-one, and I couldn't stop her. She has a little flat, and a job as a model. She has a swell boy from a nice family—name of Wordell—in love with her, but she won't give him a tumble since she's been going with Farnsworth."

He removed the cigar, examined it. "She thinks I killed him last night. She's making trouble for me."

"Why?"

"I suppose it's because I told her I would have Farnsworth's pretty face spoiled if she kept on seeing him."

"So?"

"So I have to convince her I didn't do it."

Murdock reached for a cigarette, his smile humorless. "That'll be a little tough to do, won't it? You were there last night and"—he hesitated, remembering the torn Pullman tickets, and decided to take a shot in the dark—"you knew she was about ready to run off to Florida with Farnsworth."

Murdock did not get the reaction he expected; he got no reaction at all. Nothing changed in the broad, pink face. Yates dropped his hand behind the desk, and Murdock thought it might come up with a gun. Instead of that, Yates produced a lighter and spoke between puffs.

"She thinks I did it," he said, as though there had been no interruption, "and I think you did. So do the police and that I like." He turned as the door in the side wall opened, and said, "Come in, boys."

The two men who entered, apparently in response to a buzzer Yates had pressed when he reached for the lighter, took two forward steps and stopped. One was about Murdock's height and weight, but younger, with curly brown hair and a pug nose; the other was older, heavier, and partly bald. Both watched the press photographer coldly and without interest.

"The more the police figure you," Yates continued calmly, "the more it takes the pressure off me. With my sister. And the longer you stay lost, the better I'll like it."

Murdock got it, then. He was not yet sure that Yates had killed Farnsworth, but he knew how his own disappearance would look to the police and Bennett Thatcher and the newspapers. A half hour ago he had been avoiding the authorities; now he wished he hadn't. He said, "Not even you could square a kidnapping charge, Yates."

"Kidnapping? I think not. You came here of your own accord. I have a pleasant room upstairs that you'll find quite comfortable."

"No, thanks," Murdock said, and reached behind him for the doorknob.

Yates, not stirring in his chair, said, "Take him, boys."

They were moving as Yates spoke, the big man first.

"Let's be nice, bub," he said, and then his hand lunged forward.

Murdock said nothing. He knew it would do no good, but he was too angry to care. He stepped inside the big hand and, moving forward, hooked hard with his right and followed through.

The fellow grunted and went backward, fighting to keep his balance. His legs caught the edge of a chair, and he sat down. But he came up fast, his face ugly, and as Murdock reached again for the door the curly-headed youth started to pull a gun. Then the door Murdock was reaching for banged open, knocking him aside.

Jack Fenner came in fast. He had one hand in his coat pocket, and his agate eyes took in the room in a glance. Rudy Yates was still in his chair. The big man had stopped his rush, and the gun in Curlyhead's hand was still half in his pocket.

Fenner said, "Hold it, Curly!" and smiled. He did not take his hand out of his pocket. He did not have to.

Rudy Yates sat motionless in his chair, and for the first time he looked worried. The big man still glared. Curly looked defiant, but he didn't move his hand. He spoke to Yates.

"I think we could take the two of 'em," he said.

A muscle tightened in Rudy's jaw and was still. He leaned back. He spread his hands and started to smile. "I think not . . . Shut up!" he said when Curly started to bluster. "You don't know how lucky you are. All right, Jack," he said. "It's your move."

Fenner told Curly to drop his gun, and this time the youth pulled his hand out empty. Fenner removed his own hand and jerked his head at Murdock.

"Beat it," he said. "The way you came in. I'll stick around and keep Rudy company . . . See you later, chum," he said, and winked.

Nancy Yates had a small, walk-up apartment not far from Fenner's, a shabby, gray-brick structure with uncarpeted halls and the smell of dry rot and stale food in the stairwell. Murdock, arriving at 10:30, knocked at the door, which was opened on a chain lock while he was inspected by a pair of suspicious dark eyes.

"I'm Kent Murdock," he said. "I want to talk to you about Lloyd Farnsworth."

The lashes went wide. For a moment Murdock thought she was going to slam the door. Then she said, "Just a minute," and after a brief pause she reappeared and unfastened the chain.

He thanked her, hat in hand, and went inside, hearing the door close behind him. When he turned she was leaning against the panel, her face white and her mouth set. In her right hand she held a gun and it was pointed right at him.

"You killed him," she whispered.

Murdock stood still, holding his breath. He was eight feet from the gun. He knew he could not reach it in time, and he knew from the way she held it that she was not used to guns and that was what scared him most—the thought that it could easily go off before she realized it.

He quickly put on a grin and tried to speak calmly.

"You're tougher than your brother," he said. "I've just been down to see him. I guess he's been telling you that I killed Farnsworth."

"The papers say so."

"And what're you going to do with the gun? Shoot me, or turn me over to the police?" He kept his grin constant, and when she did not reply he tossed his hat aside. "You know what Rudy told me? He told me you thought *he* did it, and I'm beginning to think he did. I know one thing—he was there last night."

Nancy Yates let the muzzle waver. She moistened her lips. "I don't believe you."

"His car was out front," Murdock said, and went on to tell about the torn tickets he had found. "I guess you were going away with Farnsworth."

"I—I was," the girl said.

"You must have loved him very much."

There was no answer to this except the tears that welled up on her eyes. She tried to blink them back and could not, and finally used the back of her hand. Murdock moved slowly toward her, offering his handkerchief.

"I don't want it," the girl said and turned her head. As she did so, Murdock reached down and gently took the gun from her hand.

When he had removed the bullets he put them and the gun on the table. She was watching him now. He produced cigarettes and handed her one. When he had given her a light he went to the couch and sat down as if it were a thing he had often done here.

She still stood at the door, a small, finely modeled girl in a skirt and blouse that made her look even younger than she was. Murdock began to talk.

"So you really think Farnsworth was in love with you," he said.

"He was."

He shook his head, smiling. "I suppose he told you he was going to marry you."

"Yes." She squared her shoulders, and her chin was set. "Next year. When he got a divorce from his wife."

"That's a long time. Why wait?"

"She was going to make a settlement. He said he'd waited this long and he might as well wait until she was thirty—that would be next year—when she got her money. Then she could pay him."

He sighed for her benefit, registering what he hoped would seem like mild amazement. "I'm a little surprised at you," he said. "You're a modern girl and you've been around a little and had a good education. You must have known about the other times and the other women who came before you. Just because he wanted to go away with you for a while is no sign that—"

"Oh!" She was outraged and furious. "You don't believe me?" she said. "Well, I'll show you."

And with that she hurried to a secretary, opened the bottom drawer, and took out a flat, green metal box measuring about nine by twelve inches.

"There," she said, eyes snapping as she thrust it toward him. "I guess that will prove he loved me. He wanted me to keep it for him, because he trusted me and . . ."

Murdock did not hear the rest of it. He was examining the box and the lock, remembering now the keys he had taken from Farnsworth. He asked what was in it. Nancy said she didn't know, she had no key.

"Maybe I have," Murdock said. He produced Farnsworth's, spreading them wide in his palm. One of them worked. He lifted the lid, and the girl dropped on the couch beside him, her head close to his as he began to remove the contents.

There were a half dozen bonds, some stock certificates. There was a red-leather notebook filled with names, dates, prices, and titles, to indicate the paintings Farnsworth had sold and to whom. There was a legal-size envelope sealed with wax. On the face of it was the name: *Rudolph Yates*.

Murdock's interest quickened. "What's in that?" he demanded.

"Papers." Nancy Yates glanced away.

"What kind of papers?"

"Well, you know—affidavits, I guess you call them. About some used-car business Rudy was once in."

Murdock remembered the indictment against Rudy Yates, the case that never came to trial. "You mean if the District Attorney had these Rudy might go to jail? How did they get here?"

The girl flushed. She bowed her head, and now her voice was barely audible. "I—I stole them," she said. "From Rudy's desk." Then, having made the admission, she raised her head, and the words rushed out. "I had to," she said. "Rudy said he'd take care of Lloyd if I didn't stop seeing him. He said he'd fix his face so no woman would ever look at him. Don't you see I—?"

"Yes," Murdock said grimly. "Rudy knew Lloyd had the envelope and what would happen if he bothered him. Only, last night, when Rudy came, the envelope wasn't there . . . All right," he said, "I guess that proves you loved him."

He did not add that the envelope might possibly make a second motive for murder, but reached for another envelope in the metal box.

This one was not sealed, and when he opened it he saw that it contained a photograph and a photostat. He looked at the photograph first, taking in its story in a glance, and then sat there, incredulous.

For the photograph showed a sidewalk scene, a hotel entrance and part of a marquee. Leaving the entrance, arm in arm, were Rhoda Farnsworth and Dr. John Carlton in his navy lieutenant's uniform. The photostat of a registration card from a hotel in San Francisco completed the story; it was signed: *Lieut. & Mrs. John Carlton.*

Murdock calmly put the picture back in the envelope and stood up. "I'll take this," he said. "And the leather notebook." He put the other things back in the box and locked it up. "You keep this," he said. "No one knows about it but us."

At the door he shook hands with her and thanked her for her help.

"We're in it together," he said. "I want to find out who killed Lloyd Farnsworth. Do you?" He saw her nod, that odd expression still in her gaze. "You'd better think it over," he said, "because it might be your brother."

He opened the door. When he turned to close it she was still watching him, her mouth slack and fear in her eyes . . .

Jack Fenner put aside the mystery book he had been reading and listened carefully to Murdock's story. When he had it all, he stood up and grunted softly, his grin crooked.

"What a guy with the dames," he said.

Murdock, busy with the drink Fenner had furnished, made no comment, and the detective began to examine Farnsworth's red-leather notebook. Presently he looked up, to eye Murdock narrowly. "You know what I think this is?"

"It's a record of sales."

"It's more than that. Rumor hath it, as we big shots often say, that Farnsworth did a bit of blackmailing. Lord knows he had opportunity enough, considering all the dames that fell for him. And my guess is that he sold a lot of paintings that way." Fenner tapped the book.

"Some of these names are legitimate collectors; maybe some bought paintings because they liked them. I think a lot of women bought them because they had to, or else. But wherever Farnsworth listed more than one sale to the same person, maybe a little blackmail was the persuader. There are three people who bought two," he said, and read off the names, which meant nothing to Murdock. "One guy bought three: Dr. John Carlton."

Murdock sat up fast and held out his hand. "Let's see." He verified the statement, and Fenner continued, "You've got two good suspects in Yates and Carlton. Both were there last night and both had motives, and I guess of the two I like Carlton's best. He's got a good practice, a nice wife, a little boy, all of which would blow higher than a kite if Farnsworth got nasty. The trouble is there are probably other people who have just as good motives that we don't know about."

He sat down with his drink, his mood reminiscent, and Murdock listened.

"I've heard plenty of stories about him," the detective said. "I don't know how true they are, but at least one dame is supposed to have committed suicide on his account, and a couple of times he was run out of town by irate husbands. He did a lot of nude jobs, so they say. I understand he'd sometimes do a nude of a lady friend and paint a different face on it so he could exhibit it. Sometimes I guess he didn't always change the face. I guess a woman might buy a picture like that later on—just to destroy it, huh?"

Fenner expected no answer. He went on, "Gene Nye had a thing in his column a couple of years ago about a husband who'd found out about one of those nudes and came up from the country to kill Farnsworth. Only, he made the mistake of telling his wife, and she phoned Farnsworth, and before the husband could get there, Farnsworth had painted a dress on the figure. He got away with that one, but right after that some guy chased him out of town. He went to Mexico City. Just got back a couple of months ago."

"He went to San Francisco, too," Murdock said.

Fenner lifted one brow. "Yeah, I guess he must have . . . Well, we still have to concentrate on Carlton and Yates. Have you heard from Thatcher?"

Murdock went to the telephone, called the lawyer, and spoke for three minutes. When he hung up he felt better. He could even smile a little. "Thatcher did all right," he said. "Tomorrow I get pinched."

"On what charge?"

"As a material witness—pending the meeting of the Grand Jury. Wyman's putting up the bail. Thatcher says it won't take more than an hour. I'm seeing him in the morning."

"Good enough," Fenner said. "Provided we crack this thing before the Grand Jury takes over. Where you going?"

Murdock had put on his hat and was reaching for his coat. "I'm going to see Rhoda."

"Now? It's almost twelve . . . Well, all right," Fenner said when Murdock belted the coat without replying. "There's just one comment I'd like to make: this Rhoda is an old friend of yours. I don't know how it used to be with you, but you can hardly expect to be objective when you're listening to her troubles."

"What about it?"

"I wondered if it ever occurred to you that a woman could have beaten Farnsworth to death—yes, and slugged you. Even a little woman—if she had a heavy candlestick to work with."

Kent Murdock did not show the photograph and photostat to Rhoda Farnsworth, nor tell her how he happened to have them; he simply described them, and knew at once from her reaction that she knew all about them.

They were in the living room of her apartment overlooking the Common, and she was sitting on the sofa, her feet curled under her, her blonde hair piled high. She wore a pastel-gray hostess gown that looked custom-made. Her gray eyes were tired, like her voice.

"I wondered what had happened to them," she said.

Murdock did not like what he had to do.

"I guess Doc Carlton knew about them, too," he said. "He bought three portraits in the past couple of years. Was that the other reason why you couldn't divorce Farnsworth?"

She looked up as though not quite understanding, and he said, "You told me it was your pride that made you stay married."

"It was. For a while. I thought I knew what I was doing, and I wouldn't listen to what they said. They told me about the other girls and the things Lloyd had done and how he drank, but I couldn't make myself believe them. You see, I loved him, Kent," she said. "I suppose it was a sort of madness."

She made a little hopeless gesture. "I don't know when it was that I finally knew. I suppose it was a gradual thing, the crumpling of this spell he'd cast over me. But there was a girl from Providence and I'd come home unexpectedly from a week-end in New York and—"

Her voice broke. She controlled it quickly and said, "It doesn't matter, does it? I finally discovered that what I took to be charm and personal magnetism was nothing but evil and sadism. I should have divorced him then, but I didn't. That was where my silly pride came in. We shared the same roof, but that was all. Not until two years ago did I finally get the courage to act, and then it was too late."

"On account of the San Francisco thing?"

She nodded. "I'd been visiting a friend and was on my way home, and I ran into John Carlton. He'd been there a week while his ship was being refitted, and he was lonely and so was I and—well, I liked him. I'd always liked him." She sighed.

"Somehow it didn't seem wrong, then, and happened in friendship rather than in passion. It would have hurt no one if it hadn't been for Lloyd."

She went on quickly, explaining how Farnsworth had happened to see them going into the hotel and checked the register, how he waited outside all the next morning, hidden in a taxi with a camera so that he could take their picture when they came out.

"You didn't see him?" Murdock said. "Or know about it?"

"Not until later, when I told him I intended to divorce him. He showed me the photograph and the photostat of the registration that he paid a clerk to let him borrow. He said if I sued for divorce he'd bring countersuit and offer those things as evidence . . . I've been paying him so much a month ever since.

"When I'm thirty I'll get perhaps three-quarters of a million, and he's agreed to give me a quiet divorce and the evidence, as he called it, for a hundred thousand. I should have been very glad to pay him," she said, "because there isn't any other way. I know Mrs. Carlton. She could not forgive John, and it would ruin his practice and his life. He really loves her."

She raised her eyes to meet his gaze, leaning forward a little as she spoke. "Will you give them to me, Kent?"

Murdock stood up, closing his mind to the haunting sound of her voice and to the pleading gray eyes. "You're awfully worried about Carlton, aren't you?"

"Because he's an awfully nice guy."

"So am I," Murdock said. "Even you thought so once."

"I still do."

"The difference is that somebody framed me for murder; I may still get tagged with it. And Doc Carlton's car was outside Farnsworth's place last night when I came out."

"Yes," Rhoda said. "I phoned him the minute I left you last night and asked him to hurry out there."

"Also, Carlton has a damned good motive and has been paying blackmail and—" Murdock stopped as the import of what she just said came to him. He leaned forward, staring hard. "What did you say?"

"I said I phoned John."

"And told him about the call I'd just got from Farnsworth?"

"Why, yes. Because I was afraid of what you might do, and I thought maybe John could do something to stop it."

She went on talking, but Murdock did not hear her. For he knew where Carlton lived, and was figuring how long it would take him to drive from there to Farnsworth's place, how long it had taken him, Murdock, to walk it, knowing now that here was one man who definitely had the chance to frame him.

His thoughts left his lean face hard, and Rhoda stood up, her gaze uncertain.

"What is it, Kent?"

"Nothing," he said. "It's all right. I'll make a deal with you," he said as he reached for his hat. "If Carlton can clear himself, you can have the pictures. If he happens to be the boy I'm looking for, he'll stand trial for murder, and then the pictures won't matter much, will they?"

He did not look at her when he had finished. He couldn't. He walked swiftly across the room, into the foyer, and let himself out.

Bennett Thatcher's estimate of the time it would take to surrender Kent Murdock and have him freed on bail was reasonably accurate. For in just seventy-five minutes Murdock was formally arrested, appeared in court before a waiting judge, and saw the bail of $5,000 supplied by T. A. Wyman.

This done, he headed for police headquarters, and, bypassing Lieutenant Bacon's office, went directly to the Bureau of Records and consulted the sergeant in charge. An hour later he had found a file photograph that satisfied him, noting that the record attached listed eight arrests on charges of extortion and assault, and one conviction.

"Guy Vernon," the sergeant said. "Meathead, they call him. Meathead Vernon."

"Did he ever work for Rudy Yates?"

"Sure. Up to a couple of years ago he was one of Rudy's regulars."

Murdock thanked the sergeant, and before he quit the building he left word with the proper official that he would sign a complaint against Vernon if the police would be good enough to pick him up. The official said he would pass the word along.

After that, Murdock went to the *Times-Clarion* and tried to work, but it was no good. Too many of his friends came into the studio and asked too many questions. What at first had been merely embarrassing became increasingly annoying as time went on.

He finally explained things to Wyman and the City Editor over the phone, and they told him to go home and take it easy.

His apartment had a stale, flat smell, but it seemed good to be back. He stripped, shaved, and took a hot shower followed by a cold one.

When he had dressed he telephoned Jack Fenner at his office and spoke of Meathead Vernon. Fenner said he knew that individual and would see what could be done to locate him. Murdock hung up and called Rudy Yates. He wasted no preliminaries. "I'm looking for Meathead Vernon," he said.

"That's interesting," Rudy Yates drawled.

"He used to work for you. I thought maybe you'd know where he is."

"Haven't seen him in months."

"But you get around. You have friends who get around," Murdock continued, his voice clipped and direct. "If you locate him, have him phone me. If you don't, I think I can dig up some new evidence for the D.A. in that used-car case that never came to trial."

He hesitated. When there was no answer, nor any disconnecting click, he knew that he had scored. He hung up as Rudy Yates was thinking it over . . .

The drone of the door buzzer heralded further developments shortly before ten that evening. Yet he was not prepared for what followed, because the man who stood in the hall was Dr. John Carlton.

Carlton's brown eyes were steady and unsmiling. He wore a gray homburg. His Oxford-gray coat was unbuttoned and he kept his hands in his pockets as he walked in. He waited until Murdock had closed the door, and then he said, "I suppose you know why I've come."

Murdock knew, all right. His mind had been racing from the instant he opened the door, for the things he saw in the tight, round face had already warned him of trouble.

"I can guess," he said. "You've been talking to Rhoda, and she told you about the photograph and stuff."

"I came to get them."

"Okay." Murdock sounded as if this was unimportant. He said, "I was about to make a drink."

"I'd like the photograph first."

Murdock studied his caller. About thirty-three, he thought, sandy-haired, just beginning to put on weight after a year and a half of civilian practice. A practice, Murdock knew, that was doing nicely, owing largely to the prominence and social standing of his wife.

"Are you going to give them to me?" The words cut sharply across Murdock's thoughts.

"No," he said flatly.

"I think you are," Carlton said, and he took a revolver from his pocket.

Murdock looked at it, his eyes dark with scorn. "Either I give you the stuff or you shoot, is that it? And then where'll you be?"

"I don't have to shoot to kill." Carlton hesitated, and for the first time seemed uncertain. "A bullet in the leg would put you down and give me a chance to search you, and every inch of this apartment."

"And for that you'd probably get five years."

"It would be worth it."

Murdock looked at him hard, measuring the whiteness of the mouth and the desperation in the eyes, and knew that Carlton meant what he said.

"Maybe it would," Kent said. "I guess Mrs. Carlton would be very much interested to know the real reason why you bought three of Farnsworth's portraits."

"Give me that photograph," Carlton said, and took a step forward.

Murdock shook his head, his anger riding him again. "You've made a stupid play, Doc. You forgot one thing. You forgot that to have a photostat made you have to have an original, and the original of that hotel card you signed is still in the hotel files. I haven't got the things you want," he added, deciding a lie would do no harm, "but if I had and you took them, the minute you closed the door I'd call police headquarters. I'd tell them all about the motive you had for murdering Lloyd Farnsworth and show them how they could prove it by checking with the hotel."

He stood up. "Now beat it," he said. "And if you bother me again I think I'll tell the police the truth, anyway, just for the hell of it—" He broke off as the telephone rang and walked quickly to the table in the inner hall.

"Murdock?" said a low, hoarse voice he did not recognize. "Meathead Vernon. I hear you been looking for me."

Murdock glanced over his shoulder. John Carlton was still standing there, the gun in his hand but no longer leveled. Murdock said, "Yes," into the telephone, hunching over it, so he would not have to speak very loud. "Where are you?"

"That comes later," the voice said, "depending on how loud your money talks. I may have to take a quick powder, and I could use some fresh scratch. What're you offering?"

Murdock thought fast, mentally counting his cash, and said he could raise a hundred dollars; possibly more later. He listened while Vernon gave him an address, repeated it to make sure he had it correct.

"Yes, I've got it," he said. "Second floor, over the paint shop."

"And get this," Vernon said. "It'll be dark up there on account I'm going to be watching for you. Anyone comes with you, or follows you, the deal is off."

"Don't worry," Murdock began.

"I won't. Come upstairs, walk in the door on the right, and wait. If it looks okay to me I'll be in.

The telephone clicked off, and Murdock turned back to the living room. He was heading for his hat and coat when he remembered John Carlton. Intent on his telephone conversation he had heard no other sound. Now, to his surprise, the room was empty. And he was suddenly grateful that there was no need for further argument.

He called Fenner and told him where he was going. Fenner wanted to give him a five-minute lead, then follow, but Murdock talked him out of it. Meathead might have a lookout, who would spot Fenner, and this was one interview Murdock didn't want interrupted.

He had to walk to Boylston before he found a taxi, and then rode out Huntington for a couple of miles, turned left finally, and told the driver to stop in a block of one- and two-story neighborhood stores, now dark and deserted.

Across the street he saw a bakery and a meat market, and the paint store next to it. Above this, three windows of the second-floor flat mirrored blackly the street shadows. There was no light behind them, but there was a faint glow beyond the doorway, and as Murdock crossed the street he saw that there was a light of some kind in the second-floor hall.

He was thankful for this as he climbed the stairs, but when he reached the hall he stopped and listened. He did not know why.

He took a step and then another, heels echoing hollowly on the bare boards. He passed under the dangling ceiling light, and on some impulse reached up and unscrewed the hot bulb.

"Just to even things up," he told himself, and felt better as the thick blackness settled about him. He walked on, groping for the door, the tightness spreading through him and every nerve alert.

He found the doorknob and went in fast, stepping aside as he slammed the door behind him. It was well that he did, though it was probably his precaution with the light that saved him.

For, in that next instant, it happened.

There was no real sound; rather, it was a whisper of some sound, the shadow of some movement ahead of him in the dark room.

He moved instantly—away from the menace of that shadow, throwing himself sideways and down as a gun blasted the silence and a pencil-point of light flicked out at him.

Three times the hammering came before he hit the floor, and he was not hurt, but knew there were other shells left and did the one thing he thought might save him.

He groaned twice, miserably. He caught his breath and let it out in a loud sigh that was drawn-out, final. Then he lay still.

There was a thin, rough carpet beneath him. The fingers of his right hand touched a chair leg. He curled his fingers around it, hoping the chair would be light enough to handle quickly. Then he heard the sound of movement to his left, the measured, faintly brushing sound of steps on the carpet.

It was hard to stay there, to lie so still.

The sound of the steps came to him again, closer, but not close enough. They were passing him on the left. He waited, ears straining for some new sound.

When it came it surprised him. He heard the click as the door opened, and then the metallic thud of some heavy object striking the floor in the direction of the windows. After that, the door closed.

He raised his head, pulled himself to his knees, and let go of the chair leg, puzzled but weak with relief. On his feet now, he oriented himself in the blackness and then stepped toward the windows.

Outside, the street stretched emptily below him. A car raced across the intersection a half block away, and then the quiet came again. He realized he was too late. His man was gone.

For another moment or two he stood there, the perspiration dampening his face and leaking down his sides. Then he groped his way back across the room and found the light switch by the door.

He snapped it on, blinking against the brightness. Then he saw Meathead Vernon.

Meathead was sitting on the floor, legs bowed and the sides of his knees touching the carpet. His thick torso was leaning back against a shabby couch, and he had been shot twice in the chest.

Three feet away a revolver lay on the floor, and Murdock knelt beside it. It was a cheap, nickel-plated model of a forgotten era, and it was this that the killer had thrown down as he left the room.

When Murdock saw that the cylinder had been designed to hold five bullets he realized why the man had not lingered. He had shot Vernon twice and kept the other three slugs for Murdock, leaving the empty gun for the police to find and interpret as they pleased.

The thought of this shocked Murdock anew. He straightened. He got out a cigarette and lit it with trembling fingers. He walked up to Vernon and made sure he was dead; then he glanced slowly about the grubby, cheaply furnished room until he spotted the telephone on the magazine-littered table.

He walked over and picked it up. Because he had nothing to lose he asked for police headquarters. When he had spoken his piece he dialed the *Times-Clarion* number, telling the City Editor to send out a reporter and a camera.

Kent Murdock had plenty of time to think during the next twelve hours. There were intervals during the police investigation of the

Vernon murder when he could isolate his thoughts and work on them, and there was additional time as he lay in bed trying to go to sleep. His brain took up the matter when he awakened the next morning, and by that time a pattern heretofore obscured began to reveal itself.

To clarify this pattern he went first to police headquarters, where he talked with Lieutenant Bacon and certain laboratory experts, and from there to one of the other city officials. At the *Times-Clarion* he checked assignments and made sure they were being covered, and then went upstairs and talked at length to some of the reporters before going into the library for further research.

After lunch he went to the *Bulletin* offices and sought out Gene Nye, the gossip columnist, who became readily cooperative and later took him into the "morgue" and told the librarian to give Murdock anything he wanted. As a result, it was nearly five when he telephoned Jack Fenner and said he would require the detective's services that evening. After that he called Thatcher.

The lawyer was still at his office, and he was immediately agreeable when Murdock outlined his plan. "I've found out quite a few things since I talked to you," Murdock said. "And if we're going to have a session with the Grand Jury next week I think you ought to know them. I want to get some people up to your place tonight and I want you to sit in while I chase them out in the open."

"I think it's a good idea," Thatcher said. "Who're you asking?"

Murdock told him, then said, "I wanted to be sure it was all right with you, and if so I thought maybe you would phone them. You carry more weight than I do."

"You talk as if you had something we could use."

"I have," Murdock said, "I hope."

And so, at nine o'clock that evening, Murdock and Jack Fenner, accompanied by a young *Times-Clarion* photographer named Eddie Geiger, pulled up in front of Thatcher's residence and piled out of the car. Other cars were already parked at the curb.

They were approaching the steps, when Fenner stopped studdenly and peered into the shadows.

"Come out of that!" he ordered; and then the bushes moved and out stepped a tall, slim figure, which, exposed to the light, proved to be that of a good-looking, bareheaded youth, wrapped in a camel's-hair coat.

"What're you doing there?" asked Fenner, taking an arm and turning the youth roughly. "What's your name?"

"Ah—Wordell," the youth said. "I'm a friend of—that is, I was just—"

"It's all right," Murdock said, remembering the name and its association. "You're a friend of Nancy Yates? . . . Good. You might as well come in."

The others were all there when Murdock stopped in the drawing-room doorway: Thatcher, spare and tall, stood in front of the fireplace, talking to Rhoda Farnsworth and Dr. Carlton, who sat on the nearby sofa; Nancy Yates and her brother, Rudy, occupied the matching sofa on the other side of the fireplace, but apparently they were not speaking, for each stared straight ahead. Murdock spoke to Eddie Geiger, turning so the others could not hear.

"Make yourself small, Eddie," he said. "I'll tell you when we're ready."

Then, as he started into the room, Nancy Yates saw Wordell, and her small mouth tightened. "You followed me," she said irritably.

Wordell colored, spoke defensively. "I wanted to know what was going on and—"

Murdock cut him off. "It's all right," he said. "I don't think she needs to stay."

"I don't mind," the girl said. "I'd like to stay." And then her words trailed off, and Murdock had her by the arm and was walking her toward the door, signaling young Wordell to follow. The bickering of young people had no place in his plan.

Rudy Yates, complete with dinner jacket and carnation, was standing up when Murdock returned to the living room. "How long is this going to take?" Rudy said. "I've got to get back to the Club. And what's this about my sister?"

Murdock sat down where he could watch both sofas, noting that Jack Fenner had taken a chair near the doorway.

"I wanted your sister to corroborate certain statements of mine," he said, "but maybe you'll take my word for them. If not, we can ask her later." He glanced at Thatcher. "I thought you ought to know about this: Lloyd Farnsworth had a green metal box. He kept some of his personal papers in it, and he gave it to Nancy Yates for safekeeping. She showed it to me the other night and I happened to have a key that opened it."

Thatcher nodded as Murdock elaborated. He made notes on a pad of paper he had on the mantel, and Murdock went on, "In that box was an envelope containing some affidavits concerning a black-market indictment on a used-car syndicate. The case never came to trial, but Rudy knows what it's all about. He also knows how Farnsworth got the envelope. I can tell you about that when we discuss it later," he said, and watched the muscles harden in Rudy's flushed face.

Then he continued, "My point is that the envelope made an additional motive for murder. His sister was in love with Farnsworth, and she was going to Florida with him. Rudy found it out and went up there the other night and tore up the Pullman tickets."

"Who says so besides you?"

"The police," Murdock said, and met Rudy's angry stare with steady eyes. "They picked up those pieces and went over them for latent fingerprints, and found yours."

Thatcher made a note of that, nodding, his thin face impassive except for the narrowed, observant eyes.

"Rudy's car was parked out front when I went in," Murdock continued. "It was gone when I came out."

"So what?" said Rudy. "So what if I did tear up the tickets?" His voice was tight now. "When I finished with Farnsworth I needed a drink. I remembered a bar a block and a half away, and I wasn't sure I'd find a place to park when I got there, so I left the car and walked. I got my drink and came back."

"Can you prove it?" Murdock waited, and when no answer came he glanced at Rhoda Farnsworth and John Carlton. "There was something else in that box," he said to Thatcher, "that concerned Carlton and Mrs. Farnsworth."

Carlton stiffened and seemed about to speak. As though sensing this, the woman put her hand on his arm. She was sitting very straight now, her face pale but composed, her gray eyes somehow no longer afraid. It was as though she realized she must finally pay for her mistake and had found sufficient inner courage to make the ordeal bearable.

Murdock had to look away. He swallowed and his face was hot as he glanced again at Thatcher.

"I can tell you the details later," he said, "but for now you can take my word for it that Carlton had a compelling motive for killing Farnsworth, and Mrs. Farnsworth had the same strong motive, because she was involved and blamed herself for what happened." He took a breath and said, "She was with me when I got the phone call from Farnsworth the night he was killed, and as soon as I left she called Carlton."

Murdock went on, explaining how he had found Carlton in his car when he came out.

"The car wasn't there when I went in," he said. "But it could have been parked around the corner. Later, after he had tipped off the police, he could have come back to watch."

"Do you deny this?" Thatcher asked, looking at Carlton.

The doctor cleared his throat, but his voice was thick. "Not all of it. Mrs. Farnsworth phoned me, yes. But when I went to get my car I found I had a flat. I went up there as soon as I changed it, and I had no more than got there when the police car came. I didn't know what had happened, but whatever it was I knew I was too late. So I came back home."

Murdock stood up. He nodded to Fenner and to Eddie Geiger, who waited with his camera in the corner. "I can tell you the rest of it privately," he said to Thatcher, and gestured toward the study door.

Thatcher caught his meaning. "If you'll excuse us," he said to the others, and led the way, closing the door when Murdock had entered. He waved the photographer to a chair opposite the desk and settled himself in the one behind it.

"That's very interesting," he said. "All of it."

"I wanted you to hear it," Murdock said. "I wanted you to know what I was up against, once I really got down to thinking things out. I didn't get anywhere at all until Vernon was killed last night. This morning I thought I had three real suspects, and then when I got working on it I decided there was really only one."

"Three?" Thatcher let his brows climb. "Rudy Yates, John Carlton, and—Mrs. Farnsworth?"

"Not Mrs. Farnsworth."

Thatcher let the brows go higher. "Not young Wordell, nor Miss Yates, certainly?"

"No."

"Then who?"

"You," Murdock said.

Thatcher let his brows come down. He squinted across the desk at

Murdock, his intent bright eyes revealing nothing. Finally he leaned back and chuckled. "You're not serious."

"You know I'm serious. You killed Farnsworth and Meathead Vernon, and if you'd taken a little more time you'd have killed me."

Thatcher passed a palm over his thinning gray-brown hair. His lips grew flat and colorless, and his voice got cold and sardonic, the way it always did when he tore into a courtroom opponent. "If you thought so," he said, "you would have come with the police."

Murdock shook his head. "I think this way is better. I had the others come"—he nodded toward the drawing room—"because I wanted to show you their motives, and why I finally had to throw them out and settle for you."

"Why did you—throw them out?"

Murdock took his time. His dark gaze was steady, his face composed; but inside he was jumpy because he was not sure his plan would work. Concentrating on the job before him he said, "Both Yates and Carlton knew Farnsworth had photographs or documents that would ruin them. With Carlton, it meant ruining his life; with Yates, it meant a jail sentence. They probably did not know where Farnsworth kept these things, but to kill him without getting them would be stupid, since on his death the evidence would surely come to light. I can understand them killing him for this evidence; I can understand Yates losing his head over his sister's infatuation and beating Farnsworth to death, anyway."

"But he didn't."

"No," Murdock said. "Because if he had—or if Carlton had—he would have looked for what he wanted. He would not have found it, because it wasn't there, but he would have looked."

Murdock leaned forward, measuring his words. "I had a chance to go over Farnsworth's apartment before the police came. It hadn't been searched. The center desk drawer was locked, but the others were neat and no attempt had been made to search them. And that's why I say neither of them killed him."

He hurried on before the lawyer could interrupt. "The man who killed him and framed me wasn't looking for papers or photographs; he was looking for just one thing—revenge. The trouble with me is that sometimes I'm not very bright. I didn't realize the importance of this until this morning. Oh, I knew I'd been framed, all right. The trouble was I didn't realize I'd been framed from the start."

He paused, but Thatcher had nothing to offer, so he said, "I guess you'd wanted to kill Farnsworth for a long time, Mr. Thatcher. And the other day you found the right way. You heard about the business at the Flamingo—or maybe you were there—and you knew I'd been seeing Rhoda Farnsworth, and you hired Meathead Vernon to do a job on me. You coached him in what to say, and you were providentially at hand to assist me and plant the idea that maybe it wasn't a mugging, while you suggested indirectly that perhaps Farnsworth was behind it. You took me to police headquarters, knowing I'd tell my story, and I think probably you waited outside and followed me home.

"After that you went to Farnsworth's with a gun, held it in his back, and made him telephone me and say what you told him to say. I doubt if he had the faintest idea of what he was doing. He was taunting me to come up and finish a job he knew nothing about, and when he hung up you hit him over the head with that candlestick. Then you finished him off and got ready for me."

Murdock laughed, an abrupt and bitter sound. "I was a pushover, wasn't I? Walked in, hotheaded, thinking Farnsworth and I were going to have it out, and you lowered the boom on me. You marked me up, skinned my knuckles, and walked out; if it hadn't been for a little break you would have got away with it."

"If the police had arrived a little sooner," Thatcher began.

"That wasn't what I meant," Murdock said. "I guess you had to get far enough away so no one would remember you before you went into a pay station to tip off the police; but the break I'm talking about is the taxi that came around the corner that first night and caught Meathead Vernon in its lights long enough for me to identify him . . . That did it, I guess," he said. "Once I knew who he was—and it was a cinch I'd find out, eventually—you had to kill him, too. And when you did, I knew Farnsworth hadn't hired him. I knew I'd been played for a sucker from the start."

Bennett Thatcher did not move. His narrowed, half-sleepy eyes never strayed from Murdock's face, but now, when he spoke, his voice had lost its bite. His tone grew softly speculative. "You said I'd probably wanted to kill Farnsworth for a long time. What makes you think so, and why didn't I?"

"Farnsworth had been back a couple of months," Murdock said. "I don't know why you waited, unless you wanted an ideal setup, but you didn't kill him before that because he wasn't in town. I think you tried to get him once before, didn't you, Mr. Thatcher? I think you've wanted to kill him ever since *the summer your wife committed suicide*—because of Farnsworth and the nude portrait he painted of her."

Kent leaned toward the desk, reaching for the telephone. "And before we go into that," he said, "it might be a good idea to get the police in and let them listen."

Murdock did not touch the telephone. His fingers were still a foot away from it when Thatcher's hand moved up from behind the desk and leveled an automatic across it. Murdock saw it coming, but he did not watch the gun; he kept his eyes on the lawyer's thin, gray face, seeing the dampness on the forehead and the way the man's jaw sagged before he tightened it.

He leaned back in his chair and let his breath out slowly, the fear beginning to build inside him—not just because of the gun, but because, having gone this far, he knew there was no turning back, nor any way out for him if he failed.

He had come here to put on his act with little more than native shrewdness to guide him, plus a psychology of his own that came from his long experience in meeting and studying people. He had facts, yes. But until this moment he had not been sure his analysis had been correct. He pretended the gun was unimportant.

"I don't think you'll need that," he said.

Thatcher did not seem to hear him. "You are right about Meathead Vernon," he said. "He was a stupid man. Someone—I believe it was Rudy Yates—got word to him yesterday afternoon that you were looking for him. He was pretty jittery when he phoned me, so I made a date with him. I told him the thing to do was telephone you and get you to his place and then take care of you. He believed me."

"He didn't talk like a man with gun in his back," Murdock said. "He sounded as if he meant what he said, and when he hung up you shot him twice. How come you missed me?"

"I don't know." Thatcher shifted his gun and wet his lips. "I didn't think I did. You gave a most convincing demonstration of a dying man. Perhaps I was confused and shot at your shadow," he said, and then his mouth dipped at the corners and his voice got sardonic again. "I think you are a little stupid, too, Murdock, for coming here like this."

"I could have come with a gun," Murdock said. "I've got Jack Fenner outside, in any case."

"He can hardly help you now."

"I don't need any help."

Murdock's voice was direct, forceful, and convincing. His confidence made Thatcher pause. "I don't follow you," the lawyer said.

"You think you've got two moves," Murdock said. "You can shoot me first and then shoot yourself—before Fenner does—or you can surrender and gamble as a lawyer that I haven't sufficient proof to convict you. All right; I'm offering you a *third* way, and I think you'll take it."

"Why should I, assuming there is a third way?"

Murdock hesitated, knowing that his life depended on what he said. "I'll have to tell this my way," he began. "It'll take a little while and I probably can't tell it in a straight line. I'll even have to guess at some things, but you'll know if I'm right or not."

He paused, arranging his thoughts, and said, "It started this morning, when I knew that Farnsworth had not hired Vernon, when I realized that neither Yates nor Carlton would have killed Farnsworth without searching for the things they wanted so badly. I began at the *Times-Clarion*," he said. "A newspaper is like a library, in a way. In its files is a history of the territory it serves and its people. Some papers call such departments 'morgues,' but all have them, and I had an idea the things I wanted would be there."

"You see, I didn't know your wife. So I started digging. I talked with reporters who had covered her death and who knew you. I used the *Bulletin's* morgue and I talked with Gene Nye, who's been covering scandal and gossip for the last ten years. And this is the picture I got.

"Your wife was twenty-two years younger than you when she married you. She came from a good middle-class family. Her folks didn't have much money, but they scraped together enough to send her to a small girls' school. They were old-fashioned, too, the way they brought her up. They were very strict. They did not encourage boy friends, and I doubt if she ever had much fun. She never really knew what boys were like, and when she got out of school she didn't know men.

"Then you came along. You had money, position, a distinguished name, and when she married you, you became the first man in her life; the only one—until Farnsworth.

"You worshipped her in your fashion, but you were strict, too, like her folks, because you were jealous and afraid. You could give her all the material things she'd ever want, but because you were so much older you worried about other things, the sort of things a man cannot buy. You were less sure of yourself than a younger man, and always you knew how beautiful she was. You saw the way other men looked at her when you were out, and you watched her, trying not to think of what might happen if she found someone she liked better.

"Well, she found the guy, finally, Farnsworth. There's no point in going into *why* she fell for him. He had the sort of charm that had fooled older and wiser women than your wife, and she had nothing in her experience that could help her, because she knew no one but you.

"You said your wife gave you that portrait for your birthday. That's a lie . . . You said she died two months later, and that also is a lie. I'll tell you what happened, Thatcher. And these are facts, a matter of record."

"On the first of three successive days during that summer you bought that portrait." He digressed to tell of Farnsworth's red-leather notebook that listed the dates of his sales. "On the second day your wife committed suicide, and on the third Farnsworth left town."

"My wife died accidentally," Thatcher said, his voice husky, but the gun steady.

"Your wife committed suicide, and you know it. Look." Murdock sat up. "I've got friends at police headquarters and at the medical examiner's office. Doc Egan didn't want to talk today until I told him how important it was. He would never repeat what he told me on a witness stand, perhaps, but he knows.

"Because of your name and position, and because there was no insurance company involved, nor any question of murder, he accepted your story that your wife suffered from migraine, had awakened after taking some pills, and, not remembering, had taken more. He says there was no suicide note—if there was, you grabbed it—but from the number of pills taken he's convinced it was suicide."

He saw Thatcher lean across the desk and tighten his hand on the gun. The lawyer wet his lips before he spoke.

"You're smarter than I thought, Murdock," he said. "The trouble is, you're too smart. If I stand trial I guess what you say will come out. I don't want it that way. I made up my mind that no one would ever speak evil of my wife. I gambled and I lost, and it looks as if I'll have to pay. I can do that, too, Murdock, but first I'm going to make sure you never talk about my wife or her reputation."

Murdock knew he meant it, knew he had only one chance left. "No," he said, and shook his head. "I told you there was a third way, Thatcher, and this is it: you're going to write out a confession and sign it."

For the first time Thatcher faltered, and his frown tempered the intent, narrowed gaze. "Why?" he said slowly.

Murdock got ready to move should the trigger finger tighten. He said, "Because if you don't, there'll be a picture of your wife on the front page of the *Times-Clarion*, which will show her as she was when Farnsworth painted her portrait—without the dress, without anything."

He went quickly on before the lawyer could interrupt. "I was with the AMG in Italy as a Monument Officer. We had to do with preserving art treasures and looking up stolen pictures. We developed an improvement on the infrared method of photographing paintings so that we could be sure just what was underneath the picture on top. In the case of an oil, once the original picture has dried, it will show up, even though another coat of paint has been applied . . . You saw the photographer I brought with me, didn't you? Well, what do you think he's been doing?"

Without moving, Bennett Thatcher seemed to sag, as though all strength had gone from his body. "How did you know?" he asked hoarsely.

Murdock began to breathe again. He watched the gun waver and dip. He moved his legs, and they felt weak and nerveless as he explained how Jack Fenner had told him the rumors about the woman who committed suicide, how Farnsworth had painted a dress on a nude portrait while an irate husband was rushing up from the country.

"I hooked the two incidents up," he said, "after I'd talked with Gene Nye and the medical examiner. And then I went on from there." Thatcher put the gun on the desk, but kept his hand on it. "Where's the photographer you brought?"

"He should be back at the office. He's supposed to phone me."

"What about the people in the drawing room?"

"There are no people in the drawing room. They've gone. There's no one there but Fenner now."

The tension had gone from Thatcher's face, leaving it flaccid and resigned. He sighed, and there was weariness and regret in the sound. Presently one corner of his mouth curled in a smile that was sardonic but without malice.

"I suppose you know I had every intention of killing you."

"It was a chance I had to take," Murdock said. "You protected your wife's name and reputation two years ago, and you've protected it since. I had an idea, feeling as you did about her, that you'd want to go on protecting her, once you knew there was no way out for you."

"You're right, of course." Thatcher unlocked a desk drawer and took out a folded sheet of paper. He struck a match, touched the flame to the paper, and as it burned in the ashtray he said, "That was the note she left me." He took out a small bottle, half filled with little pills.

"Yes," he said quietly, "I was the irate husband. She'd been seeing Farnsworth for over three months when I discovered it. I knew what he was like, and I'd heard about the nudes he sometimes did. I didn't accuse her then, but I said I was going up and find out. She must have telephoned him the minute I left—we were on the Cape that summer and it took me two hours to drive it—because when I got there the picture I saw was the one I have over the mantel."

He said, "I bought it on the spot, gave him a check, and called the express company to have it delivered. I did nothing more, then, but I was nearly out of my mind, thinking of the time it had taken her to pose for him and how they had been together, and when I got home I started in again."

He fell silent, distance in his gaze. After a minute, he exhaled softly and said, "What happened then was my fault. I was tortured by jealousy and rage and I accused her of everything I could think of. I guess she must have still been infatuated with him, because finally she turned on me. She became hysterical—I had driven her too far—and suddenly she not only admitted everything but taunted me with Farnsworth's cleverness in painting the dress on the portrait. I hadn't known until then, you see, but she told me how she'd posed and said she was glad.

"I got a gun. I brought her to town with me. I took her upstairs and locked her in her room and told her I was going to kill him . . . I would have," he said, "if I could have found him. I looked for hours, until nearly daylight, and then I came back and found her unconscious, with the note on the table. I drove her to the hospital, but she was too far gone; they couldn't save her." He rubbed his hand over his face and said, "The next day when I went looking for Farnsworth I found he'd left town."

The telephone rang as he finished and he picked it up. "For you," he said.

Murdock said, "Hello," and listened to what Eddie Geiger had to say. He put his hand over the mouthpiece and turned to Thatcher. "What about it?" he said.

"Has he developed the negatives?"

"No. His orders were to develop them only in case I didn't show up."

"Then he doesn't know," Thatcher said. "No one knows but you and me? How much time do I have?"

Murdock thought it over. "An hour after I leave with your confession."

"And I have your word that you will destroy the negatives? . . . Very well. It's a deal."

Murdock spoke into the telephone. "Okay, Eddie," he said. "Just sit tight until I get there . . . No, I don't want them developed." He put the telephone aside and found Thatcher examining the bottle of pills.

"I guess I can't use these," the lawyer said. "With this new benzedrine antidote they'd probably pull me out of it." He stood up, taking the gun with him. He got some paper and walked to the typewriter table in the corner. "Do you want to write it, or shall I?"

"You write it," Murdock said. "You're a lawyer and you know how to make it stand up. You don't have to put in anything about your wife—just say the motive was a personal one that developed between you and Farnsworth since he returned. Tell how and why you framed me, and how and why you had to kill Meathead Vernon. I'll settle for that. I think the police will, too."

Thatcher sat down and began to write. For five minutes he hammered steadily at the typewriter; then he stopped and glanced up.

"I want you to know one thing," he said. "I never intended that you should pay with your life for Farnsworth's murder. With the setup I had I felt pretty sure I could get you an acquittal, and if T. A. Wyman hadn't called me in I would have offered my services." He grunted softly, a disparaging sound. "Most men in a spot like that would have been satisfied with an acquittal, but you had a stubbornness and integrity I hadn't counted on. You had to have a clean bill."

He sighed again and bent over the machine. Presently he began to type again . . .

Jack Fenner rode back to the *Times-Clarion* with Murdock, but he went only as far as the corner bar. Here they had a quick one and said good night, and then Murdock went to the studio. Eddie Geiger was waiting, and when he had turned over the film-holder Murdock told him he could go home.

That left him alone in the studio, and he took the two-page confession from his pocket and read it once more before opening the film-holder and exposing the negatives. He got out his lighter, touched the flame to the film, and watched it sputter and curl up into ash. He took the photograph of Rhoda Farnsworth and Dr. Carlton and added it to the fire, and when it was going again he put on the photostat of the hotel register.

When the flame and smoke were gone, he lit a cigarette and leaned back in his chair. He thought about Nancy Yates and young Wordell. He was happy that Rhoda Farnsworth could have another chance. He tried not to think about Bennett Thatcher, for he knew that before the night was over, the police would find him dead, slumped over his desk, and the papers would pounce on the story.

He was glad he would not have to cover the case. Tomorrow he could be philosophical and know that this was much the best way for everyone concerned, even for Thatcher; but tonight he felt lousy, and he knew that presently he would go downstairs to the bar and get another drink or two, and then go home and have a few more in the hope that he could forget for a little while everything that had happened.

But first there was another job to do. He glanced at his watch. Then, because he had no choice but to face the issue as he would any other unpleasant assignment, he picked up the telephone and asked for police headquarters.

ABOUT THE AUTHORS

David Alexander

Journalist David Alexander is the author of fifteen mystery novels and one short story collection (*Hangman's Dozen*, Roy, 1961). He claims to be the only mystery writer to have a race horse named after him. Born in Kentucky in 1907, he was educated at the University of Kentucky (1927-28) and Columbia (1928), worked as a tour director and then reporter and sportswriter for *Blood-Horse* and *Thoroughbred Record* eventually to become the managing editor of America's first sporting newspaper, the New York *Morning Telegraph*. His best-known detective is Bart Hardin, also editor of a sporting paper, the *Broadway Times*. Hardin appears in eight novels, including *Terror on Broadway* (Random House, 1954), about a modern Jack the Ripper who stalks his victims on Broadway's crowded sidewalks at night, and *The Death of Humpty Dumpty* (Random House, 1957), in which a man in a clown costume leaps from the ninth floor of a Times Square hotel at midnight on New Year's Eve—and vanishes into thin air. Alexander has written non-fiction books on subjects as diverse as the Wall Street crash and the history of racing. His short story "The Man Who Went to Taltavul's" (included in this volume) was a winner—Second Prize—in Ellery Queen's Mystery Contest for 1956.

Linda J. Barnes

Playwright Linda Barnes branched out into the detective field with her first novel, *Blood Will Have Blood* (Avon, 1982), in which actor and private eye Michael Spraggue, scion of an old and distinguished Boston family, investigates when murder strikes during a revival of *Dracula* in Boston. *Dead Heat* (1984), the third Spraggue novel, features murder in the famous Boston Marathon. "Lucky Penny," her short story featuring Carlotta Carlyle, a six-foot-one, red-headed Boston cab driver, was runner-up for the Shamus Award of the Private Eye Writers of America for Best Short Story of 1985 (included in this volume).

George Harmon Coxe

The king of medium-boiled mystery, Coxe maintained a remarkably high level of quality throughout his long and prolific career. Born in Olean, New York, he was educated at Purdue (1919-20) and Cornell (1920-21), worked for five years as a newspaper reporter, three as an advertising salesman, and two as a scriptwriter for Metro-Goldwyn-Mayer, following which he became a freelance writer, selling in quantity to major pulps such as *Black Mask*. Beginning in 1935 he wrote *Murder with Pictures,* the first of no fewer than sixty mystery novels, all published in hardcover by Knopf. Half were series novels, most featuring Kent Murdock, photographer for Boston's *Herald-Courier*. Two other Bostonians were popular Coxe characters, "Flash" Casey of the *Express* and private eye Jack Fenner. In 1964 the Mystery Writers of America awarded Coxe their coveted Grand Master Award. He died on January 30, 1984.

David Ely

Not a prolific producer, Ely creates short stories and novels that, carefully crafted and polished, are memorable. Chicago-born (1927), Ely was educated at the University of North Carolina (1945), Harvard (A.B., 1949), and was a graduate student at St. Anthony's College at Oxford, England (1954-55). From 1949 to 1967, he worked as a reporter and rewrite man, with time out for military service in both the Navy (1945-6) and the Army (1950-52). Many of his works have a slightly fantastic touch. His best known novel, *Seconds* (Pantheon, 1963), is about an aging man who is medically given his youth back and what he does with it. His short story "The Sailing Club" won the Mystery Writers of America's "Edgar" for the Best Short Story, 1962.

* * *

Robert L. Fish

A world-travelling engineer, Robert L. Fish turned to writing only late in life, but made up quickly for lost time. His first novel, *The Fugitive* (Simon & Schuster) won the MWA Award for Best Novel of 1962. He went on to write thirty mystery novels, three collections of short stories, and edit two MWA anthologies. Fish was born in Cleveland, Ohio, August 21, 1912, and was educated at Case Western Reserve University (B.A., 1933).

His series detectives include the colorful and popular Capt. Jose da Silva, Brazilian liaison with Interpol, in such cases as *Isle of Snakes* (Simon & Schuster 1963), and *The Shrunken Head* (Simon & Schuster, 1963); Clancy, a police lieutenant in New York's Fifty-second Precinct with a heart of gold, in *Mute Witness* (Doubleday, 1963; filmed as *Bullitt*); and Lt. Jim Reardon, a tougher Columbo, in such novels as *Deadline: 2 A.M.* (Doubleday, 1976). Fish also completed Jack London's unfinished novel, *The Assassination Bureau, Ltd.* (McGraw Hill, 1961; later filmed). He is especially noted for two collections of the best Sherlock Holmes parodies ever done, *The Incredible Schlock Homes* (Simon & Schuster, 1966) and *The Memoirs of Schlock Homes* (Bobbs Merrill, 1974). Fish died in 1981.

Jacques Futrelle

Born in Georgia in 1875, Futrelle worked as a reporter in Virginia and then as theatrical manager before moving to Boston to become a member of the staff of the *Boston American*. There, on October 30, 1905, he created one of mystery fiction's greatest detectives, Professor Augustus S. F. X. Van Dusen, The Thinking Machine, in one of that field's greatest stories, the classic "Problem of Cell 13." At a dinner party of Boston society, Professor Van Dusen, a little man with a large head and domed forehead, states that no jail can hold a man who knows how to think. A fellow guest turns out to be the warden of a new prison and takes him up on his claim. Locked in, Van Dusen sets to work to think his way out of an escape-proof prison. Futrelle's Thinking Machine stories, many gathered from fading newspaper files by editor E. F. Bleiler, appear in two volumes, *Best "Thinking Machine" Stories* and *Great Cases of the Thinking Machine* (Dover, 1971 and 1976 respectively). Futrelle and his wife, May, also a writer, were passengers aboard the Titanic in 1912. Heroically, Futrelle placed his wife in a lifeboat and went down with the mighty ship.

George V. Higgins

Boston attorney Higgins is unique among mystery writers for his knowledge of crimes in high places of society. As a Federal Prosecutor he helped send many people in the Nixon administration to jail for Watergate-related crimes. Born in Brockton, Mass., November 13, 1939, he was educated at Boston College (A.B., 1961) and Stanford (M.A., 1965). After two years as an AP reporter he entered Boston College Law School and was admitted to the bar in 1967, becoming Assistant U.S. Attorney for Massachusetts in 1970-73 and assisting in the Watergate investigation as Special Assistant 1973-74. His first novel, *The Friends of Eddie Coyle* (Knopf, 1972), was a best-seller and was made into a movie starring Robert Mitchum. His Watergate investigations are recounted in *The Friends of Richard Nixon* (Little, Brown, 1975). His eleven novels (nine of them crime stories) have been both critical and financial successes, praised for their phonographic accuracy of dialogue and insider's knowledge of the criminal justice system. In addition to practicing law, Higgins is a columnist for the *Boston Globe* and the *Wall Street Journal*.

Edward D. Hoch

Unusually for a professional writer, Hoch specializes not only in short stories, but also in short detective stories of the classical, fair-play kind. Born in Rochester, New York, on February 22, 1930, and educated at the University of Rochester (1947-49), he served in the U.S. Army for the next two years. After some years of editorial and advertising work, he became a full-time writer in 1968. The author of some 700 short stories, he has been a mainstay of *Ellery Queen's Mystery Magazine* for nearly two decades. In 1968 he received the coveted Edgar of the Mystery Writers of America for the Best Short Story of the Year, "The Oblong Room," and became MWA president in 1982. His best known series detectives include small-town New England physician Dr. Sam Hawthorne, specialist in impossible crimes; the semi-occult Simon Ark, said to be a two-thousand-year-old Coptic priest in whose life good and evil are so evenly balanced that even God cannot decide if Ark belongs in Heaven or Hell (God sends him back to walk the Earth again until his acts settle the matter one way or the other); and Capt. Leopold, violent crimes specialist of the East Coast. Hoch's "Village of the Dead," in which an entire religious community commits suicide, is a remarkable precursor of the Jonestown massacre. Collections include *The Quests of Simon Ark* (Mysterious Press, 1984) and *Leopold's Way* (Southern Illinois University Press, 1986).

Hayden Howard

Best known for his science fiction, Howard began his writing career with mysteries. His first short story, "Pass the Bottle," won a Special Award in Ellery Queen's Eighth Annual Contest in 1953. He studied engineering at UCLA for two years before switching to the University of California for a degree in social science. During graduate study he began writing for relaxation. A group of his novelettes from *Galaxy Science Fiction* (1965-67) appeared as *The Eskimo Invasion* (Ballantine, 1967). His second story, "The Dipping of the Candlemaker" (included in this volume), was also a winner (Third Prize) in Ellery Queen's Ninth Annual Contest.

Charlotte MacLeod

A rising star in the mystery sky, Boston advertising agency executive Charlotte MacLeod writes popular mysteries with likable central characters. An American born in Canada (Bath, New Brunswick, November 12, 1922), she was educated at the Boston Art Institute, later joining (and becoming vice president of) Boston's N. H. Miller Advertising Agency (1952-82). Her series character, Peter Shandy, professor of agriculture at Balaclava College, first appears in *Rest You Merry* (Doubleday, 1978), in which Shandy turns detective when a killer tries to hide his victim's body by leaving it inside the absent Shandy's home on Christmas Eve. Sarah Kelling, down-on-her-luck scion of upper-class Boston society, investigates murder on Beacon Hill in such novels as *The Family Vault* (Doubleday, 1979) and *The Withdrawing Room* (Doubleday, 1980). MacLeod also writes under the pen-name of Alissa Craig. Her story in this volume comes from her first collection of mystery stories, *Grab Bag* (Avon, 1987).

S. S. Rafferty (John J. Hurley)

The creator of Cork of the Colonies, S. S. Rafferty was born in New Haven, Connecticut, on August 4, 1930, received his education at

Columbia and the University of Bridgeport, Connecticut, served in the U.S. Marines, worked as a reporter (Bridgeport *Post Telegram,* 1955-57) and then entered the advertising field, advancing to senior vice-president. In the early seventies he began writing detective short stories, most of them in two surprisingly contrasting series published in *Ellery Queen's Mystery Magazine.* One features Captain Cork, who investigates murder in thirteen well-researched stories, each set in a different colony just before the American Revolution, and collected in *Fatal Flourishes* (Avon, 1979). The other features nightclub standup comic Chick Kelly, whose tales are as modern as neon on Broadway and are told in today's showbiz slang.

Phoebe Atwood Taylor

Boston born mystery writer Taylor is currently undergoing a revival of her popular and numerous novels. Born May 18, 1909, she was educated at Barnard College (B.A., 1930), and promptly began a career as a full-time writer. Her best-known series detective, Asey Mayo, former seaman, racing car driver, auto company president, and Yankee *par excellence*, appears in her first book, *The Cape Cod Mystery* (Bobbs Merrill, 1931). "The Codfish Sherlock," as the newspapers call him, stars in twenty-three novels and two collections of novellas, all filled with local color and well-observed custom, and told with a humorous touch. Many of the Mayo novels are being reprinted by Countryman Press. The cases of her second series detective, the man who looks like Shakespeare, Professor Leonidas Witherall, are all set in Boston. Witherall first appeared in *Beginning with a Bash* (Collins, London, 1937). The story by her included in this volume comes from *Three Plots for Asey Mayo* (Norton, 1942).

Donald E. Westlake

Author of perhaps the best series of novels ever written about a professional criminal, Westlake works under almost as many false identities as the crooks he writes about. Born in New York on July 12, 1933, he was educated at New York University (1949-50), and SUNY Binghamton (1956-57), a period interrupted by his Air Force service (1954-1956). Beginning with novels much in the *Black Mask* vein, Westlake soon began his most famous series, about professional thief Parker, with *The Hunter* (Pocket, 1962). Including *The Seventh*

(Pocket, 1966) and *The Green Eagle Score* (Fawcett, 1967), it ran for sixteen novels (five of which were made into films, notably *Point Blank*, 1967, with Lee Marvin) ending with *Butcher's Moon* (1974), all under his Richard Stark pen name. Concurrently Westlake began a series of crime comedies such as *God Save the Mark* (Random House, 1967), which won a Mystery Writers of America Award for that year as Best Novel, and beginning with *The Hot Rock* (Simon & Schuster, 1970), a series about the inept crooked cop Dortmunder, none of whose capers turned out right. Very different in mood are his five somber novels about guilt-ridden cop Mitch Tobin, whose partner is killed when Tobin leaves his post for a romantic if adulterous interlude.